DURCH STARTEN

ENGLISCH
GYMNASIUM

ÜBUNGSBUCH

10

Verfasserinnen: Sonja Häusler und Katrin Pürer

Diesem Buch ist ein Lösungsheft zu den Übungen beigelegt.

Entspricht der Rechtschreibreform 2006

Bibliografische Information der Deutschen Bibliothek:
Die Deutsche Bibliothek verzeichnet diese Publikation in der
Deutschen Nationalbibliografie; detaillierte bibliografische Daten
sind im Internet über http://dnb.ddb.de abrufbar.

VERITAS-VERLAG, Linz
www.durchstarten.at
Alle Rechte vorbehalten,
insbesondere das Recht der Verbreitung
(*auch durch Film, Fernsehen, Internet,
fotomechanische Wiedergabe, Bild-,
Ton- und Datenträger jeder Art*) oder
der auszugsweise Nachdruck

Lektorat: Klaus Kopinitsch
Grafische Gestaltung: Gottfried Moritz
Illustrationen: Helmut »Dino« Breneis
Satz: Toni Froschauer
Herstellung: Julia Bamberger

Auf umweltfreundlichem Papier gedruckt bei:
siehe https://produkt.veritas.at/26849#additional

7. Auflage 2023   ISBN 978-3-7058-8853-1

VERITAS
Gemeinsam besser lernen

INHALTSVERZEICHNIS

VORWORT

Herzlich willkommen in der 6. Klasse! Was wird dich in diesem Jahr erwarten? Nun, grundsätzlich hast du die Routine der Oberstufe ja bereits kennengelernt. Es wird also (so nicht ein unerwarteter Lehrerinnen- oder Lehrerwechsel bevorsteht) weitestgehend keine Überraschungen und wesentliche Neuerungen in diesem Schuljahr geben. Zumindest was das Fach Englisch betrifft. Die erste mehrstündige Schularbeit solltest du bereits in der 5. Klasse hinter dich gebracht haben und auch die neuen Testformate bei den *reading* und *listening comprehensions* sollten keine Überraschung mehr sein. Um es kurz zu machen: In der 6. Klasse wartet viel harte Arbeit auf dich, nichts allerdings, mit dem du nicht schon vertraut bist. Du musst einfach weiter bereit sein, deinen eingeschlagenen Weg (zur Matura) fortzusetzen und dafür entsprechend Leistung zu erbringen. Auch wenn dieses Ziel noch ein Stück weit weg ist, vermeide es, in ein Motivationsloch zu fallen, denn sonst verpasst du zu viel Wichtiges, das du vielleicht nicht mehr aufholen kannst. In diesem Sinn wünschen wir dir schon jetzt viel positive Energie und Durchhaltevermögen!

Was kannst du von diesem Übungsbuch erwarten?

Ebenso wie „DURCHSTARTEN für die 5. KLASSE" ist auch dieses Übungsbuch in unterschiedliche Abschnitte unterteilt, um möglichst viele der (in diesem Schuljahr und bei der Matura) geforderten Fertigkeiten abzudecken.

Den Anfang machen erneut die **Hörübungen** (*listening comprehensions*), die allesamt von *native speakers* mit verschiedenen Akzenten gesprochen werden. Die Aufgabenstellungen hierzu **entsprechen der standardisierten Reifeprüfung** und der modularisierten Oberstufe. Gleiches gilt für den zweiten großen Abschnitt, die **Leseübungen** (*reading comprehensions*). Am Anfang dieser beiden Abschnitte findest du nochmals kurze Erläuterungen zu den Testformaten. Solltest du genauere und detailliertere Erklärungen brauchen, so findest du diese im Durchstartenband für die 5. Klasse.

Der darauffolgende *Writing*-Teil darf natürlich auch in diesem Übungsbuch nicht fehlen. Während in Durchstarten 5 die gängigen Textsorten (*letters, mail, report, essays*) besprochen wurden, findest du in diesem Übungsbuch erneut *tasks* und *exercises* dazu. Du solltest das theoretische Wissen zu den einzelnen Textsorten bereits verinnerlicht haben und kannst dich bei den aktuellen Übungen nun zum Beispiel auf Fehlersuche begeben oder einen Text korrigieren.

Gleich im Anschluss daran findest du den **Grammatik**-Teil. Nachdem im Übungsbuch der 5. Klasse der Schwerpunkt auf den englischen Zeiten lag, ist die 6. Klasse von Grammatikkapiteln wie *conditionals*, *modal verbs* oder auch *adjectives/ adverbs* gekennzeichnet. Am Anfang jedes Kapitels findest du wieder kurze Erklärungen, und dann ist es bereits *your turn*. Bitte denk daran: Je fleißiger und regelmäßiger du übst, desto schneller wird sich der Erfolg einstellen.

Auch der nächste Teil **basiert** bereits **auf der standardisierten Reifeprüfung**, es ist dies *Language in Use*. Hier findest du wieder verschiedene Zeitungsartikel und Texte, bei welchen du dein sprachliches Wissen testen und verbessern kannst. Die Texte sind inhaltlich **auf den Lehrplan der 10. Schulstufe abgestimmt** und hoffentlich auch für dich von Interesse.

Den nächsten Abschnitt bildet das **Vokabular (*vocabulary work*)**. Hier bekommst du Unterstützung, um deinen Wortschatz und deine sprachliche Ausdrucksfähigkeit verbessern zu können. Du kannst Synonyme, Homonyme, *collocations* und Adjektive bearbeiten – und falls du jetzt keine Ahnung hast, was das alles ist, dann mach dich einfach schlau und entdecke, wie du dein Vokabelwissen *pushen* und *boosten* kannst.

Last but not least: Im Anhang findest du wieder eine Reihe von **Probeschularbeiten** (*testing section*), welche sich erneut als zusätzliche Schularbeitsvorbereitung anbieten. Sie bestehen jeweils aus einer *listening comprehension*, einer *reading comprehension,* einer Übung zur *Language in Use* sowie unterschiedlicher Grammatik. Mit einem vorgegebenen Punkteschlüssel kannst du dir deine Note errechnen und weißt somit ganz genau, bei welchen Teilbereichen du vielleicht noch ein bisschen üben und nachhelfen musst.

Wie profitierst du am besten von diesem Buch?

Grundsätzlich kannst du an jeder beliebigen Stelle dieses Buches zu üben beginnen. Natürlich empfiehlt es sich aber, die Art der Übungen abzuwechseln, damit nicht eine Fertigkeit mehr geschult wird als eine andere. Im Idealfall nimmst du also in einem bestimmten Zeitraum aus jedem Teilbereich eine gewisse Anzahl von Übungen durch. Auf diese Art und Weise stellst du sicher, dass dir keine Übungsart entgeht, und du hast viel Abwechslung beim Üben. Nachdem du eine Übung beendet hast, kannst du dich mit dem beigelegten **Lösungsheft** selbst korrigieren. In diesem findest du die Lösungen zu sämtlichen Übungen und außerdem Muster- und Beispieltexte sowie die *Tapescripts* zu den Hörübungen.

Kennst du deinen Lerntyp?

Von der Existenz der vier Lerntypen hast du bestimmt schon gehört. Wahrscheinlich weißt du mittlerweile auch sehr genau, wie du am besten lernst. Solltest du aber noch nicht die optimale Methode für dich entdeckt haben, dann schau dir doch mal den folgenden Überblick an. Vielleicht kannst du daraus ja für dich etwas mitnehmen, was dir in Zukunft das Lernen ein wenig erleichtert. ☺

▣ Der auditive Lerntyp

… kann leicht gehörte Informationen aufnehmen, sie behalten und anschließend wiedergeben. Erklärungen hören sich für ihn stimmig und logisch an und er lernt am leichtesten, wenn er sich den Stoff laut vorsagen oder ihn wiederholt von einer CD/DVD oder einem MP3-Player abspielen kann. Der auditive Lerntyp ist Meister im Auswendiglernen. Selbstgespräche während der Lernphasen sind daher keine Seltenheit. Nebengeräusche irritieren diesen Lerntyp eher leicht, daher am besten Türe zu, Musik aus und ran an die Materie!

▣ Der visuelle Lerntyp

… lernt am besten durch das Lesen von Informationen und das Beobachten von Handlungsabläufen. Inhalte können leichter behalten werden, wenn sie in Form von Grafiken, Illustrationen oder Bildern veranschaulicht sind. Für diesen Lerntyp ist es besonders wichtig, visuelle Vorstellungen (Bilder) im Kopf zu haben, um so Eselsbrücken zu bilden. Hilfreich hierbei ist es, sich Skizzen, Bilder, Lernposter, *mindmaps* oder Lernkarteien anzulegen.

▣ Der kommunikative Lerntyp

… merkt sich Inhalte am ehesten in Form von Diskussionen und Gesprächen. Für ihn ist die sprachliche Auseinandersetzung mit dem Lernstoff und folglich das Verstehen im Dialog von großer Bedeutung. Er muss Erklärungen (entweder von der Lehrerin/dem Lehrer oder von Mitschülerinnen und Mitschülern) durchbesprechen, diskutieren und hinterfragen, damit sie für ihn logisch und schlüssig sind. Hilfreich und wichtig für diesen Lerntyp sind neben Diskussionen vor allem auch Frage-Antwort-Spiele sowie Lerngruppen. Gemeinsames Lernen kann für den kommunikativen Typ der Schlüssel zum Erfolg sein.

▣ Der motorische Lerntyp

… profitiert am meisten, wenn er Handlungsabläufe selbst durchführt und auf diese Weise nachvollzieht. Für ihn ist ganz wichtig, am Lernprozess unmittelbar beteiligt zu sein, durch *learning by doing* eigenständige Erfahrungen zu sammeln und den Inhalt im wahrsten Sinne des Wortes zu begreifen. Themen werden relativ selbstständig von ihm erkundet und bearbeitet, und dabei hat das Ausprobieren einen hohen Stellenwert. Bewegung ist für den motorischen Lerntyp sehr wichtig, also habe keine Hemmungen, im Zimmer auf und ab zu gehen, während du lernst.

Zum Schluss bleibt uns wie immer nur, dir viel Erfolg, Motivation und vor allem Spaß an Englisch zu wünschen!

Sonja Häusler & Katrin Pürer

LISTENING COMPREHENSION

INTRODUCTION

Du bist mit dem Format der *listening comprehensions* ja schon seit „DURCHSTARTEN für die 5. KLASSE" vertraut. Auch in diesem Buch findest du wieder eine große Anzahl an Hörübungen, die dich in Richtung Zentralmatura trainieren. Folgende Übungsformate erwarten dich:

Answer the questions (key words).

Beantworte die Fragen in maximal 4 Wörtern. Diese müssen grammatikalisch nicht korrekt angeordnet sein. Es zählt einzig eine dem Sinn entsprechende Wiedergabe des Gehörten.

a.	When did Lauryn Silverman's eating problems start?	*three years ago*

Multiple choice

Finde die beste von vier möglichen Antworten bzw. die beste Möglichkeit, den Satz zu vollenden. Kreuze diese an.

a.	Britain's problem in the middle of the 19th century was that	
	A the British loved tea.	☐
	B China challenged Britain as an empire.	☐
	C China controlled the world's tea production.	☐
	D Britain had grown too big and could not get enough tea to serve all people.	☐

Sentence completion

Vervollständige den Satz mit dem exakten Wortlaut.

a.	This year, there is an _____ of "A Christmas Carol" in our cinemas.	*animated version*

True or false?

Hake bzw. kreuze die richtige Antwort an.

		T	F
a.	The 1980s TV commercial warns people on the effects of drugs on their brain.	☐	☐

Who says what?

Ordne die Sätze den Sprechern zu.

A	So sometimes it's like something urgent that you have to really quickly respond to.
B	They won't come to you and speak face to face.

Melissa Block (host)	
Jennifer Ludden (interviewer)	
Daniel Epstein (schoolboy)	

Kleine Checkliste für Hörübungen

1. Lies dir die Aufgabenstellung aufmerksam durch.	**6.** Nimm dir eine Minute Zeit zum Durchlesen.
2. Löse die *pre-listening* Aufgabe.	**7.** Höre dir den Hörtext ein zweites Mal an.
3. Höre dir den Hörtext einmal an.	**8.** Kontrolliere, ob du alle Fragen gelöst hast.
4. Beantworte so viele Fragen wie möglich.	**9.** Vergleiche mit den Antworten im Lösungsheft.
5. Lass keine Frage aus. Rate im Notfall.	**10.** Lies dir den Hörtext im Lösungsheft durch.

LC 1: STRUGGLING TO OVERCOME ANOREXIA

Introduction

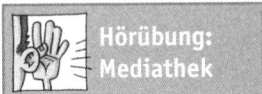

More and more teenagers are affected by eating disorders. In the following presentation you are going to hear the story of a young girl who wants to share her experiences with us.

1. Pre-listening: Word matching

Match the words with the definitions by writing the numbers in the boxes.

1. anorexia nervosa	☐	eating only a very limited choice of foods
2. restrictive diet	☐	specialist on the studies of nutrition (food)
3. nutritionist	☐	pressure of blood against walls of blood vessels
4. heart rate	☐	electric blanket that keeps people warm
5. heat blanket	☐	type of eating disorder: people stop eating
6. blood pressure	☐	number of heartbeats per minute

2. Answer the questions (key words).

a.	When did Lauryn Silverman's eating problems start?	*three years ago*
b.	What are people suffering from anorexia nervosa afraid of?	
c.	Why did Lauryn start eating less?	
d.	Which positive feeling did Lauryn associate with not eating?	
e.	What was the first alarming sign that made Lauryn's parents send her to a nutritionist?	
f.	What did the doctor say about Lauryn's pulse and heart rate?	
g.	What did Lauryn think was happening to her on March 21st?	
h.	When Lauryn came back home, how did she at first consider the food on her plate?	
i.	What did Lauryn realize having started doing after having taken her first bites of food?	

LC 2: THE TEA THIEVES: HOW A DRINK SHAPED AN EMPIRE

Introduction

Hörübung:
Mediathek

You might have heard that tea has always played an important role in British history.
The following interview tells you a surprising story how Britain helped India to become the dominating tea power.

1. **Pre-listening: Fill in the words from the box into the gaps.**
   The first letter will help you.

   > unchallenged – spy – confiscated – keep pace – horticulturalist – travelogue – merchant

   a. A m_____ is a person who makes trade with other people or businesses.

   b. My car was c_____ because the police thought that I had caused an accident with it.

   c. I'm sorry that you have to wait for me, but I just can't k_____ with you.

   d. Gina is the only one who can really dance salsa. Her performance is u_____.

   e. I read your t_____ on your round-the-world trip. Jamaica must have been fantastic!

   f. A s_____ is a person who tries to find out secret information for governments or companies.

   g. A h_____ is a person who designs and plans gardens and green areas.

2. **Multiple choice**
   Find the solution. Tick the correct box.

   a. Britain's problem in the middle of the 19th century was that

     A the British loved tea. ❑

     B China challenged Britain as an empire. ❑

     C China controlled the world's tea production. ❑

     D Britain had grown too big and could not get enough tea to serve all people. ❑

   b. Britain wanted to set up a tea industry in India because

     A there were already huge tea plantations there. ❑

     B India was a British colony. ❑

     C India was huge enough to serve all British with tea. ❑

     D the best experts on tea production came from India. ❑

   c. Why did the tea-opium trade between Britain and China come to a halt?

     A Because Britain started a war with China. ❑

     B Because the Chinese emperor did not want his people to become drug addicts. ❑

     C Because China confiscated the British opium without paying for it. ❑

     D Because the British were not satisfied with the quality of Chinese tea. ❑

   d. Robert Fortune

     A knew a lot about gardening and plants because he read a lot of books. ❑

     B travelled with pirates and bandits to China to spy on Chinese tea plants. ❑

     C saw himself as a thief who stole Chinese tea for British plantations in India. ❑

     D faced a lot of challenges, like illnesses, to learn about Chinese plants. ❑

LC 3: FROM DICKENS HIMSELF, NOTES ON "A CHRISTMAS CAROL"

Introduction

Hörübung:
Mediathek

One of the most popular Christmas stories is "A Christmas Carol" written by Charles Dickens. You might have already heard about the three ghosts that visit mean and grumpy Scrooge on Christmas Eve to show him his past, his present and his gloomy future. When Scrooge remembers his happy childhood and realizes that if he does not change, he will die alone and unloved, he opens his heart and learns to cherish the blessings of celebrating Christmas with a loving and caring family. The following radio show illustrates how Dickens himself commented on how to read and perform his own story.

1. Pre-listening: Collocations

Find the words that go together. Write the correct numbers on the lines provided.

1. animated   _____ reading   = CD or mp3 version of a book

2. audio   _____ margin   = empty space on the right side of a page

3. reading   _____ rendition = conventional performance of a play

4. public   _____ room   = place where you can read books

5. right-hand   _____ reading   = a book is read in front of an audience

6. classic   _____ version   = cartoon film

2. Sentence completion (exact words)

Fill in the missing words or phrases.

a.	This year, there is an _____ of "A Christmas Carol" in our cinemas.	*animated version*
b.	On _____ old Scrooge sat busy in his counting-house.	
c.	The promptbook of "A Christmas Carol" is on the _____ of the New York Public Library.	
d.	In Dickens' day, public readings of fiction and poetry _____.	
e.	Charles Dickens gave _____ public readings of "A Christmas Carol".	
f.	In Dickens' readings, complex sentences _____ with simple ones.	
g.	In the right-hand margins, Dickens wrote down many kinds of clues, like what kind of _____ at the time.	

LC 4: THIS IS "YOUR FACE ON METH", KIDS

Introduction

Hörübung:
Mediathek

Have you ever heard of the drug methamphetamine, also known as meth or Crystal meth?
It is one of the most addictive substances in the world that has devastating effects on those who take it.
The following interview presents a new deterrence strategy.

1. Pre-listening: Find the correct order of the words. The first letter is written in bold.

mecialomrc	*commercial*	noun: TV advertisement, spot
apcmnaig		noun: strategy in advertising to promote a product or idea
vagrae		verb: to bring great destruction, to ruin, to wreck
pohmr		verb: to change into, to turn into
ologphsiicaly		adjective: bodily, not psychological
itvayn		noun: pride in one's appearance, conceitedness
tdevstaaing		adjective: destructive, damaging, shocking
lexicompon		noun: natural colour, appearance, texture, tone of skin

2. True or false?

Tick the correct box.

	T	F
a. The 1980s TV commercial warns people on the effects of drugs on their brain.	❏	❏
b. In the 1980s the abuse of meth increased.	❏	❏
c. Meth is a drug primarily used in urban areas.	❏	❏
d. Tom Allman designed a computer program showing the effects of meth on your face.	❏	❏
e. The program "Your face on meth" appeals to young people's sense of beauty.	❏	❏
f. More than 90 percent of the people who try meth only once get addicted to it.	❏	❏
g. The interviewed sheriff says that nearly everybody in Willits has tried meth.	❏	❏
h. Most teenagers start crying when they see what meth could do to them.	❏	❏
i. Kids who have tried the program will definitely be too afraid to try meth in the future.	❏	❏
j. Successful strategies against drug abuse were scare tactics and "Just Say No" campaigns.	❏	❏
k. "Your face on meth" has been the most successful anti-drug campaign so far.	❏	❏

LC 5: IN BRITAIN, LIGHTS COME UP ON CLUBBERS' DRUG

Introduction

Hörübung:
Mediathek

In the last exercise you heard about an extremely dangerous drug called meth.
The following radio show talks about a new designer drug called mephedrone that is on the rise in Britain.

1. Pre-listening

What do the colloquial expressions (umgangssprachlich) mean? Match them with the explanations.

colloquial term		explanation	
1.	street name	**A**	to take drugs
2.	to sweep the scene	**B**	drug that can be legally purchased
3.	to do drugs	**C**	to give sb. a kick
4.	to rave about	**D**	to appear the first time
5.	to give sb. a buzz	**E**	to request or demand for sth.
6.	to push for	**F**	slang term for an illegal drug
7.	legal high	**G**	to be mad/crazy about sth.
8.	to hit the scene	**H**	to have a very high impact

1.	
2.	
3.	
4.	
5.	
6.	
7.	
8.	

2. Multiple choice

Complete the sentences with the appropriate ending. Tick the correct box.

a. Mephedrone is
- **A** an illegal substance that can be bought online. ❑
- **B** a new, harmless designer drug. ❑
- **C** a party drug that is becoming more and more popular. ❑
- **D** a drug used by schoolkids to better concentrate. ❑

b. Many teenagers think that mephedrone is safe because
- **A** it has no side-effects. ❑
- **B** it is not officially banned. ❑
- **C** it makes you feel good. ❑
- **D** it is used by many people. ❑

c. Jessie Farragher thinks
- **A** that broader actions than banning mephedrone must be taken. ❑
- **B** that Facebook makes the problem worse. ❑
- **C** that banning mephedrone would solve the problem. ❑
- **D** that it is stupid to make mephedrone illegal. ❑

d. It is a fact
- **A** that 26 people died because of mephedrone. ❑
- **B** that teachers are not allowed to confiscate illegal substances. ❑
- **C** that meph is a class B drug, like cannabis. ❑
- **D** that meph is sold as plant food. ❑

e. Les Iversen thinks
- **A** that banning meph is useless because then other drugs would come along. ❑
- **B** that doing drugs should just be discussed as a public health problem. ❑
- **C** that meph is safe and legal. ❑
- **D** that the fact that meph can be easily purchased seduces people to take it. ❑

LC 6: CHINA UPROOTS CHILD SLAVE LABOR RING AT BRICK PLANT

Introduction

Hörübung:
Mediathek

In the 19th century, child labour was common practice. Kids were forced to work extremely long hours in highly dangerous conditions for low wages. The following interview illustrates that in some parts of the world, the situation for children has not changed much in the last 150 years.

1. Pre-listening: Fill in the words from the box into the gaps.

unscrupulous – kiln – brick – ordeal – starvation – prosecution – exploitation

a. A _____ is a block of clay that is moulded and hardened in a kiln.

b. An _____ is a difficult and painful experience a person has to go through.

c. An _____ person is someone without principles who does not care about what is right.

d. _____ means that you die due to a lack of food.

e. _____ means that a person is used by someone for selfish purposes without being rewarded.

f. A _____ is an oven for hardening, burning or drying a substance.

g. _____ means that a person is being investigated on a crime.

2. Sentence completion (exact words)

a.	8-year-old boys have been sold and _____ 14 to 16 hours a day making bricks in primitive kilns.	*forced to work*
b.	Several kids have tried to escape and some of them reportedly _____.	
c.	Someone, apparently trying to get _____, had destroyed the places where the workers were living.	
d.	Anthony Kuhn understood that the brick kiln was run by the son of the _____.	
e.	In many cases, the mine or brick kiln owners got _____ beforehand and found ways of obstructing search.	
f.	Someone has told the parents _____ and so they are in a very tough position.	
g.	Some of the smarter, tougher children managed _____.	
h.	All this wealth that's being generated has to be generated by _____.	

LC 7: BECOMING CLOSE: THE GEOGRAPHY OF FRIENDSHIP

Introduction

Have you ever thought of the reasons why your best friend is your best friend?
The following radio show presents some new insights into the phenomenon of friendship.

1. Pre-listening: Collocations

Find the words that go together. Write the correct numbers on the lines provided.

1. social   _____ program   = first years at university, studying for your B.A.

2. mental   _____ background = having made common or similar past experiences

3. undergraduate   _____ connection = relationships with other people

4. chance   _____ quad   = dormitory rooms at university: quadrangle

5. shared   _____ encounter = you happen to meet someone

6. campus   _____ time   = time spent together in the same location

7. face   _____ health   = healthy state of mind

2. Answer the questions (key words).

Do not use more than four words!

a.	According to new research, which aspects are important for maintaining mental health?	*friendships and social connections*
b.	What did Bipin Sen want to start in Chicago?	
c.	What did Bipin Sen ask the guy he met on the plane when he saw him again on campus?	
d.	Why did Leila Holtsman think that Sally and her were quite different?	
e.	Which difference did Sally strike?	
f.	How did Sally describe Leila?	
g.	According to Prof. Sacerdote, which two aspects are the big determents for kindling friendship?	
h.	According to Greg Eells, what are friends expected to do, as exemplified with Sally and Leila?	
i.	According to Greg Eells, what does the big amount of shared time of college roommates help to develop?	

LC 8: SORRY CHARLIE: "TWO AND A HALF MEN" MAY GO ON

Introduction

Hörübung:
Mediathek

The US sitcom "Two and a Half Men" has been one of the most successful TV shows ever.
However, in 2011, a discussion about firing Charlie Sheen hit the news. Listen to the radio show of 2010, which already discusses a scenario where Sheen may lose his job.

1. Pre-listening

What do the phrasal verbs mean? Match them with the explanations.

	phrasal verb		explanation		
1.	to make good on sth.	A	jemanden in der Hand haben	1.	
2.	to have sb. over a barrel	B	ausscheiden aus	2.	
3.	to brush up on sth.	C	etwas einlösen	3.	
4.	to drop out of	D	austauschen	4.	
5.	to swap out	E	etwas auffrischen	5.	

Now, fill in the appropriate phrasal verb.

a. I wonder if Steve really _____ his threat to leave Moira.

b. Have you heard that Gina _____ our cheerleading team?

c. You should really _____ your dating skills! That was lame.

d. Alicia really thinks she has got me _____, but I won't let her put pressure on me!

e. My school has _____ teachers so fast, I do not even remember all my teachers' names.

2. True or false?

Tick the correct box.

	T	F
a. Charlie Sheen is the highest paid TV star in the world.	❏	❏
b. He wants to leave "Two and a Half Men" because he wants to work on other projects.	❏	❏
c. The sitcom's producers are willing to raise Sheen's pay to make him stay.	❏	❏
d. When Sheen took over Michael J. Fox' role in "Spin City", the sitcom got more popular.	❏	❏
e. In 1969, Kirstie Alley replaced Shelley Long in "Cheers".	❏	❏
f. A good comedy lives primarily from its stars.	❏	❏
g. There are some comedies which could perhaps not survive without their stars.	❏	❏
h. It is likely that Charlie Sheen will be replaced by a no-name actor.	❏	❏

LC 9: TEEN TEXTING SOARS: WILL SOCIAL SKILLS SUFFER?

Introduction

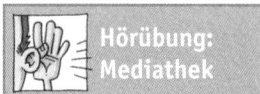

How many text messages do you get a day? And how many do you send? Have you ever had the feeling that you spend more time texting than actually talking to your friends?

1. Pre-listening

In the following text, some words are missing. Choose the correct answer (A, B, C or D) for each gap (1–5) in the text. Write your answer in the boxes provided. The first one (0) has been done for you.

I prefer (0) ... a text message to talking on the phone. I start (1) ... on my phone even before I get on the school bus. Sometimes I (2) ... texting while I am talking to my friends face to face! But I am not the only one who is (3) ... to the cell phone! Have a look at all those guys at school always having their phone on their (4) ... . My mum has already tried to set a (5) ... to my texting, but nothing can keep me from doing it.

0	A	texting	B	sending	C	emitting	D	giving
1	A	clapping	B	tipping	C	tapping	D	hammering
2	A	stay	B	avoid	C	want	D	keep
3	A	addicted	B	fascinated	C	spellbound	D	overcome
4	A	hands	B	fingertips	C	arms	D	mouth
5	A	test	B	punishment	C	menace	D	limit

0	1	2	3	4	5
B					

2. Who says what?

Match the speakers with the sentences. There are some extra sentences.

0	Melissa Block (host)	F, G
1	Jennifer Ludden (interviewer)	
2	Daniel Epstein (schoolboy)	
3	Amanda Lenhart (Pew center)	
4	Nini Halkett (teacher)	

A	So sometimes it's like something urgent that you have to really quickly respond to.
B	They won't come and speak to you face to face.
C	If it's somebody in front of you and you don't want them to know you're talking about them.
D	The average teen sends about 50 texts a day.
E	We found that 58 percent of teens who go to schools where the phone is forbidden say they've sent a text message in class.
F	Three out of four teenagers now have cell phones.
G	Do you think texting hurts your child's social skills?

LC 10: TEENS, SEX AND TV: A RISKY MIX?

Introduction

Hörübung:
Mediathek

What is your favourite TV series? Have you ever had the idea that what you watch on TV could influence your life? The following radio show discusses quite a provocative claim.

1. **Pre-listening: Collocations**

   Find the words that go together. Write the correct numbers on the lines provided.

   1. striking _____ high schoolers = rich high school kids

   2. privileged _____ ad = commercial that is too exciting, explicit, sexy

   3. dramatic _____ culprits = apparently those who are to be blamed

   4. obvious _____ assumption = rational and logical belief or idea

   5. provocative _____ repercussions = hard consequences

   6. reasonable _____ number = a surprisingly high number

2. **Multiple choice**

   Complete the sentences with the appropriate ending. Tick the correct box.

   a. Michelle Norris introduces "Gossip Girl" as a series

   A that gives a lot of answers on questions about sex. ❑

   B that is the most notorious of young and sexy teenage TV shows. ❑

   C that circles around rich New York teenagers. ❑

   D that seems to propel teenage pregnancies. ❑

   b. Another TV show that deals with teenage lust is

   A The Secret Love Life of the American Teenager. ❑

   B The Sexual Life of the American Teenager. ❑

   C The Secret Lives of American Teenagers. ❑

   D The Secret Life of the American Teenager. ❑

   c. Amanda Krzepicki thinks

   A that the show affects teen behaviour. ❑

   B that the show does a lot to herself. ❑

   C that the show might have an effect on teens' attitudes. ❑

   D that the show is not very entertaining. ❑

   d. According to Stephanie Savage, the fact that Blair in "Gossip Girl" fears being pregnant

   A was supposed to show that immoral behaviour carries consequences. ❑

   B shows that the TV show wanted to draw attention to the dangers of sex. ❑

   C illustrates the lifestyle of wealthy and spoilt Upper East Side girls like Blair. ❑

   D marks a significant moment in Blair's life. ❑

   e. Rebecca Colins thinks that television sitcoms are the worst sex-offenders

   A because they picture far more sex than TV shows like "Gossip Girl". ❑

   B because there are a lot of provocative ads displayed. ❑

   C because they show adults displaying their excessive sex life. ❑

   D because there people talk a lot about sex. ❑

LC 11: ONE TEEN'S STRUGGLE TO QUIT SMOKING

Introduction

Hörübung:
Mediathek

You might have heard that sentence a thousand times, "Don't start smoking. It kills you."
But do you take these warnings seriously? The following interview tells the story of one young girl and her experiences with smoking.

1. Pre-listening: Synonyms

Find the words that mean the same. Write the numbers in the box.

	original word		synonym
1.	to decline	**A**	to stop, to pause, to come to a halt
2.	to stall	**B**	to keep from doing
3.	to avoid	**C**	to forbid
4.	to prohibit	**D**	to give up, to refrain from, to stop
5.	to quit	**E**	to fall, to decrease, to become less
6.	to prevent	**F**	to evade, to dodge, to try not to do

1.	
2.	
3.	
4.	
5.	
6.	

2. Sentence completion (exact words)

The first one has been done for you.

a.	The USA has _____ in youth smoking over the past decade.	*seen a decline*
b.	Kindra Tanner says that she started smoking at the age of 13 and she says it was _____.	
c.	Pediatrician Jonathan Klein says that a lot of kids view smoking as _____.	
d.	According to Jonathan Klein one reason why kids start to smoke is that many are following the _____.	
e.	Klein says that if you, as a parent, can't quit smoking you have to _____ children.	
f.	He says that teens often _____ of beating a nicotine addiction.	
g.	Parents can help kids notice when TV and movies leave out the real _____, like cancer.	
h.	Nearly all adults who smoke started _____.	

LC 12: CONTROVERSY OVER THE WORLD CUP SOCCER BALL

Introduction

Hörübung: Mediathek

Are you interested in soccer? Perhaps you even play in a team? Or do you prefer enjoying a good game in the stadium? In June and July 2010, the world cup took place in South Africa and before the games started, a big discussion started. Listen to the radio show and find out what the players were most concerned about ...

1. Pre-listening: Fill in the words from the box into the gaps.

> score – nickname – penalty kick – to mourn – defenders

a. Tina's _____ is "Purple" because of the colour of her hair.

b. When did you last _____ a goal?

c. When you lose an important person, it is important _____ and to cry.

d. In a football game, those players who are not in possession of the ball are the _____.

e. When a player violates the rules, the other team can perform a _____.

2. Answer the questions (key words).

Do not use more than four words!

a.	What does the name of the World Cup ball "Jabulani" mean in English?	*celebrate*
b.	What does the ball, according to a keeper from South Africa, have?	
c.	What do Adidas and their designers say about the soccer ball?	
d.	What happened to the ball on Saturday's game between the U.S. and England when the goalkeeper wanted to catch it?	
e.	Who discusses most about the ball's behaviour?	
f.	What happened to the ball in the game Serbia – Ghana and consequently caused a penalty kick?	
g.	What do the grooves in the ball supposedly do and therefore make the ball move unpredictably?	
h.	Players, especially the losing ones, usually complain about the World Cup ball. But why is the situation different this time?	

LC 13: SOCCER FANS URGE FIFA TO USE VIDEO REVIEW

Introduction

Sunday, 27th of June, 2010: The soccer World Cup has reached the round of 16 – millions of people are looking forward to two thrilling games of splendid football. First game: Germany versus England. The German team quickly scores two goals, but then the English take up the chase. 2:1, 2:2 – oh no, sorry. 2:1 – Why? The ball was behind the line! Sorry, but the referee didn't see it. So the game goes on and the Germans win 4:1. Second game: Argentina versus Mexico. 26th minute, Messi passes to Tevez, he scores, but: is offside. The referee doesn't see that offence, the game goes on, Argentina wins 3:0. Listen to the following interview and find out what people say about these two wrong decisions.

1. Pre-listening

Before you listen to the interview, read the following sentences and then find out what function the "do" carries.

a. "I thought you don't like mango ice cream?" "Oh, you're wrong. I **do** like mango, but I hate papaya."

b. Imagine!! Yesterday, Steve rang up Gina and ... he **did** ask her out! Finally ...

c. The referee must be blind! The ball **did** cross the line – you saw it too, didn't you?

d. I **do** want to see you today. Believe me!

e. I tell you, the cat **did** open the door! I saw it with my own eyes.

2. Now, tick the correct box.

a. The "do" is a grammatical necessity that you have to use in positive present simple sentences. ❑

b. The "do" stresses the truthfulness of the sentence. It can be translated with "tatsächlich". ❑

3. True or false?

Tick the correct box.

	T	F
a. The referee Frank Lampard did not see the 2:2 goal in the Germany-England game.	❑	❑
b. This wrong decision was made in a moment when the game was nearly decided.	❑	❑
c. A solution would be to use a technology that sends signals from the goal-line.	❑	❑
d. As they have to run up to 12 miles per game, referees want a second referee on the field.	❑	❑
e. In American football, assistants help the referee to make important decisions.	❑	❑
f. According to the FIFA, the referee should stay the official, final authority.	❑	❑
g. People fear that replay technology could spoil the characteristic flow of football games.	❑	❑
h. In ice hockey, the game comes to a halt, the goal is checked, and then the game goes on.	❑	❑

LC 14: HOMEWORK: OVERCOMING FEAR

Introduction

Hörübung:
Mediathek

Is there anything you are especially afraid of? Have you ever tried to overcome a certain fear? How did you do that? The following radio show presents two people who talk freely about their biggest fear and how they dealt with it.

1. Pre-listening: Fill in the words from the box into the gaps.

> triathlon – borrow – snorkel gear – overcome – lend – face – arachnophobia – cure

a. I have never been able to _____ my fear of rats!

b. You have to _____ your biggest fear: Try to touch the snake!

c. May I _____ your car? Mine is at the mechanic's.

d. A _____ consists of a mask, a snorkel and, optionally, flippers.

e. When you do a _____ you have to swim, cycle and run.

f. _____ means that you are afraid of spiders.

g. Can you _____ me your pen? Mine doesn't work.

h. When you want to _____ a phobia you need to see a psychologist.

2. Who says what?

Listen to the radio show and find out who says what. There are some extra sentences.

1	Andrea Seabrook	F		
2	Meg Rawlings			
3	Lizbeth Alt			

A	Sharks patrol this water!
B	She dragged her mother to the movie theatre.
C	I ended up curled in a foetal position and hanging on to her.
D	I borrowed some snorkel gear.
E	They're swarming!
F	It turns out we have some seriously brave listeners.
G	It wasn't like I was cured, but it did help.
H	We may just put you on the air.
I	I had to jump off a boat that was right near Alcatraz Island.

LC 15: LADY GAGA VS. ACE OF BASE

Introduction

Hörübung:
Mediathek

You turn on the radio, a supposedly new song is presented, but you think, "Where have I heard that song before?" In fact, it's not only annoying to hear the same old thing again and again, it can also be against the law. The following radio show discusses the vague limits between inspired new creation and mere theft.

1. Pre-listening: Antonyms

Find the words that have the opposite meaning. Write the number in the box.

original word		antonym	
1.	sunset	**A**	monophonic
2.	bright	**B**	innocent
3.	polyphonic	**C**	original
4.	culpable	**D**	to follow
5.	derivative	**E**	sunrise
6.	to precede	**F**	dark

1.	
2.	
3.	
4.	
5.	
6.	

2. Multiple choice

Complete the sentences with the appropriate ending. Tick the correct box.

a. "Don't turn around"

  A is the new single by Lady Gaga. ❏

  B is a 60-year-old dance hit. ❏

  C is the new Ace of Base hit single. ❏

  D shows parallels to the song "Alejandro". ❏

b. Maura Johnston

  A doesn't think that "Alejandro" is influenced by a song by Shakira. ❏

  B sees parallels between ABBA's "Fernando" and the hit single "Alejandro". ❏

  C thinks that "Alejandro" reminds her of Madonna's "La isla bonita". ❏

  D hears a lot of different influences in the song "Alejandro". ❏

c. Jay Smooth

  A thinks that copying ideas from other songs is stealing. ❏

  B argues that every song is influenced by songs that have existed before. ❏

  C appreciates the reggae influence in modern songs. ❏

  D complains that there are always people who say that artists steal ideas. ❏

d. Lady Gaga

  A cannot be blamed for stealing as no one can prove her offense. ❏

  B should list all the songs that influence her new hits. ❏

  C should not be blamed for stealing as Ace of Base was influenced by other bands. ❏

  D can definitely be accused of stealing in her new song. ❏

LC 16: THAT NOT-SO-HEALTHY GLOW: THE DANGERS OF TANNING

Introduction

Hörübung: Mediathek

A healthy looking tanned glow – or a leathery orange texture that reminds you of grilled chicken? Both scenarios can be the consequence of the same procedure: entering the tanning studio, lying down on the tanning bed and enjoying the warm beams that surround your sun-deprived body. But what are the long-term effects of artificial tanning? Listen to the interview and find out more on that "hot" issue!

1. Pre-listening: Find the correct order of the words. The first letter is written in bold.

cecarn	*cancer*	uncontrolled growth of cells causing serious diseases
n**a**ec		oily skin that leads to inflamed spots
le**pa-s**kedinn		of/with light skin colour
le**mo**		dark, intensely pigmented part of your skin
o**mm**aelan		most dangerous form of skin cancer
inog**c**ariccen		causing cancer, carcinomas (adjective)
na**b**		prohibition by official decree

2. Find the mistakes!

Read the sentences. Tick the correct ones and correct the wrong ones. The first one has been done for you.

a.	Brittany Cicala's prom night was seven years ago.	*eight years*
b.	Brittany wanted to tan because she wanted to look better in her silver prom dress.	
c.	She got addicted to tanning and called herself a "tanorexic".	
d.	Catherine Mosher did a survey on alcohol addiction.	
e.	In 2004, Catherine's mother found a mole on her daughter's neck.	
f.	This mole turned out to be a melanoma, but it was her only suspicious mole.	
g.	A tan is a protection response to ultraviolet light damage.	
h.	In the USA, tanning under the age of 18 is banned.	

LC 17: E-BOOK READERS EXPECTED TO GROW IN POPULARITY

Introduction

You are lying on the beach, a thrilling book in your hands, enjoying the pleasure of what you are reading. Everything is perfect: the sun is shining, a light breeze is rustling through the palm tree above you, the smell of the fresh seawater fills your lungs, but: your back hurts because you can't find the perfect reading position, small grains of sand make a creaking and gnashing sound every time you turn a page and you think: Why the hell haven't I bought an e-book reader? The following radio show tells you more about that fascinating gadget.

1. **Pre-listening: Word formation**

   Find the missing words.

	NOUN	VERB	ADJECTIVE
1.	commuter		
2.			different
3.		to access	
4.		to expect	
5.			expanding
6.		to compare	

2. **Answer the questions (key words).**

   Do not use more than four words!

a.	What's new about the hardware of the Nook eReader?	*colour display*
b.	What can you do with the new feature "Lend Me"?	
c.	In the past two years, who primarily bought the Kindle eReader?	
d.	Which advantage of regular books does Omar Gallaga mention compared to the portability and convenience of e-books?	
e.	What will you be able to do with the Windows eReader application that Amazon is going to introduce?	
f.	In which situation does Robert Siegel consider the mobility of the e-book a big advantage?	
g.	In addition to books, what else can you read on e-books according to Omar Gallaga?	

LC 18: SCHOOL DESEGREGATION: AT WHICH PRICE?

Introduction

Hörübung: Mediathek

In Austria, it is a common thing to hear different languages in one classroom, to see children of various cultures and skin colours in one school. In the United States, the fact that black and white people share classes has not always been as natural as it is today. In the following interview, S. Pearl Sharp, a contemporary witness of school desegregation, talks about her experiences, feelings and doubts.

1. Pre-listening

What do the following proverbs, sayings and concepts mean? Match them with the correct meaning.

	proverb/saying/concept		meaning		
1.	to lift a yoke off your shoulders	**A**	absorption of minority, loss of differences	**1.**	
2.	to be on your agenda	**B**	abolishing racial segregation (separation)	**2.**	
3.	to be the foot soldier	**C**	to gain access to, to become a part of	**3.**	
4.	to find your entry door into	**D**	to be blamed of having copied ideas	**4.**	
5.	to be accused of plagiarism	**E**	to be relieved of a problem	**5.**	
6.	desegregation	**F**	to act according to other people's plans	**6.**	
7.	assimilation	**G**	to have on your mind, to plan	**7.**	

2. True or false?

Tick the correct box.

        T   F

a. In September 2007, Central High School in Little Rock celebrated its 50th anniversary. ❏ ❏

b. The first black students in Central High School in Arkansas were called Little Rock Nine. ❏ ❏

c. S. Pearl Sharp was one of the first black students in Arkansas' Central High School. ❏ ❏

d. In her youth, S. Pearl Sharp had to follow the orders and plans of her parents. ❏ ❏

e. As a black girl in a predominantly white school, she had to face prejudices and violence. ❏ ❏

f. Integrated black school kids had a harder time in the South of the USA than in the North. ❏ ❏

g. Pearl has always had doubts whether integration was worth the pain black kids had to face. ❏ ❏

h. Desegregation often turned into assimilation and into the loss of black community ties. ❏ ❏

i. The Little Rock Nine made it, but many other black kids suffered due to integration. ❏ ❏

LC 19: WHO WILL LIVE TO BE 100? GENETIC TEST MIGHT TELL

Introduction

Hörübung: Mediathek

Would you like to know how long you are going to live? If there was a test that might tell you your life expectancy, would you take it? The following interview tells you more about this topic.

1. Pre-listening: Fill in the words from the box into the gaps.

> genetic signatures – geneticist – dementia – longevity – hypertension –
> genetic marker – centenarian

a. People endowed with _____ get very old.

b. A _____ is a person who is 100 or more years old.

c. A _____ is a specific bit of DNA that produces a certain characteristic or trait.

d. _____ are gene patterns of people.

e. _____ is a disease that causes the loss of cognitive abilities.

f. _____ means that your blood pressure is too high.

g. A _____ is a scientist who specialises in studying the structure of genes.

2. Who says what?

Listen to the interview and match the speakers with the sentences. There are extra sentences.

Renee Montagne (host)	A	
Joe Palca (interviewer)		
Dr. Thomas Perls		
Dr. Paola Sebastiani		

A	Scientists are hoping their test will lead to a better understanding of the genetics of why some people live longer than others.
B	Not only did those people live long lives; they lived long, healthy lives.
C	A lot of work has to be done to then understand what is the biology. (...) So this is a first step.
D	The accuracy of the model is 77 percent.
E	You have a hint – and that's better than having nothing.
F	Longevity definitely runs in families, but which genes and how they work was a mystery.
G	If there were a medical test that could tell you whether you would live to be 100, would you take it?
H	The oldest subject in our study was 119.

LC 20: THIS YEAR, SMART PHONES ARE HOLIDAY MUST-HAVE

Introduction

Hörübung: Mediathek

Downloading videos, checking your friends' status on Facebook, playing games, listening to music, watching films, ... No, I'm not talking about you sitting in front of your computer in your room, I'm talking about you sitting at the bus stop, holding your phone in your hands. Listen to the following radio programme on what's on the list for Santa this year.

1. Pre-listening: Jumbled words

Find the correct order of the words. The first letter is written in bold.

gegadt	*gadget*	electronic device
ckBla ayFrid		day after Thanksgiving: start of Christmas shopping season
leswires caerrri		telephone company that provides services for mobile phones
ybCer ndaMoy		another important shopping day in the USA – mainly online shopping
ckbris-nda-rtmoar restos		a company that possesses a building or a store, contrasts online shopping

2. Sentence completion (exact words)

The first one has been done for you.

a.	This year, _____ of smart phones	*it's the turn*
b.	Every year, there seems to be some kind of gadget that everybody _____.	
c.	Marshmallow Shooters are sort of like Nerf guns that _____.	
d.	There's been a lot of _____ over the weekend about Google's phone called the Nexus One.	
e.	Some people might want to think about waiting and see what Google does before you _____ contract on a phone.	
f.	Even Twitter is a good place to _____ that are coming directly from companies like Dell.	
g.	Don't _____ that are not retailers that you're comfortable shopping with.	
h.	There might be a phishing scheme to _____ or your credit card information.	

READING COMPREHENSION

INTRODUCTION

Über die Wichtigkeit der Leseverständnisübungen solltest du in der 6. Klasse bereits Bescheid wissen. Ebenso über die gängigen Testformate, die dich bei der Zentralmatura erwarten. DURCHSTARTEN für die 5. KLASSE hat dich darauf bereits bestmöglich vorbereitet und dir eine detaillierte Beschreibung der Testformate geliefert. Der nachfolgende Überblick ist also nicht neu für dich. Ebenso wenig neu ist die Tatsache, dass dich bei den *reading comprehensions* in diesem Übungsbuch zwischendurch auch wieder Übungen erwarten, die nicht Teil der Zentralmatura sind. Sie dienen einerseits der Auflockerung, andererseits dem Textverständnis. Um sicherzugehen, dass du mit eventuell neuem Vokabular keine Schwierigkeiten hast, finden sich oft *word matching*-Übungen am Beginn der *readings*. Hier kannst du vorab schwierige Wörter oder Phrasen mit den entsprechenden englischen Erklärungen verbinden.

BESCHREIBUNG DER TESTFORMATE

- **Multiple choice**

  Verständnisfragen zum Inhalt eines Textes/Artikels werden gestellt und vier Antwortmöglichkeiten zur Auswahl gegeben. Vergiss nicht, es gibt immer nur EINE richtige Antwort. *Study the example*:

  > **1.** Why is it not so important to understand every single word in a newspaper article?
  >
  > **A** Because the meaning of familiar words becomes clear anyway. ❑
  >
  > **B** Because there's mostly a vocabulary section at the end explaining difficult words. ❑
  >
  > **C** Because the meaning of unfamiliar words often becomes clear through the context. ☑
  >
  > **D** Because it's completely enough to understand only half of the article. ❑
  >
  > Answer C is the correct solution so you tick the respective box!

- **Gapped Text**

  Fehlende Sätze müssen an den richtigen Stellen im Text eingefügt werden. Beim Lesen des Textes ignorierst du vorläufig die Lücken. Danach entscheidest du, welcher Satz wohin gehört. Aber Vorsicht: Du hast mindestens zwei Sätze mehr zur Auswahl als Lücken vorhanden sind. *Study the example*:

Climbing Mount Everest has always fascinated and attracted alpinists all over the world.	A
But for sure, the dangers of avalanches must not be underestimated because they can be lethal.	B

- **Note taking**

  Auf eine gestellte Frage musst du – in nicht mehr als VIER WÖRTERN – die richtige Antwort geben. Hierbei kommt es weder auf grammatikalische Richtigkeit noch korrekte Rechtschreibung an, sondern du sollst zeigen, welche die wichtigsten vier Wörter sind, um die Frage korrekt zu beantworten. *Study the example*:

1.	What are reasons for teenagers to make their first experiences with drugs?	*curiosity, peer-pressure, interest*
2.	What is most dangerous when mixing drugs with alcohol?	

■ **Matching headlines**

Überschriften müssen entsprechenden Textpassagen zugeordnet werden. Auch hier ignorierst du anfangs die Lücken. Vorsicht: Es gibt wieder mindestens zwei Überschriften mehr, als du brauchst. Also achte darauf, welche *headlines* du ausschließen kannst! *Study the example*:

Dealing with violent behaviour	**A**
Getting rid of one's aggressions	**B**

■ **Sequencing**

Ein Text/Eine Geschichte wird gelesen. Danach sollst du eine Zusammenfassung in die richtige Reihenfolge bringen und entsprechend nummerieren. *Study the example*:

2	Though first aid for the most dangerously injured victims had been given immediately, the number of deaths is beyond imagination.
4	A mourning ceremony, including a parade honouring the victims, is going to take place next Friday.
1	The news of yesterday's airplane crash came unexpected and surprising for everybody concerned.
3	The government as well as Britain's Prime Minister have promised to shed light into this sad affair as soon as possible.

■ **True/False/Justification**

Zunächst wird eine gestellte Frage mit „wahr" oder „falsch" beantwortet (angehakt). Danach müssen die ersten vier Wörter jenes Satzes aus dem Text gefunden und notiert werden, welche dich zu der Entscheidung *true* oder *false* geführt habe. *Study the example*:

		T	F	Justification
1.	It's proven that torture exists today, primarily in Third World countries.	☑	☐	*Nowadays torture still exists …*
2.	The methods of how to torture people have not changed throughout the years.	☐	☑	*Today different techniques are …*

KLEINE CHECKLISTE FÜR READING COMPREHENSIONS

■ Bei der Zentralmatura hast du für die Leseverständnisübungen 75 Minuten Zeit. Es müssen vier Testformate zu voneinander unabhängigen Texten bearbeitet werden.

■ Es dürfen keine Wörterbücher verwendet werden. Lies über unbekannte Wörter einfach hinweg, du wirst sehen, am Ende des Textes sind diese durch den Kontext klar geworden.

■ Meist hast du bei der Zentralmatura einen Bildimpuls zum Text. Schau dir diesen im Vorhinein an. Zusammen mit der Überschrift ist es dann meist relativ leicht, Vermutungen über den Inhalt des Textes anzustellen. Tu dies, damit du ungefähr weißt, was thematisch auf dich zukommen wird.

■ Eliminiere nach dem Ausschlussprinzip Überschriften und Sätze, die nicht zum Text gehören. Je weniger Möglichkeiten du zur Auswahl hast, desto leichter kommst du zu einer (richtigen) Entscheidung.

■ Nachdem du alle Aufgaben gelöst hast, schau dir noch einmal alles durch und hinterfrage deine eigenen Lösungen und Antworten kritisch.

■ Nicht vergessen: Eine falsche Antwort bringt genauso viel Abzug wie gar keine Antwort. Bevor du also eine Lücke leer stehen lässt, ist es besser, zumindest einen Tipp abzugeben.

Auf den folgenden Seiten findest du nun jede Menge *reading comprehensions*. Diese sind auf den Lehrplan der 6. Klasse AHS abgestimmt und entsprechen somit den Themengebieten, die deine Lehrerin/dein Lehrer im Laufe dieses Schuljahres behandeln wird. So kannst du also immer zu den Themen, die in der Schule gerade auf der Tagesordnung stehen, entsprechende Leseverständnisübungen machen und dir zusätzliches Wissen verschaffen, das du wiederum vielleicht in einen Schularbeitstext einbauen kannst.

Also, viel Spaß beim Lesen und Lösen der Übungen! ☺

RC 1: 50 CENT: MILLIONAIRE RAP STAR

Task 1 **Pre-reading: Word matching**

Match the nouns with the corresponding verbs or adjectives by writing the numbers in the boxes.

1. addiction	[ ] to be amazed	7. success	[ ] to introduce
2. criminal	[ ] to produce	8. talent	[ ] to manage
3. poverty	[ ] to commit a crime	9. decision	[ ] to be successful
4. signature	[ ] to be addicted to	10. adolescence	[ ] to be talented
5. amazement	[ ] to sign	11. introduction	[ ] to decide
6. producer	[ ] to be poor	12. management	[ ] to be an adult

Task 2 **Reading**

Read about the American gangsta rapper 50 Cent, then do the exercises on the next page.

You have surely already heard about 50 Cent, one of America's most famous rappers. Songs like *In Da Club* or *Candy Shop* have made this musician popular all over the world. But what else do you know about him? Go on reading in order to inform yourself about his life and his career.

Basically 50 Cent's life is an amazing story about somebody who has managed to overcome a very poor childhood to finally become top of the music business thanks to talent, hard work and a little bit of luck. The rap star was originally born Curtis James Jackson III in Queens, New York on July 6th, 1975. His childhood and early adolescence were characterised by the loss of his parents. He actually didn't know his father and his mother, a drug dealer, was killed when Jackson was only eight years old. Consequently he was brought up by his grandparents, also living together with numerous uncles and aunts.

At the age of 12 Curtis Jackson got in touch with drugs, a topic that was very popular in Black America at that time. In order to support his family and to obtain some money for himself, he started to sell crack, spending most of his days on the streets. He also took up boxing around that time. He loved doing that sport and he was really good at it. Unfortunately he permanently had to deal with the police. He was once arrested for having and keeping a gun and when he was found to sell drugs, he was sent to a boot camp for six months.

As far as music is concerned his first real breakthrough was in 2000. As Jackson had a real talent for music, and especially for rapping, he nearly signed a contract with Columbia Records. When he was involved in a shooting, however, Columbia decided to stop and cancel the contract as Jackson presented too much of a risk.

Jackson's next big chance came almost two years later. Rap superstar Eminem, who had spotted 50 Cent's huge talent, introduced him to a famous producer who immediately arranged a record deal. As a consequence his first commercial album *Get Rich Or Die Tryin* was released in February 2003 and became an immediate success. By now it has sold 13 million copies.

Of course, his tough and hard past is part of 50 Cent's image today. But there is much more to this gangsta rapper. He is a rather clever and successful businessman who managed to set up his own drinks company called Formula 50. Later on it was sold to Coca-Cola and 50 Cent got $ 100 million out of this deal. Other projects related to 50 Cent include video games, trainers and sport clothes, a body spray and even an autobiography.

Task 3　True/False/Justification

Tick the correct box and write down the first four words of the sentence supporting your decision!

		T	F	Justification
1.	When he was still young the rapper used to spend a lot of time with both his parents.	❏	❏	
2.	During his early childhood 50 Cent was basically raised by his father.	❏	❏	
3.	When he was 12 years old 50 Cent wanted to contribute to the family income by selling drugs.	❏	❏	
4.	Luckily the musician hardly ever got in touch with the police.	❏	❏	
5.	50 Cent's musical career was not really boosted before the millennium.	❏	❏	
6.	His first record company didn't want to work together with him as his behaviour was too unpredictable.	❏	❏	
7.	It was due to another famous rapper that 50 Cent finally signed his first record contract.	❏	❏	
8.	50 Cent's first album was only a modest and very moderate success.	❏	❏	
9.	By now the rapper has also brilliantly managed to set up other businesses.	❏	❏	

Task 4　Word matching

Match the words related to the topic of crime with the corresponding expressions by writing the numbers in the boxes.

1. gun ☐ to take something that doesn't belong to you without asking

2. murder ☐ a crime in which someone is killed with a gun

3. tough ☐ a place with strict discipline for young criminals

4. arrest ☐ to kill somebody

5. steal ☐ a weapon that fires bullets

6. boot camp ☐ this is what the police do with a person who has done something wrong

7. shooting ☐ a person who is rough, not kind and gentle

RC 2: ROBIN HOOD – BRITAIN'S BEST KNOWN MYSTERY MAN

Task 1 **Reading**

Read the following article, ignoring the gaps in the text.

Every nation has its heroes and gentlemen robbers. **1**_____ But Britain surely has the greatest one: Robin Hood, the noble thief who stole money from the rich in order to give it to the poor. He has been the country's number one folk hero for at least 600 years but who actually is – or rather said *was* – this mysterious man?

That's of course a tricky question to answer. **2**_____ So tracing back the name doesn't really solve the mystery. Also "Hood" was a widespread surname and consequently historians don't really know where to start. Secondly, the number of people who doubt Robin Hood's existence at all is countless and many are sceptical and deny that such a noble thief has ever existed. And if he really existed, the real Robin Hood has long been overtaken by the legend and the stories told about his brave and courageous actions.

But still, so far numerous poems, ballads and books have been written about him and he even appears in Shakespeare's play *The Two Gentlemen of Verona* (1590). For sure, Robin Hood is also part of our modern world as he features in at least six blockbuster movies, one of the last ones starring Russell Crowe, Cate Blanchett and Max von Sydow. As far as his popularity is concerned one is even tempted to compare him with Santa Clause. **3**_____

So what does the fictional Robin Hood look like and what does he do? **4**_____ It depends on the storyteller so no wonder that significant differences concerning his behaviour and his characteristics turn up if you read different stories or watch different movies. What they all have in common, however, is that they present a man who was believed to have lived during the time of King Richard the Lionheart (1157–1199). He was said to have owned a little farm near Sherwood Forest and he was supposed to spend most of his freetime hunting. When King Richard went on a crusade and his brother came to power, greedy men took away Robin Hood's farm.

5_____ Land was taken away from them and given to the Saxons and the whole power system turned out to be very unfair. As a result of all that Robin Hood fled to the forest where he started a new life – a life which he devoted to helping the poor. Soon he was joined by other men who were equally disappointed with these living conditions and on the basis of regular intervals the gang robbed wealthy people, stole their money and distributed it among the poor.

Robin Hood and his men were never caught. **6**_____ But whenever they robbed somebody, they came out of the forest like invisible creatures and disappeared like ghosts. No matter how hard the King's men tried to catch and arrest this noble thief, they didn't have the slightest chance against this man full of myth and mythos.

Task 2 **Summarising the theme**

Which of the following statements (A, B or C) best summarises the article above?

A	The article deals with Robin Hood's presentation in history books and ancient films.
B	The article presents a basic overview of Robin Hood's life, his actions and his doings.
C	The article describes in detail how Robin Hood robbed rich and wealthy people and distributed the money among the poor.

Task 3   Gap filling

You now find eight sentences (A–H). Six out of these eight sentences belong to the text. Read the article again and try to find out which ones they are and match them with the correct gap (numbers 1–6).

First of all because Robin or Robert was a common name in the Middle Ages.	A
It was the first time that brave men stood up for their rights and fought for the poor.	B
Unfortunately that's another difficult question to answer.	C
And every nation is proud to tell stories and myths about them.	D
King Richard's brother started several attempts to stop the thieving gang.	E
No child, at least not in Britain, is unfamiliar with Robin Hood.	F
Robin Hood never wanted to live a life like that so he was rather unhappy.	G
With this change in power the situation became worse for the poor people.	H

Task 4   Comprehension

Answer the questions in full and correct English sentences.

1. Why is Robin Hood called a "noble" thief?

2. In the Middle Ages, what was the problem with popular first names like Robin or Robert?

3. How do we see that Robin Hood is still popular in today's world?

4. Why do people compare Robin Hood with Santa Clause?

5. At what time do people believe Robin Hood lived?

6. Why was it never possible for the King's men to catch Robin Hood and his gang?

Task 5   Opposites

Find the correct opposites by writing the numbers in the boxes.

1. poor   ☐ afraid
2. courageous ☐ unimportant
3. fictional   ☐ wealthy
4. significant ☐ real

5. numerous   ☐ limited
6. countless ☐ admit
7. deny   ☐ same
8. different ☐ few

RC 3: TYPICALLY AMERICAN – STARBUCKS COFFEE

Task 1   Guessing the facts

You are going to read an article about Starbucks, the world's biggest coffee chain. Before you do so test your knowledge about coffee and complete the following sentences with the words from the box. Mind that this is only a guessing activity so don't worry if you don't get all the words correct!

bitter – taste – rainy – species – caffeine – coffee beans – half – density – beverages – roasted

1. Coffee is a brewed drink prepared from roasted seeds commonly called _____.

2. Due to its _____ content, coffee usually has a stimulating effect on humans.

3. Today coffee is one of the most popular _____ in the world.

4. The traditional method of planting coffee is to put about 20 coffee seeds into a hole at the beginning of the

   _____ season and then wait and watch them grow.

5. About _____ of them are eliminated naturally.

6. Usually there are two main _____ of coffee grown: arabica and robusta.

7. Robusta coffee tends to be _____ and has less flavour but a better body.

8. Coffee is usually sold and consumed in a _____ state.

9. The roasting process influences the _____ and changes the coffee bean.

10. The _____ of the coffee bean influences the strength of the coffee drink.

Task 2   Pre-reading: Word matching

Match the words with their definitions by writing the numbers in the boxes.

1. chain	☐	the place where a company has its headquarter
2. to be based in	☐	sweet stuff like cookies or brownies
3. panini	☐	a colloquial (slang) expression for glass
4. pastry	☐	it grants you access to university without paying for it
5. mug	☐	a group of stores belonging to the same company
6. tumbler	☐	small soft sandwiches filled for example with ham and cheese
7. nappy	☐	first layer of cloth worn by babies
8. scholarship	☐	a colloquial (slang) expression for cup

Task 3 Reading

If you think about Starbucks, what comes to your mind? Exactly! It's the association of a good cup of coffee probably flavoured with vanilla or hazelnut and some whipped cream. Yummy. You think about the comfortable ambiente and maybe a good chat with your friends. You recall the green round logo featuring the words "Starbucks Coffee" in big letters. And it strikes you that wherever you are, there is a Starbucks shop, too. But have you ever thought about why Starbucks is so successful and who the man responsible for this success actually is? Here we go with the facts:

Starbucks is an international coffee and coffeehouse chain based in Seattle, Washington, United States. It is the largest coffeehouse company in the world with 17.133 stores in 49 countries, including 11.068 in the United States, nearly 1.000 in Canada and more than 800 in Japan. The chain is popular for selling drip-brewed coffee, espresso-based hot drinks, other hot and cold drinks, coffee beans, ice cream, salads, hot and cold sandwiches and panini, pastry, snacks and items such as mugs and tumblers. Besides the company also markets books and music and many of the products are seasonal or specific to the location of the store.

But who has made and turned the company into what it is today? It's a man called Howard Schultz, nowadays almost 60 years old. The former quarterback with his big grin grew up in a low-income household with a very ambitious but poorly educated father who floated from job to job. One of the worst was delivering and picking up used nappies. However, Howard really learned from his father how to be a hard and honest worker and how to be able to look in the mirror each night and be proud of yourself and the things you have achieved. Time went by and due to a football scholarship Howard was able to attend and finish university. Soon afterwards he first set foot in a Starbucks shop and the moment he did so he had a vision. What followed were numerous years of nonstop success, rising sales figures and Howard was long considered a hero at Wall Street.

But times have changed and so has Starbucks. Due to the economic crisis expansion had to be stopped and consequently nearly 1.000 stores (mainly in the US) were closed. Today the idea is to individually design each store to fit with its local area. The former trend of unifying the Starbucks shops has reversed and now the goal is to give each store its individual characteristic and design.

For sure, nobody knows how Starbucks will develop in the future but one thing is certain indeed (and that's also one of the slogans on Starbucks' homepage):
Every day, we go to work hoping to do two things: share great coffee with our friends and help make the world a little better.

Task 4 Note taking

Answer the questions in not more than FOUR words. Don't try to form sentences, just write key words.

1.	What are common associations people have with Starbucks? Name at least three!	
2.	Where exactly could the first Starbucks shop be found?	
3.	Which kinds of food can be found and bought at a Starbucks shop?	
4.	Apart from food and beverages, which other things can be purchased at a Starbucks shop?	
5.	Why exactly was Howard Schultz' childhood problematic?	
6.	What has nowadays changed in the concept of the Starbucks shops?	

RC 4: HAVING NO MONEY DESTROYS YOUR LIFE

Task 1 **Reading**

Read the interview with Helen Shepherd, a social worker in Milwaukee, and the magazine Public Affairs.

Public Affairs: Mrs Shepherd, first of all thank you for taking some time to join us and for informing us about one of the most pressing issues these days: poverty among black women. You have been working as a social worker for more than two decades and you have surely experienced a lot. What would you say was the most unforgettable incident for you in all these years?

Helen Shepherd: At first, many thanks for giving me the opportunity to talk about this serious and important matter in public. You've asked for an unforgettable incident ... let me think. Well, actually it's impossible to only come up with one special happening that has remained unforgettable. There have been so many in the course of the last twenty years – good ones as well as bad ones. What I would like to start with, however, is one of my last cases in order to show you what it really means to be poor and how poverty can destroy your whole life. One of my last challenges was trying to help a black single mother of three. Her children were 9, 11 and 16 and she had been left by her husband after the birth of their youngest child. He had never really wanted to raise a family so no wonder he finally packed his stuff and disappeared.

Public Affairs: That really sounds hard. What was the name of the woman and how old was she?

Helen Shepherd: Clarissa was about 36 years old when I met her for the first time. It was shortly after the displacement from her house. She actually had a job at a supermarket where she really worked very hard for very little money. But she kind of liked doing that job and was not particularly unhappy. One day, however, a colleague accused her of having stolen some goods, nothing special, just some cosmetic items and a few magazines. She denied it and to tell the truth, I can't really say if she did it or not. It doesn't matter anyway.

Public Affairs: What happened next with her and especially the children?

Helen Shepherd: To make a long story short: Clarissa lost her job and couldn't pay the rent for her apartment. And after three months, in which she desperately tried to find a new job – she had to leave her home. The eviction (*Zwangsräumung*) didn't take long as the family didn't really possess a lot. What the people from the moving company did was basically carrying all the family's belongings out of the house and putting a "for rent" sign up. The rest was Clarissa's problem and she was left with it completely on her own.

Public Affairs: It's unbelievable to imagine something like that. What would you say is worst at such a moment?

Helen Shepherd: I've often heard that the hopelessness and frustration is the worst. The women feel like having ruined not only their but also their children's lives. Many turn to drugs and/or alcohol, others become depressive. And sometimes families fall apart as the children can't stand their mother's condition any longer.

Public Affairs: Is eviction especially a problem for black women or does that also affect men?

Helen Shepherd: It absolutely is a problem related to women. A recently published survey revealed that one of every 25 renter-occupied households in the city is evicted each year. In black neighbourhoods, the rate is one in 14. Besides eviction has become typical in the lives of poor black women as they are frequently left alone with their children.

Public Affairs: Mrs Shepherd, one last question: what has happened to Clarissa and her three children?

Helen Shepherd: Fortunately I could finally place them at an asylum for poor black women but we will have to see how the whole situation develops.

Public Affairs: Thank you for talking to us and all the best for your future and your next cases.

Helen Shepherd: You're welcome!

Task 2 **Multiple choice**

Tick the appropriate box so that your answer is correct according to the text.

1. For how long has Helen Shepherd been working as social worker?
   A For nearly 20 years. ❏
   B For exactly 20 years. ❏
   C For more than 20 years. ❏
   D For far more than 20 years. ❏

2. It's quite difficult for Helen Shepherd to just remember one unforgettable incident because ...
   A ... she has experienced so many good and bad things in her career. ❏
   B ... she has forgotten most of the former cases. ❏
   C ... she just remembers those cases that ended successfully. ❏
   D ... she doesn't want to think about former cases, no matter if good or bad ones. ❏

3. Why did Clarissa lose her job?
   A Because she accused a colleague of having stolen something. ❏
   B Because a colleague accused her of having stolen something. ❏
   C Because the manager saw her stealing something. ❏
   D Because she confessed that she had stolen something. ❏

4. What did the moving company do with Clarissa's stuff?
   A They sold her stuff and used the money for the last three months of rent. ❏
   B They put her stuff outside the house and then organised some self-storage for her. ❏
   C They emptied the house and then they tried to help Clarissa find something new. ❏
   D They just put Clarissa's things outside on the pavement and tried to hire the house again. ❏

5. Who is particularly affected by eviction?
   A Poor white women who don't want to have a husband. ❏
   B Poor white women who are being left by their husbands and have to care for children. ❏
   C Poor black women who have to care for their husbands. ❏
   D Poor black women who don't have a husband but have to care for children. ❏

6. How did Clarissa's case end?
   A She was sent to an asylum where she had to work hard. ❏
   B She was sent to an asylum for blacks who had been at prison before. ❏
   C She was sent to an asylum for poor black women who need help. ❏
   D She was sent to an asylum for poor white women who didn't want to work. ❏

7. What is the worst aspect about eviction?
   A That the mothers have to start looking for a new place where to live. ❏
   B That the families are sometimes torn apart and the mothers are hopeless. ❏
   C That the children don't want to move anywhere else. ❏
   D That the fathers might lose contact with their children. ❏

8. What happened to Clarissa's husband?
   A After the third child had been born he packed his stuff and left. ❏
   B After the second child had been born he packed his stuff and left. ❏
   C After the eviction had taken place he packed his stuff and left. ❏
   D He left before the birth of the third child as he didn't want to have three kids. ❏

RC 5: WHEN MOUNTAINEERING TURNS INTO AN OBSESSION

Task 1 High, higher, the highest

Look at the following names of mountains. Have you heard about any of them? Guess which one the highest is and number them. Start with the highest mountain, giving it number 1.

Dhaulagiri ☐   Makalu ☐

Lhotse ☐   K2 ☐

Mount Everest ☐   Kangchenjunga ☐

Nanga Parbat ☐   Cho Oyu ☐

Task 2 Pre-reading: Word matching

Match the words with the corresponding definitions by writing the numbers in the boxes.

1. mountaineering ☐   part of a very high mountain where there is only ice, also in summer

2. glacier ☐   height

3. crampon ☐   at least two people walking on a glacier and being connected with a rope

4. altitude ☐   the feeling of being sick when you are on very high mountains

5. altitude sickness ☐   to climb (high) mountains

6. rope team ☐   metallic pieces you put on your shoes to have good grip on snow and ice

Task 3 Reading

Read this autobiographic text, ignoring the gaps for the headlines.

1_____

I can remember when I was a kid I was absolutely not keen on walking or hiking. But, like every child, I kind of had to from time to time. However, I grew older and could finally decide on my own whether I wanted to go to the mountains or rather stay at home. At that time I mostly, if not to say always, opted for the second possibility. But times have changed, I turned into an adult and consequently also my hobbies, passions and interests have changed. By the way ... hello I'm Sonja and I'm 30 years old.

2_____

Actually I've always been keen on sports but until three years ago outdoor activities never used to be attractive for me. I prefered indoor sports and mostly did aerobics. Until, one day, I met an old school friend of mine whose passion was mountaineering. So he asked me if I wanted to join him on a tour in Styria. I thought why not giving it a try and was even looking forward to doing it. So I packed my backpack, put on my Nike sport shoes and was convinced to be perfectly equipped.

3_____

The tour onto the mountain in Styria really taught me a lesson. The things I had in my backpack were absolutely not the stuff I needed, I had the wrong food with me (imagine I had a pineapple cut into pieces with me and I almost starved while going up the mountain) and my super perfect Nike shoes were wet already after ten minutes. What a success! But still, it was fascinating and simply wonderful from the beginning to the end and I was really sad when we reached the car again and I had to go home.

4 _____

I knew that mountaineering was the thing I wanted to do. It had a fascination for me which I'm still today not able to describe. It's probably this mixture of very hard physical exercise and the silence and nature around you. As I wanted to improve my performance I started to do courses and trainings where I was taught how to use crampons, how to behave when you walk along a glacier in a rope team and how to save somebody on a glacier. I was so enthusiastic about all that and I would have liked to spend all my free time in the mountains. I also changed my equipment and bought the clothes I needed for really high mountains.

5 _____

In summer 2010 I finally fulfilled one of my greatest dreams – climbing the Mont Blanc (4.810 m) in France. It was actually not planned but the conditions and the circumstances were perfect for doing it. So I said yes and my partner and I started to plan the tour. It was a three-day trip to the summit and on the fourth day we returned. We didn't use the cable car but climbed the mountain from the valley. I didn't wash myself or brush my teeth for four days and we even spent one night outside in a bivvy (that's a small tent which you usually use for emergency situations in the mountains). And for sure, it was the greatest adventure I've ever experienced!

6 _____

Summarising I have to say that physically and mentally this was the hardest mountain I have ever climbed and at the very top I also had enormous problems with altitude sickness. I had a terrible headache, could hardly concentrate and felt sick all the time. But I would do it again without hesitating for a minute. My goal now is to go on discovering the Austrian mountains as they are also worth climbing and seeing. If I'm lucky, I might as well get the chance to climb the Matterhorn in Switzerland next summer. Let's see ... But who knows, maybe some time in the future I will get again the chance to climb a REALLY high mountain. ☺

Task 4 Matching headlines

In the text there are six gaps for the headlines of the paragraphs. Take a look at the headlines below and decide which headline (A–I) goes together with which paragraph (1–6). Mind that there are three headlines that do not fit.

Fulfilling my personal dream	A
Discovering myself and my passion	B
Improving my physical condition	C
Learning by doing	D
Being impatient with myself	E
Early beginnings	F
Putting it in a nutshell	G
Facing reality and experiencing what it's like	H
Failing the highest mountain of the Alps	I

RC 6: SWEATSHOPS – THE PRICE FOR YOUR CLOTHES IS HUMANITY

Task 1 Pre-reading: Word matching

Match the words with the corresponding definitions by writing the numbers in the boxes.

1. sweatshop	☐	to nag all the time/to talk about all the things you don't like
2. developing country	☐	killing and removing your unborn baby from your body
3. health insurance	☐	the person who is your boss and who pays your wages/salary
4. abortion	☐	a person who goes shopping somewhere and buys something
5. employer	☐	a problem that affects many other areas as well
6. refugee	☐	a factory with very poor and unfair working conditions
7. to complain	☐	makes it possible for you to go to the doctor without paying for it
8. customer	☐	it's another term for 3rd world country
9. a widespread problem	☐	a person who fled to another country

Task 2 Reading

Have you ever asked yourself where the clothes you are wearing come from and under which conditions they were produced? No? Well then read this report and find out about some unpleasant details.

First of all, most of the things we wear everyday were produced in so called developing or third world countries. As the name already indicates, these are poor countries where the living standard is not comparable to the one we enjoy here. The people there usually don't have a really good education and for some, especially for women, it's rather problematic to find a job. Many of them end up in places called sweatshops.

A sweatshop is a factory where the working conditions are extremely poor, unfair and in most cases even inhuman. The employers often employ refugees who have come to the respective country illegally. So usually they neither have any papers nor any rights. As a rule they are exploited, don't have any holidays and no health insurance. If they fall ill, they simply lose their job and are replaced. It's not seldom that sweatshop workers have to work far more than 12 hours per day and it's usually very sticky, smelly and hot inside the factory. Furthermore, women are regularly forced to have an abortion once they are pregnant. All that sounds barbarous and it's hardly possible to imagine how the workers can endure these conditions. There is also no use to complain as people only risk to lose their salary or, in worst case, their job.

Some years ago sweatshops were a widespread problem. Popular brands like *Nike* or *Levi's* had their goods produced in cheap sweatshops and then sold their products for expensive money to European customers. But luckily a lot has changed since then. During the last years strict regulations were introduced by the single governments and by now almost all the big companies take care about their image and try not to get in touch with the sweatshop topic. When talking about their production most companies say that fairness and human working conditions are those key words that are most important.

Let's hope that we can believe these companies. The only thing every single customer can do is to be a bit attentive and to watch out where the stuff we are wearing was produced. Maybe sometimes it's better to buy the more expensive T-shirt but to also have the knowledge that it was produced under fair conditions.

Task 3 True/False/Justification

Tick the correct box and write down the first four words of the sentence supporting your decision!

		T	F	Justification
1.	Developing countries are the same as industrialised countries; there's no difference.	❏	❏	
2.	The majority of our everyday clothes comes from poor, not industrialised countries.	❏	❏	
3.	A high number of workers (in developing countries) have no other chance than working in a sweatshop.	❏	❏	
4.	Usually refugees have the same rights as legal immigrants.	❏	❏	
5.	As a rule female sweatshop workers are treated better than male ones.	❏	❏	
6.	Only no-name labels are associated with the problem of producing their goods in sweatshops.	❏	❏	
7.	Famous brands don't care about the sweatshop topic.	❏	❏	

Task 4 Text completion

Read the summary of the article above and complete it with the words given (mind the extra words!).

> health insurance – cheaper – rules – new – controls – inhuman – human being – salary – denied – more expensive – rights – old

Sweatshops are not a _____ phenomenon. On the contrary, they have been existing for quite some

time. In earlier times, however, the problem was largely _____ and governments hardly

cared for the workers' rights. Fortunately this has changed and the workers' well-being and the observation of their

_____ are a major concern nowadays. It's also no longer possible for a worker not to have

a _____ _____. This ensures that once you fall ill or you have to go to a

hospital, you don't have to pay extra for it.

But still, regular _____ are necessary to make sure that the big companies really stick to

the rules. For the company it's of course much _____ to have their goods manufactured in a

sweatshop and because of this the profit they can make afterwards is enormous.

Nevertheless, it should be the _____ _____ that counts most and

not the profit and the money.

RC 7: PLASTIC SURGERY – AN ADDICTION?

Task 1 Prepositions and word matching

Complete with the correct prepositions and match the phrases with the translations by writing the numbers in the boxes provided.

1. to be addicted _____ something

2. to be responsible _____ something

3. to long _____ something

4. to crave _____ something

5. to carry _____ something

6. to be discontent _____ something

☐	sich nach etwas sehnen, etwas wollen
☐	von etwas abhängig sein, süchtig sein
☐	etwas durchführen, ausführen
☐	für etwas verantwortlich sein
☐	mit etwas unzufrieden sein
☐	sich nach etwas sehnen, etwas wollen

Task 2 Pre-reading: Text completion

Fill in the words from the box into the gaps. The first letter will help you but mind the extra words again.

> beauty ideal – dissatisfied – wealth – injecting – anaesthesia – liposuction – real – wrinkles – hurting pain –
> injection – risky – disturbed – pain killers – accident – lifting – cosmetic surgeon

1. The doctor who carries out plastic surgery is called a c_____ s_____.

2. Before any operation the patient is given an a_____.

3. Quite often patients feel a h_____ p_____ after an operation.

4. Sometimes patients are also d_____ with the result of the plastic surgery.

5. If you have a l_____, fat is removed from parts of your body.

6. These days body or face l_____ is also very popular to get rid of one's wrinkles.

7. Older people also often have their w_____ removed to look younger.

8. In the last few years the number of people i_____ Botox has increased largely.

9. Especially for young girls it's important to fit to the b_____ i_____.

10. P_____ k_____ should limit the patient's pain.

11. Some people have plastic surgery due to deformation after a car a_____.

12. In any case, plastic surgery is always a r_____ business.

Task 3   Reading

Read this newspaper article about the dangers of plastic surgery, ignoring the gaps in the text.

While just a few years ago it was a complete taboo topic, plastic surgery is nowadays fully accepted and accredited. Not only stars and celebrities have their faces lifted, Botox injected, fat removed and other smaller or bigger parts of their bodies changed. **1**_____ But at what point does having plastic surgery turn into an addiction? Read the report by Louisa Lowridge.

Plastic surgery has never been more popular before and these days people use to talk about it openly and in public. **2**_____ But first of all it's essential to distinguish between two types of plastic surgery: the one carried out after, let's say, an accident and the one carried out for pure cosmetical purposes. As far as the first type is concerned Dr. Antony Jenkins, plastic surgeon at the Medical Centre in Milwaukee, says, "It's fully understandable that those patients who had an accident and who consequently have to live with scars or body deformations want to carry out plastic surgery. For them it's usually the way back to their former lives and they need the surgery to feel self-confident and comfortable with their bodies again." **3**_____ But this need not always be the case and strongly depends on how severe the injuries and deformations are.

The second type of plastic surgery, however, is only and exclusively carried out because of people's vanity. Magazines and TV constantly put especially women under very much pressure as they permanently present current beauty ideals. **4**_____ For normal ordinary women it's almost impossible to live up to this ideal. What some of them do instead is helping mother nature and carrying out plastic surgery. According to Dr. Jenkins patients are most hesitant before the first plastic surgery. They have doubts concerning possible health risks and the financial burden. Once the first operation has been carried out successfully, these doubts are usually put aside and further operations follow. "I really have a big pool of patients, again primarily women, who come again and again and really get hooked on the feeling of improving their appearances", says Dr. Jenkins. "They long for the perfect body and are willing to do everything."

It's no surprise that unsuccessful plastic surgery is usually not talked about. "There are numerous doctors in the Czech Republic, Slovenia or Hungary who pretend to be plastic surgeons. In fact most of them have never carried out liposuction, breast enlargement or similar stuff in their careers. The problem with them is that they offer these operations at much cheaper prices and promise the patients the same result", Dr. Jenkins explains. **5**_____ If plastic surgery goes wrong, it can turn out to be life threatening and this, of course, must not be underestimated. So a basically easy operation – if not carried out in the right environment and by the right person – can turn into a life-threatening affair.

In the end it's up to everybody himself/herself whether he/she wants to have plastic surgery carried out. **6**_____ If they live a happier life afterwards or not, remains most probably unanswered.

Task 4   Gap filling

You now find eight sentences (A–H). Six out of these eight sentences belong to the text. Read the article again and try to find out which ones they are. Match them with the correct gaps (numbers 1–6).

When this type of plastic surgery is carried out, some parts of the expenses are covered by the patient's health insurance.	A
Also more and more ordinary people save all their money to be able to afford a change in their physical appearance.	B
If plastic surgery fails, the patients are often disfigured and depressed for the rest of their lives.	C
It's a phenomenon fully accepted by society.	D
Unfortunately nobody warns the patients that they expose themselves to significant health risks.	E
It's actually really understandable that women want to look like these beauty ideals.	F
Unfortunately these ideals feature very thin and skinny models that really seem to have the perfect body.	G
Without doubt, several risks remain and patients should at least inform themselves about potential dangers.	H

RC 8: WHAT MAKES TEENAGERS REALLY HAPPY?

Task 1 **Warm up**

Look at the following list of words. What makes YOU happy? Tick the things that are true for you. If you feel like, you might also make a ranking giving numbers from 1–10. Start with the one that is most important for you and mark it number 1.

- [ ] A caring family who always supports me.
- [ ] Friends I can really rely on.
- [ ] Going to parties every weekend.
- [ ] Drinking alcohol whenever I am out.
- [ ] Smoking cigarettes.

- [ ] Having a pet and caring for it.
- [ ] Having time for myself and my hobbies.
- [ ] Having enough pocket money.
- [ ] Being independent.
- [ ] Trying out new and crazy things.

Task 2 **Pre-reading: Word matching**

Match the words with the corresponding definitions by writing the numbers in the boxes.

1. party-pooper (slang)   [ ] somebody who is always afraid and frightened and doesn't take any risks

2. kidney and liver   [ ] somebody who has never fun and always worries about possible problems

3. coward   [ ] you are forced to always do what your friends do, even if you don't want

4. dehydration   [ ] inner organs of the human body

5. peer pressure   [ ] if you don't drink enough and your body doesn't have enough water

Task 3 **Reading**

The following article, taken from a youth magazine, deals with the different aspects that make teens happy.

Everybody wants to be happy. Everybody longs for happiness and the quest and search for it is most probably a life-long venture. If you ask people of different age what exactly it is that makes them happy, you will get very different answers. What we want to discuss here, however, is the question what makes teenagers happy. And still, even among teenagers the range of possible answers to this question is really wide.

According to a nation-wide survey carried out by Toronto's Youth Academy, an intact and good family background is important for almost 87% of all teenagers. The number rises of course, the younger the teens are. Generally it is to say that a loving and caring family environment contributes to feelings of safety and well-being. If they grow up in an intact family, teens feel like having somebody they can rely on in every situation and that gives them a feeling of happiness.

What else? It's hardly a surprise that friendship ranks second in the factors accounting for happiness. Having friends and being part of a group are essential for teens as that further develops their social skills. If a child grows up without close friends, he or she will soon realise a lack in social interaction. What is interesting in this context, by the way, is that the number of close friends does not play any role. It's the existence of friends at all that either makes us happy or – in case of absence – unhappy.

Finding an answer to what makes teenagers unhappy is at least as interesting as posing the question the other way round. Several aspects can lead to teenagers' unhappiness. The first, and probably most surprising one, is the fact that teens whose parents smoke tend to be unhappy (if they don't smoke themselves of course).

Quite often the use – or rather the abuse – of drugs makes teens feel miserable. Many teenagers feel like they have to give it a try taking drugs simply due to peer pressure. They are afraid to be regarded as party-poopers or losers if they don't follow the crowd's mainstream.

Trying out drugs (this can also be in the form of alcohol) sometimes also happens out of pure curiosity. Teenagers are nosy about the effects of certain party drugs or alcohol and they want to experience this feeling for themselves.

There's actually nothing to say against trying out certain things and in a certain limit. It only turns out to be problematic if the teens take the wrong type of drug or simply don't know when to stop. *Ecstasy* (short form is only *E*) is an example for this. The dangerous aspect about that drug is that it blocks your blood vessels so if you dance and sweat a lot, and if you don't drink enough water, you are dehydrated and collapse. *Ecstasy* can also strongly damage your liver and kidneys and can even lead to coma. So you better don't play around with that one.

Task 4 Note taking

Answer the questions in not more than FOUR words. Don't try to form sentences, just write key words.

1.	How long does it usually take to find out what makes people happy?	
2.	Why is the family for most of the teens the number one happiness factor?	
3.	Why is friendship also very important for the teenagers?	
4.	What happens to a child that grows up in a limited and isolated environment?	
5.	Which negative impact does peer pressure have on single teenagers?	
6.	Name two factors why teenagers try out drugs (no matter in which form).	
7.	When does taking drugs turn into a problem? Give two reasons!	
8.	While being under the influence of *Ecstasy*, when is it likely that your body dehydrates?	
9.	What are the worst side effects of taking (too much) *Ecstasy*? Name at least two!	

RC 9: IMPOSSIBLE TO BE HAPPY – YOUTH UNEMPLOYMENT

Task 1 Pre-reading: Word matching

Match the phrases with the corresponding explanations by writing the numbers in the boxes.

1. unemployment	☐	to have a job and earn money regularly
2. to be employed	☐	to deliver newspapers to people's houses
3. employer	☐	the money you get for your work
4. wages/salary	☐	to give somebody a job
5. to have a paper route	☐	the state of not having a job and not receiving any money
6. to employ somebody	☐	the person who is your boss

Task 2 Reading

Read about one of the most hot-spot topics for young Americans these days.

Think about the following scene: an American teenager cycling happily along the streets of a pretty green suburb and throwing newspapers onto people's front porches. That sounds familiar, doesn't it? But it's a scene that tends to disappear these days as since the financial crisis, unemployment has risen dramatically, especially among young people.

When just considering America, unemployment has increased by 10% since 2009. 16–24 year old teenagers were particularly hit by this crisis as the unemployment rates have almost doubled for them. There are basically two reasons for this phenomenon. One is that jobs carried out by teens or people in their early twenties are often in industries like manufacturing, building and retails. The problem is that especially these industries were hit by the recession very hard. Banks no longer gave credits, so businesses and individuals had less

money to spend. Whole companies had to close down and the number of highly qualified workers who lost their jobs was incredible. This directly led to the second reason for youth unemployment: these experienced workers started to take over jobs that were usually carried out by teens. They had to do that in order to be able to nourish their families. When having the choice between a job candidate with lots of work experience and an inexperienced teenager, employers of course opted for the qualified staff. Poor luck for the teens …

Nowadays even newspaper routes are done by actually well-educated adults. In the 1990s nearly 60% of newspaper routes were taken by teenagers, compared with just 20% today. So times have obviously really changed.

Sometimes the difficulty of finding a job also depends on your origin and culture. Nationally, some 17% of high

school students have part-time jobs, but the figure for African-Americans is lower than 9%. Furthermore, teens from poor families are less likely to find jobs than those whose parents are well off. It seems as if, at least for some teenagers, it's not enough to handle and come to terms with the economic crisis but they also have to deal with racial and social prejudices and face them during their struggle to find work. What a hard and unfair life!

Fortunately teens have realised all these problems and the changing trends and they react to this situation. Nowadays many decide not to directly enter the job market after high school but stay on to further improve their qualifications. Today, 83% of 16–19-year-olds are still at school, compared with 78% ten years ago. In the end, this could be good for the economy because when businesses start to expand again, they are going to need qualified people.

Task 3 True/False/Justification

Tick the correct box and write down the first four words of the sentence supporting your decision!

		T	F	Justification
1.	There has been a significant rise in American unemployment rates since 2010.	❏	❏	
2.	Youth unemployment can basically be explained by two major reasons.	❏	❏	
3.	Jobs in manufacturing, building and retail were hardly affected by the crisis and cuts.	❏	❏	
4.	Only businesses and companies had problems and shortcuts due to the economic crisis.	❏	❏	
5.	Skilled workers carried out jobs meant for teens because otherwise they wouldn't have been able to nourish their families.	❏	❏	
6.	Your background and your origin often simplify your chances to find a job.	❏	❏	
7.	Coming from a wealthy family background is definitely helpful when looking for a job.	❏	❏	
8.	The majority of the young generation is ignorant towards the difficulties related to finding a decent job.	❏	❏	
9.	In the long run businesses will need skilled and qualified employees.	❏	❏	
10.	The latest tendency among teens is to try to achieve extra qualifications after high school.	❏	❏	

Task 4 Which job at which age?

Look at the following jobs. Which job can you carry out from which age on (in Austria)? Write 13 (at the age of 13), 14 (at the age of 14), 16 (at the age of 16) or 18 (at the age of 18) into the corresponding boxes.

❏	work in a grocery store	❏	work in a restaurant
❏	work in an office	❏	work at your parents' company
❏	deliver magazines	❏	work at a gas station
❏	work as security guard	❏	work at a baseball park
❏	work as a baby-sitter	❏	deliver parcels by car
❏	sell cinema tickets	❏	wash your dad's car
❏	give tutoring lessons	❏	give swimming lessons
❏	deliver newspapers	❏	mow your neighbour's lawn
❏	do any work at night	❏	animate tourists

RC 10: HAPPY AND LUCKY: BEYONCÉ – TODAY'S BIGGEST POP STAR

Task 1 Pre-reading: Word matching

Match the phrases with the corresponding explanations by writing the numbers in the boxes.

1. achievement   ☐   a prize for the things you have achieved in your life

2. inauguration   ☐   to have a gig on TV

3. medical equipment   ☐   to put an album on the market/ready for the audience

4. to appear on TV   ☐   to write your name below an important document

5. to rename   ☐   positive things you have already reached in your life

6. an award   ☐   to change a name

7. to rehearse   ☐   to be part of something/to be associated with something

8. to sign   ☐   celebration that officially turned Obama into the president of the USA

9. to release an album   ☐   things doctors and nurses need in hospitals and for surgeries

10. to be involved in sth.   ☐   to train/to practise

Task 2 Reading

The following article is going to present a portrait of top musician Beyoncé Knowles.

She is young, charismatic and more than good looking. She not only has the perfect body and face, but also the perfect voice. **1**_____ Clearly, who is being talked about is Beyoncé Giselle Knowles. The American R&B, pop, funk and soul singer was born in Texas (Houston) in September 1981. With her still young age she has reached enormous success turning her into a superstar.

No doubt, Beyoncé is one of the biggest names in music today. **2**_____ She has sold more than 120 million records, has won nearly 100 awards including 16 Grammys. She has also got her own fashion house (it's called *Deréon* by the way) and she has acted in films like *Dreamgirls*.

No wonder that a superstar like her has got millions of fans all over the world. **3**_____ The tickets for live concerts are usually sold within a few minutes and her live performances are a real experience.

But let's take a closer look at the beginning of her career. Beyoncé's father, Mathew, was a salesman for medical equipment and her mother, Tina, was a hair stylist. **4**_____ With seven years she surprised everybody singing John Lennon's *Imagine*. She joined her first rock group at the early age of eight. The group consisted of six girls and they called themselves *Girlz Tyme*. Soon they appeared on a star search show on TV and it didn't take long until the group renamed themselves as *Destiny's Child*. Beyoncé's father became the girls' manager.

Success, however, didn't come overnight and they really had to work hard. Rehearsing four hours per day was not seldom and not even after having signed the contract with Columbia did they stop to work so tirelessly. Even though their first album was quite successful, their second album (released in 1999) turned the girl group into real superstars and idols. **5**_____ Nevertheless, problems between the group's members and Beyoncé's father increased and consequently they split up in 2005. Beyoncé's solo career already started in 2003.

In public, the pretty American singer is of course the centre of attention. Her private life presents a contrast to this glamorous image: she keeps her private life strictly private and tries not to be involved in any scandals. She has been together with rapper Jay-Z (his real name is Shawn Carter) since 2002 and the couple married in 2008. **6**_____

Beyoncé seems to have it all – a fantastic career, lots of money, wonderful houses, good looks and a famous husband. She definitely belongs to the happy and lucky ones. If anything is missing in her life? Well, probably only the fact that she can't live an ordinary, everyday life. In an interview in 2008 she kind of complained that sometimes she feels trapped in her own life. She also admits that it's sometimes difficult to switch between the vamp she is on stage and the nice and well-behaved young woman she is in reality. Well, if these are her only worries, we can probably really call her happy!

Task 3   Gap filling

You now find eight sentences (A–H). Six out of these eight sentences belong to the text. Read the article again and try to find out which ones they are. Match them with the correct gaps (numbers 1–6).

We only have to take a closer look at her achievements to realise that.	A
They kept the wedding in New York secret and reporters only found out about the ceremony six months later.	B
Beyoncé's musical talent was clear from a very early age onwards.	C
It's not clear whether Beyoncé is happily married but she is going to give an interview discussing the matter in detail in a few weeks.	D
Do you already ask yourself who this person might be?	E
US President Barack Obama is one of them and she even sang at his inauguration in 2009.	F
It took quite a long time for Beyoncé's parents to find out about her talent and love for music.	G
Their third album, however, went straight to number one in the US charts.	H

Task 4   Summarising the theme

Which of the following statements (A, B or C) best summarises the article? Tick the correct box!

A	The article presents a detailed description of Beyoncé's career, from early age onwards until today.	
B	The article deals with a personal presentation of Beyoncé's private life and her affairs.	
C	The article gives a general overview about the superstar's life and the milestones in her career.	

Task 5   Defining the audience

Where do you think would an article like that be most likely published? Tick the correct box!

A	The article might be found on Beyoncé's homepage.	
B	The article is probably published in a youth magazine with a possible focus on music.	
C	The article could possibly be found in an online Newsletter for classical and alternative music.	

RC 11: ELECTRONIC WASTE: A 21ST CENTURY PROBLEM

Task 1 **Reading**

Read the following interview between Dr. Michael Stains, an expert on the topic of environment, and the magazine "Go Green" which appears once a month to inform people about environmental dangers.

Go Green: Dr. Stains, first of all thank you for doing this interview with us. Let me get straight to the point: today's topic is waste. There are lots and lots of English words for the things we throw away but what's actually the difference between them? Or is there no difference at all?

Dr. Stains: Well, rubbish includes food you throw away, old newspapers, empty tins and bottles – everything you put in a dustbin or recycling bin. Garbage is simply the American word for rubbish and trash is yet another one, also American. Waste is the word you use to describe material that is no longer used, or which comes from producing something. We talk about nuclear waste or industrial waste, just to give you two examples.

Go Green: Or about electronic waste which is the topic of this month's special series. What actually is electronic waste? Can you explain that for our readers?

Dr. Stains: That's easy to explain. Many people in developed or industrial countries need a new computer or laptop every two or three years. The lifespan for mobile phones and smart phones is even shorter. This means that Europeans and Americans produce approximately 14 kilograms of electronic waste per person every year. And China is not far behind. Adding up their electronic waste as

well, we end up with about 20 to 50 million tons globally. It's useless to say that this is incredible and actually unbelieveable!

Go Green: Where does all that electronic waste go? I mean, what happens with it?

Dr. Stains: Some of this hi-tech trash is dumped in landfills but most of it is shipped to the Third World in order to be recycled cheaply. The biggest problem of e-waste, however, is the fact that it is not even half as green and clean as it looks like.

Go Green: What do you mean? Recycling e-waste sounds good, doesn't it? Are there any problems or dangers related to it? And if yes, which ones?

Dr. Stains: Actually there are loads of dangers. This electronic waste should be handled with extreme care but in fact it is not. Backyard recycling firms in India and Nigeria do not even know about the ecological risks. What they do is simply burn the electronic hardware to separate the plastic from the metals.

Go Green: Which effects does that have, on the environment as well as on the humans?

Dr. Stains: Well the burning process sends clouds of dioxins and other toxins into the air and I think there's no need to say that this is

fatal for our atmosphere and the ozone layers. As far as the humans are concerned who breathe in all these fumes on a regular basis, they are in danger of suffering from cancer, liver diseases, kidney failure, asthma and eczemas. And I'm sure that there are also numerous other undetected illnesses!

Go Green: So why do they go on working with these substances?

Dr. Stains: Because they simply need the money. Electronic waste is a big business in the world's poorest countries and thousands of poor adults and children are forced to work in this recycling industry because they don't have any other chances. For sure, they are happy to make some money and be able to nourish their families but workers often pay with their health, ignoring the dangers and the harm they do to themselves and their bodies.

Go Green: Is there a way out of this dilemma?

Dr. Stains: One way of making electronic waste safer would of course be to invest money and build adequat recycling factories. Another one would be to develop more eco-friendly products which is already happening.

Go Green: Thank you Dr. Stains for this interesting and informative interview.

Task 2 Sequencing

Put the sentences into the correct order to get a short summary of the interview you've just read.

	This is basically due to the fact that people in rich countries regularly need new computers and mobiles.
	Unfortunately they don't know how dangerous that is, for the humans as well as the nature.
	But the people in these poor countries don't know how to recycle e-waste correctly.
1	The problem that these days too much waste is produced is not new.
	The useless electronic stuff is shipped to Third World Countries where it is recycled.
	But they won't stop doing that as they urgently need the money to support their families.
	They expose themselves to poisonous fumes and risk to get cancer or other incurable diseases.
	What they do is to burn the stuff to separate the plastic from the metal.
	What is new, however, is the fact that the amount of electronic waste has risen dramatically.

Task 3 Finding out people's opinions

Read through the short comments people give on the topic of recycling and environmental protection. Then decide which of the three statements (A, B, or C) best summarises the person's opinion.

Eva Meyers: I do think that we have to take care of the environment. I mean if we ruin our planet, what will happen to the next generations? What will their lives look like? And apart from that I think that we simply don't have the right to be so ignorant concerning environmental problems.

A In Mrs. Meyers' opinion people should protect the environment so that they have a good lifetime.

B Mrs. Meyers thinks that, for future generations, it would be unfair not to protect the environment.

C The woman is uncertain what to think about a topic that has such wide-reaching consequences.

Jacob Ronald: Personally I think that protecting the environment is extremely important. I do as much as I can like going to work by bus and recycling my waste. I separate paper, glass bottles, organic waste and metal. I don't understand people who are not interested in environmental matters.

A Mr. Ronald separates his waste but apart from that he is not really enthusiastic about that matter.

B The man avoids going by bus on a regular basis.

C He thinks about how to save the environment and tries to behave and act environmentally friendly.

Marc Sleigh: To tell the truth there's actually nothing that interests me less that saving the environment and recycling my waste. Mother Earth will outlive us anyway so why should we bother? There are much more important things to care about.

A Marc Sleigh almost always tries to protect and save the environment.

B He hardly ever worries about what can be done to improve the state of Mother Earth.

C The man actually never thinks about possible solutions for environmental problems.

RC 12: WHAT'S AN NGO? ... TALKING ABOUT AMNESTY

Task 1 Warm up

How much do you already know about Amnesty International? Look at the following sentences and tick the ones that you think are true for the organisation.

❏ Amnesty helps endangered animals.

❏ They fight to stop violence against women.

❏ Amnesty defends poor people's rights.

❏ It is their goal to abolish death penalty.

❏ They care for everybody having a decent job.

❏ Amnesty protects the rights of immigrants.

❏ Amnesty regularly distributes food.

❏ They are against any kind of torture.

❏ They care about the rights of refugees.

❏ Amnesty only protects the rights of children.

Task 2 Pre-reading: Facts and figures about Amnesty International

Test your knowledge about Amnesty. Can you complete the sentences with the words from the box?

lobbying – non-profit – United Kingdom – 2.2 – lawyer – independent – candle – human – headquarters

1. Amnesty International is a well-known _____ rights organisation.

2. As it is _____ from the government, Amnesty is a non-governmental organisation.

3. It was founded in the _____ _____ in July 1961.

4. Amnesty's _____ are in London.

5. They have about _____ million members and supporters worldwide.

6. Their methods range from media attention to _____ and campaigns.

7. Amnesty's motto is as follows: *It's better to light a* _____ *than to curse the darkness.*

8. It's characteristic for Amnesty that they are a _____-_____ organisation.

9. Peter Benenson, a labour _____, founded Amnesty International.

Task 3 Reading

Read the following text taken from an information brochure about Amnesty International. Ignore the gaps.

1_____

Amnesty International is a worldwide movement which is independent of any government (that's why it's called NGO ... non-governmental organisation), any political party, ideology, economic interest or religious belief. Their mission is to prevent and terminate abuses of human rights and to demand justice for those whose rights have been violated. Among other aspects they take action against any type of human rights violation, no matter if the people in question are immigrants or poor.

2_____

Amnesty seeks the release of so-called "prisoners of conscience". These are men and women imprisoned for their political beliefs, race or religion even though they are not guilty of any violence or wrongdoing. They demand fair and early trials for all such prisoners and also fight against death penalty which is, unfortunately, still carried out in many countries. Furthermore they oppose torture and any other kind of inhuman and humiliating treatment or punishment of prisoners. Besides Amnesty tries to find out about people who have "disappeared", probably out of political or religious reasons.

3_____

As mentioned above, Amnesty is strictly against torture which is still very common in certain countries. Amnesty International and other human rights organisations have been campaigning against torture for almost 40 years in more than 60 countries. While in earlier times torture was purely physical punishment, it has now taken up a completely different form. Nowadays torture is basically carried out on a mental level. This means that people are, for example, deprived of sleep until they finally go crazy. Or they are locked up in completely dark and silent chambers until they lose their senses. Yet another form is to make the victims listen to dripping water until they eventually go mad. The methods these days are unlimited and even though no physical harm is done to them, they have to endure enormous distress.

4_____

It's extremely hard, if not to say impossible, for people who have experienced torture to live a normal life again afterwards. Usually they turn into very frightened and sceptical individuals who even mistrust their own families. It's not uncommon that couples break up, children are neglected and the people who were tortured end up leading a life in frustration and isolation. Seen from this point of view, torture also creates long-term damages (traumatic disorders, anxiety disorders) that must not be underestimated.

5_____

When help is needed, campaigns are organised to mobilise public opinion. These can take the form of individual, country or thematic campaigns. Throughout the years many techniques have been developed, such as direct appeals (letter writing for example), media and publicity work and public demonstrations. Quite often fund raising goes hand in hand with campaigning. In urgent situations Amnesty calls on existing networks or crisis response networks. For all other matters it relies on its members.

6_____

Finally, in the field of international human rights organisation (of which there are far more than 300) Amnesty has the longest history and the broadest name recognition and is believed by many to set standards for the movement as a whole. So, let's never stop supporting this organisation that has already changed so many lives to the positive! And who knows – maybe one day you also work for Amnesty and the realisation of its goals.

Task 4 **Matching headlines**

In the text there are six gaps for the headlines of the paragraphs. Now take a look at the headlines below and decide which headline (A–H) goes together with which paragraph (1–6). Mind that there are two headlines that do not fit.

The different forms torture can take	A
Amnesty and the "prisoners of conscience"	B
Torture and the change on human behaviour	C
What's the use of Amnesty International?	D
Being innovative – defining the standard	E
Giving the correct definition	F
How is help actually organised?	G
Torture methods in earlier times	H

RC 13: AMNESTY INTERNATIONAL: DID YOU KNOW THAT ...?

Task 1 **Pre-reading: Combining sentences**

Combine the following sentences by writing the correct numbers into the boxes.

1. If you work on a voluntary basis, you □ that you can make the world a better place.

2. People who work for free mostly □ their help and support is needed and helpful.

3. If you have an idealistic attitude, you believe □ don't get any money for the things you do.

4. In case you join Amnesty International you □ you give it to a charity organisation to help.

5. Amnesty members are fully convinced that □ usually have to pay a membership fee.

6. If you donate money, □ do that out of very idealistic reasons.

Task 2 **Reading**

Read the interview with 32 year old Jeremy Coldham, a voluntary member of Amnesty International, and the reporter of a human rights magazine called "Just Fair".

Just Fair: Jeremy, in "real life" you work with computer hardware and special Internet features in a British computer company. Apart from that you have been a voluntary member of Amnesty International for eight years. What can you first of all tell us about Amnesty's foundation?

Jeremy: Amnesty International was started in 1961 with a newspaper article by the British lawyer Peter Benenson. He called on people everywhere to work for the release of thousands of men and women imprisoned all over the world because of their political and religious beliefs. There was an enormous response to his work and Amnesty International soon became the world's largest human rights organisation.

Just Fair: Interesting. But what actually happens when somebody is arrested out of unfair reasons? How does Amnesty react in such a case?

Jeremy: When news of an arrest reach Amnesty, they talk with the person in question and try to find out if the arrested is a prisoner of conscience. Then the prisoner is "adopted" by one member of the Amnesty group. As a next step letters and telegrams are sent to the government, signatures for international petitions are collected and money is raised which is then needed to get the arrested out of prison.

Just Fair: Jeremy, you've just mentioned money. I think it might be interesting to get some more information about where Amnesty actually gets its money from. How exactly does that work?

Jeremy: First of all, Amnesty International is a completely independent organisation and they trust in broad public support. This means that the group gets no money from governments or political parties. The hundreds of thousands of bounties that sustain Amnesty's work come from the pockets of its members, that means people like me, as well as the public, other organisations, foundations and companies. The money available is then spent on research and action, campaigning costs, human rights meetings and administration costs.

Just Fair: Does the organisation also receive donations?

Jeremy: Yes, sure. Donations are extremely important and I think if people stopped donating money, Amnesty would have a big problem.

Just Fair: I see. Jeremy, my last question is about the voluntary members. Who are these people and what exactly is their motivation to work without receiving payment?

Jeremy: Amnesty International members are very different from each other and you can find all types of people joining the organisation. They are young and old, black and white and have the most different jobs you can imagine. You may find politicians, factory workers, doctors, housewives, farmers, journalists, teachers and students. Simply everybody. And their motivation is easy to explain: these are people who are very idealistic and who want to help that every person lives in freedom. Today there are more than 2.2 million members in 150 countries.

Just Fair: Thanks a lot for talking to us Jeremy and all the best for your future!

Task 3 True/False/Justification

Tick the correct box and write down the first four words of the sentence supporting your decision!

		T	F	Justification
1.	With a newspaper article Peter Benenson wanted to activate and motivate people to help others who were in trouble.	❑	❑	
2.	But unfortunately hardly anybody was really interested in working for Amnesty.	❑	❑	
3.	Usually the government "adopts" prisoners (of consciousness).	❑	❑	
4.	Amnesty is financed by its members and (public) organisations.	❑	❑	
5.	Instead of spending it Amnesty usually saves the money for urgent crisis.	❑	❑	
6.	In order to operate sufficiently Amnesty also largely relies on people's donations.	❑	❑	
7.	Voluntary Amnesty members are all people working in social jobs.	❑	❑	
8.	Anybody can work for and support Amnesty International.	❑	❑	
9.	It's essential that Amnesty members are not egoistic and selfish.	❑	❑	
10.	Today there are almost 3 million members working for Amnesty.	❑	❑	
11.	Originally Jeremy works with computer software and special Internet features.	❑	❑	

RC 14: FACING MULTICULTURAL BRITAIN

Task 1 Pre-reading: Word formation

The following nouns are taken from the article below. Complete the chart with the missing words.

ADJECTIVE	NOUN	GERMAN TRANSLATION (of the noun)
	patience	
	tolerance	
	adaption	
	poverty	
	persecution	
	abundance	

Task 2 Reading

Read the article about what life is like when people from different origins live together.

1_____

Life in a multicultural country like Britain is not always easy. Culture clashes and divided opinions about lifestyle are part of the daily life and the different ethnic groups and communities need lots of patience and tolerance to handle this situation. Report by Cathrine Magpie.

2_____

Something like a "united Britain" does actually not exist because too many foreign influences dominated this country in the past. Through conquest, trade, migration, travel and asylum the country constantly changed and is still today in a state of permanent adaption.

3_____

Nowadays, there are more than 37 different ethnic groups, each presenting more than 10.000 people. So currently more than 300 languages are spoken in a relatively small country like Great Britain. Despite these high numbers of ethnic groups, they are all well-integrated in and part of British society. The countries where the immigrants originally come from are very different. These are for example India, the Caribbean, Ireland, Iraq, Afghanistan or Bosnia. The reasons for moving to another country are mostly the same: people want to flee from poverty or persecution, or they search for abundance and a better life.

4_____

Even though Great Britain needs its immigrants and they make up an essential and important part of society, there are also difficulties and problems. In fact, lots of immigrants are faced with rejection, racism and segregation. This is especially the case when it is obvious that they are not from England (for example black people). For them it's very hard to find a decent housing and a job and they are permanently exposed to ridiculous prejudices.

5_____

The situation is much easier for their children. Once settled in the new country (in this case Great Britain) children of immigrants grow up like locals. They take up the new language (English) from the very beginning and they usually receive a good general education. It's easy for them to make friends and finding a job later on doesn't present the slightest challenge. The problem they have to face, however, is that sometimes they are torn between the two cultures. On the one hand they grow up being taught their original native culture. They experience this culture within family boundaries. But on the other hand they are part of modern English society. This sometimes leads to tremendous discrepancies.

6_____

In order to fight against racism some Brits discussed changing their national flag called Union Jack. The idea was to include the colour black in order to represent the black people living in the UK and to symbolise that society is open-minded towards immigrants (not only blacks of course). This, however, just remained an idea. But still, the message is clear: it's a country of equal opportunities for everyone.

Task 3 Matching headlines

In the text there are six gaps for the headlines of the paragraphs. Take a look at the headlines below and decide which headline (A–H) goes together with which paragraph (1–6). Mind that there are two headlines that do not fit.

Ethnic groups today	A
The lives of second generation immigrants	B
Making blacks happy: the British flag	C
Problems immigrants have to face	D
First generation versus second generation	E
The British flag as solution	F
The past influencing the present	G
When different cultures come together	H

Task 4 Text completion

Based on what you have just read, complete the following text with the correct information. The first letter of the missing words is given and should help you.

Nowadays the number of immigrants living in Great Britain is very h_____. They come from

d_____ countries but their reasons to immigrate are very s_____: they hope to live a

b_____ life, to be able to nourish their families and to f_____ a good job. Sometimes immigrants

also had to leave their country because of w_____ or religious/political p_____. However, once

they arrived in the n_____ country, they often have to deal with a very different life. They have to get used

to d_____ morals and customs. They also have to learn the new l_____ which is sometimes more

difficult than originally expected. Quite often immigrant families stay there for the rest of their l_____.

Their c_____ grow up being so-called second generation immigrants. They usually have a much

e_____ life than their parents but they also have to face and handle certain p_____.

Unfortunately d_____ is still widespread, not only in the UK but also in many other countries.

RC 15: NEW LAWS TO REGULATE ALCOHOL CONSUMPTION

Task 1 **Pre-reading: Jumbled expressions**

Find the correct combinations to get some phrases and expressions related to the topic of alcohol.

A	B
drink alcohol – get addicted – risk severe being under – dead – a bunch to sober – alcohol – to be – to feel	the influence of alcohol – drunk – intoxicated to drinking – up – consumption – sick regularly – health damages – of drunks

_____	_____
_____	_____
_____	_____
_____	_____
_____	_____

Task 2 **Reading**

In the following article you are going to find out about consequences of too much alcohol consumption.

Every little child knows that too much alcohol is bad for you. Nevertheless the number of British teenagers (and even children) who regularly consume alcohol rises constantly, making it hardly possible for them to spend a night out without getting drunk. The government has observed this tendency for quite some time and is now planning to introduce stricter laws to regulate alcohol in pubs, restaurants and advertising campaigns.

Especially so-called alcopops have enjoyed immense popularity in the last time. These are sweet alcoholic drinks (e.g. *Barcardi Breezer*) that teenagers particularly like. Different flavours are on offer and the tricky aspect is that – because of the big amount of sugar – many teens don't realise in the first place that they are already drunk. Only after some time, when they go to the toilet for example, do they find out about their critical condition.

But what can be done against more and more teenagers frequently consuming alcohol? How can this innocuous behaviour be stopped? There has already been a call for warning labels to be stuck on bottles containing alcohol, similar to those used on cigarette packs. Whether this would have a deterrent effect or not is uncertain. Another option is a complete ban on advertising, including cinemas and posters. According to experts, drastically putting up the prices for alcohol would also help limiting the number of addicted youngsters. Checking pubs and shops, if they stick to the rule of not selling alcohol to under-18s, is also an option officials plan to carry out.

Especially doctors are also worried. They start to see a rapide increase in serious liver diseases in young people because of alcohol. And the treatment for this is very expensive for the health service. A recently published report of the government states that the alcohol misuse costs Britain 20 billion Pounds each year and led to 600,000 violent crimes, 360,000 cases of domestic violence, 22,000 premature deaths and at least 1,000 suicides.

Finally, we must not forget that whatever alcohol we drink, only ten minutes after having consumed the drink, more than 50% of the alcohol will be in our bloodstream. And after one hour all the alcohol will have been absorbed. Last but not least, being fully tanked up kills thousands of brain cells.

Task 3 **Multiple choice**

Tick the appropriate box so that your answer is correct according to the text.

1. What is an alcopop?

   A It is a popular non-alcoholic drink that contains lots of sugar. ❏

   B It is an unpopular alcoholic drink that contains little sugar. ❏

   C It is a popular alcoholic drink that contains huge amounts of sugar. ❏

   D It's an unpopular alcoholic drink that contains less sugar than other drinks. ❏

2. After having drunk alcopops, when do the teenagers usually find out that they are drunk?

   A Immediately afterwards, no matter if they stand up or remain seated. ❏

   B Shortly afterwards but only if they stand up to go to the toilet. ❏

   C A long time afterwards as alcopops take hours until they are absorbed. ❏

   D Some time later, when the teens stand up again, for example. ❏

3. Why is getting drunk on a regular basis described as "innocuous behaviour"?

   A Because youngsters often neglect their duties for school. ❏

   B Because teenagers quite often (and people in general) don't realise how serious getting drunk might be. ❏

   C Because alcohol addiction cannot be treated and is therefore incurable. ❏

   D Because only teens can die of an overdose of alcohol. ❏

4. Which measures can be taken to make teenagers (and people in general) aware of alcohol's dangers?

   A You could forbid alcohol at all, no matter if it's in private or public places. ❏

   B You could forbid alcohol for people under the age of 21. ❏

   C You could check the government's website and inform yourself. ❏

   D You could make stricter regulations, introduce limitations and control them. ❏

5. Why do doctors worry so much when it comes to the topic of alcohol consumption among teens?

   A Because teenagers more and more often suffer from liver damages. ❏

   B Because teenagers more and more often suffer from brain damages. ❏

   C Because teenagers more and more often suffer from domestic violence. ❏

   D Because teenagers more and more often suffer from suicide attacks. ❏

6. Why is a rise in alcohol consumption related to a rise in the costs for the health service?

   A Because other aspects (like domestic violence) must be treated as well. ❏

   B Because usually a brain damage caused by alcohol must also be treated. ❏

   C Because rising suicide rates lead to rising funeral costs. ❏

   D Because violent crimes lead to higher costs for prisons. ❏

7. How long does it take until all the alcohol drunk has been absorbed?

   A It usually doesn't take long – up to one hour at a maximum. ❏

   B It takes quite long – usually up to two hours. ❏

   C It's hardly possible to predict as it depends on the type of alcohol. ❏

   D It only takes ten minutes until all the alcohol has entered your bloodstream. ❏

8. Being completely drunk ...

   A reduces the number of your brain cells, but only if you do it regularly. ❏

   B doesn't have the slightest effect on your brain cells. ❏

   C kills numerous of your brain cells, no matter how often that happens. ❏

   D is responsible for the loss of about thousand brain cells. ❏

RC 16: PLAGUE OF COCAINE

Task 1   Pre-reading: Word matching

Match the phrases with the corresponding explanations by writing the numbers in the boxes.

1. to struggle	☐	harbour
2. customs	☐	to whitewash black and illegal money
3. prearranged	☐	policemen not dressed in uniforms but casual clothes
4. plainclothes police	☐	a very nice and pleasant place where you feel comfortable
5. to be delighted	☐	something that was fixed and planned some time ago
6. port	☐	an area you have to pass when entering a foreign country
7. money-laundering	☐	to strongly fight/to have difficulties with something
8. to confiscate	☐	to be extremely happy
9. an eldorado	☐	to fight very hard and with full enthusiasm
10. to fight vigorously	☐	to take something away

Task 2   Reading

Read the article about how the deadly white powder is flooding Europe.

When Viasa airlines Flight 728 arrived at Rome's Airport coming from Caracas (capital of Venezuela), flight attendant Monica Garcias, 26, was the last person off the plane. Struggling with three heavy suitcases she passed through customs without inspection, climbed into a prearranged taxicab and rode to the outskirts of the city for a rendezvous with a man named Enrico Fericosa. The moment she handed her suitcases over to him, plainclothes police, including the cabdriver, closed in. In the luggage they found 8 kg of pure cocaine, worth about 10 million Dollars on the European retail market. The "Monica Gang" as the newspapers entitled their headlines, was broken.

While Rome police were delighted to put Monica out of business – her gang had carried out approximately 15 of such drug shipments to Italy – no one pretends that this is the end of drug dealing. On the contrary, a new and very profitable industry has developed in the last years: cocaine trafficking. With the help of the Sicilian Mafia, Colombian drug runners are flooding Europe's ports and air terminals with tons of the deadly white powder. "There is so much cocaine floating around the oceans", says David Brisbane of Interpol, "that they even forget to unload it sometimes. Shipments get mixed up or forgotten and end up in unintended places like Sri Lanka."

Just a few years ago, Europe's main contact with the cocaine trade was as a money-laundering centre and as a source of chemicals for the processing of coca leaves into the final product. The dominant drug of choice in Europe was heroin at that time. Cocaine was considered to be an American problem. This is obviously no longer the case. Only last August experts from Interpol warned that "a white plague was hitting the Continent". Cocaine confiscations in 20 European nations rose from 1.500 kg to 12.900 kg, figures for some individual countries are equally dramatic.

Only some years ago Europeans used to think that a capture of five to six kilos was big stuff. Now they see 1- and 2-ton shipments and ask themselves how that much cocaine has got there. The answer is relatively simple: by ship, by fishing boat, by plane, by mail, by human carriers and many more. And creativity is not limited as far as smuggling is concerned. Only look at the following variety of possible methods but keep in mind that this is only a small selection of the possible methods in use: Cocaine is either hidden in computers or agricultural equipment, can be injected into coconuts, or smuggled in the stomachs of racehorses and even humans. It's absolutely useless to say that especially the latter method is more than dangerous and these days more and more kids are used for this job, as they cannot really be arrested and no harm can be done to them.

Experts say there are several factors why Europe has turned into the new eldorado for dealers. First of all, because smuggling cocaine to the U.S. becomes harder and prevention efforts carried out in the country only show some modest success. So the demand for cocaine has currently been relatively flat. Secondly, Europe seems to offer endless coastlines that make it rather easy and attractive to smuggle the stuff into the single countries. Besides, Western Europe alone, with its 350 million people, is a bigger potential market than the U.S.

However, police and special forces will go on fighting vigorously against this tendency of flooding Europe with the white powder. Stricter regulations, consequent checks and strong punishment are hoped and expected to be the best solution.

Note taking

Answer the questions in not more than FOUR words. Don't try to form sentences, just write key words.

1.	What did Monica Garcias have problems with when leaving the airplane? Why was it difficult for her?	
2.	Why did nobody at the airport check her luggage?	
3.	How did the cabdriver know where to take Monica Garcias after the flight?	
4.	Why did the policemen who arrested Monica not wear their normal uniforms?	
5.	What exactly is Cocaine trafficking? What does that term mean?	
6.	Whose problem was Cocaine in earlier times?	
7.	How is Cocaine usually smuggled? Name four different possibilities!	
8.	Give two reasons why Europe is so popular for Cocaine trafficking!	

EXTRA READING – SHORT STORY: LEAVING

Reading

Read the story about Kate, a young girl, whose drugs experiences were fatal for her.

She woke up at the first ring of the telephone. Her body was tight and she realised that she was fully covered in sweat. *Ring. Ring.* She was hardly able to breathe and was lying in her bed like paralysed. *Ring. Ring.* She slowly turned her head, checking the alarm clock. 4 am. *Ring. Ring.* Her hands were trembling while she checked her bedside table to find the mobile. *Ring. Ring.* She suddenly heard glass breaking. "Damn it", she whispered into the darkness. The glass of water, which she had put on the bedside table when going to bed, had fallen down. *Ring. Ring.* Finally. There it was. She took the mobile and brought it to her ear. "Hello", she heard herself say in a far too silent voice. "Yea, that's me." Moira was still lying in her bed, desperately trying to understand what the man on the phone was talking about. "An accident?", she repeated the man's words. And then it struck Moira and her eyes were suddenly wide open. She was fully awake.

The things that followed were carried out by Moira completely automatically. She felt like being in trance. She changed her pyjamas for jogging trousers and a sweater and put on her Puma sneakers. The Puma sneakers. She was holding them in her hands waiting for a minute. She looked at them almost tenderly, remembering the shopping tour last week when she had bought them. The shopping tour with Kate. "Alright", she said to herself, "no time to lose." She sighed, dwelled in the memory of the shopping tour for another few seconds and then rushed to her car.

Moira is an accountant in her mid-forties and since the birth of her only child, Kate, she has been working for Stripfield Consultant in Goansville. Moira and her husband broke up shortly after their daughter had been born. Chester, Moira's husband, left the family when Kate was still a baby and Kate actually doesn't have any memory concerning her father. She was still too young when he decided to start a new life with a much younger woman. Anyway. Moira and Kate always had a good life and Kate was obviously a happy and satisfied child. Time has passed and has turned Kate into a teenager. One that is still nowadays happy and satisfied. Moira has always come along with her daughter quite well and she often had the impression that their relationship resembled more one between friends that one between mother and daughter. However, things have changed. Things always change and mostly these changes are to the worse.

Shortly before she reached her blue Toyota, her car key fell down. Moira almost lost her nerves and was desperately looking for the key. Tears came to her eyes while her hands were touching the wet ground in search for the key. She tried to calm down, telling herself repeatedly that everything will be fine again. Moira knew the way to the hospital. She often had to go there when she was pregnant. At that time Chester accompanied her and at that time she still believed that they would be a happy, little family for the rest of their lives. Anyway. Losing her husband to another woman was something Moira could handle although it hurt a lot. Of course it did and Moira had times in her life when she thought she couldn't go on. When she thought she didn't have the strength to bring up a child on her own. But she has always carried on and even now, being in such a desperate situation, Moira didn't think of giving up.

The hospital entry was only dimly lit at that time of the night. There were hardly any people, only a young man was standing close to the door, smoking nervously a cigarette and looking uncomfortable. Moira only realized him out of the corner of her eyes while she was walking inside. The smell of disinfection lotion hit her nostrils at once. It's a smell that immediately makes you feel sick and depressed. Moira felt like being in a trap. She would have liked to turn around and run away if only she could. But no, she had to be strong once again in her life. A life that has always presented challenges, difficulties and problems. She was so fed up with all of these.

Moira turned right, following the seemingly endless aisle with its endless white walls. The soles of her Puma sneakers were squeaking on the grey hospital floor. She was almost running when she passed some wooden chairs, an old-fashioned coffee machine and the paintings of unknown artists. All that didn't matter at that moment, all her thoughts were devoted to her daughter Kate. Finally she reached an information counter where she could ask a middle-aged nurse for the way to the Intensive Care Unit. The woman pointed to the elevators, telling Moira to get out on the third floor. Moira rushed to the elevator in the middle, pushing the button impatiently and counting the seconds in her mind. "One – two – three … come on … why doesn't this damn thing work?" She couldn't stand it any longer and pushed open the door to the stairs.

Moira was out of breath when she reached the third floor. The atmosphere at the ICU was strange. Everything was completely silent as if nobody was alive there. She looked around, quickly spotting a nurse removing some bedpans. While walking towards her, she imagined which state Kate would be in. She asked herself how seriously people must be injured to come to the ICU. "Excuse me", she said softly, tapping the woman with the bedpans on her shoulder. "Sorry Ma'am, no visitors at that time." The nurse had already turned around again, occupying herself with some bed sheets. "I got a call. My daughter is here", Moira tried again. Now the nurse stopped folding the bed sheets, looked at Moira intensely and went over to a rather old-fashioned computer. "Alright. What's the name?", she eventually asked. "Pilkington. Kate Pilkington." The nurse tapped something on the computer and after what seemed an eternity, she finally said, "She's in room 2B. I'll call Dr Flinch to fill you in about the details." The nurse didn't wait for any reaction. She just stood up from her chair and disappeared in the room directly behind the white chart-board. Now Moira was alone. Nervously she moved her hand through her dark long hair.

Moira was an exceedingly beautiful woman for her age and there were many men – friends, colleagues and others – who would have liked to date her. But Moira never showed any sign of interest. After the disappointment with Chester she tried to concentrate on her daughter, excluding men completely from her life. This tactic hadn't made her happy but at least it hadn't made her unhappy. Or more unhappy than she has been in her life so far.

"Mrs Pilkington?", a man asked coming directly towards her. "Yes, that's me. How is my daughter, Dr …". Moira tried to find the little name-tag that doctors have usually pinned to their white coats. "Flinch", the man answered, obviously realizing Moira's intention. "Well Mrs Pilkington, your daughter Kate has been here now for three hours and we have finished the first set of tests." Moira breathed in deeply, still not knowing what had happened. But she didn't dare say a word, patiently waiting for Dr Flinch to go on. He slowly thumbed through his papers, checking the results of the last blood tests. "Kate suffers from a toxic shock caused by too much adrenaline in her body. The result was a shortness of breath, followed by a cardiovascular blockage which means a kind of heart attack." Moira didn't understand anything. Why was that doctor talking about a heart attack? With her 16 years Kate was only a teenager. And she had always been fit and healthy. Moira looked up from the floor, her eyes directly meeting Dr Flinch's, pressing her two eyebrows together. The moment she opened her mouth to ask that doctor how the hell it was possible that Kate had had a heart attack, Dr Flinch only said "drugs". He waited for a few seconds before he went on. "A young man took her to hospital, shortly after midnight. He said that they had been at a party and that he had put some Crack into her cocktail. Then everything had gone out of control. She had drunk way too much alcohol and then she had suddenly collapsed. The guy is waiting downstairs, smoking a cigarette."

Like in a bad Hollywood movie Moira saw pictures passing her inner eye, pictures of her daughter getting drunk and collapsing on any dirty dance floor in any shabby bar. "The guy is waiting downstairs, smoking a cigarette", Moira remembered Dr Flinch's words. "Had that been the guy she had noticed when entering the hospital?", she asked herself. Anyway. That didn't have priority now.

She nervously shifted from one foot to the other, trying to think clearly. Which was definitely difficult at that moment. Drugs. Her daughter had taken drugs. But why? And who was that guy who had given her that stuff? Had he forced her to take it? Had she taken drugs before? Thousands of questions came to Moira's mind but as she knew that Dr Flinch could answer none of them, she simply said, "Can I see her?" "Sure", he just said. "Follow me. She's asleep now." Dr Flinch turned around leading the way to room 2B. His steps were fast and Moira had to hurry to keep up with him. Shortly before opening the door of room 2B he turned around once more, directly facing Moira. His expression was very serious. "Kate stopped breathing during the heart attack, that's why she has a tube in her lung. At the moment we can't exactly say when, and if at all, she might start breathing again. Her collapse has led to considerable brain damage and right now we can't predict how her condition will develop. The situation is very serious, Mrs Pilkington." After having said the last word, he swung the door open and entered the room.

Moira didn't even have time to fully realize the doctor's words. But they were unimportant the moment she saw her daughter. Kate, poor little Kate. Oh my God. Moira hesitated coming closer to her daughter. She looked so young and innocent, like a little child that must be protected. Three big grey machines were stationed around her bed, each indicating and showing colourful lines in rhythmic movement. A big white tube connected one of the machines directly with Kate's mouth, another one was placed below the nostrils. Kate's face had a strange, calm expression. "She can't hear you but nevertheless talk with her. Tell her some news, nice stories or whatever. Psychologists say that hearing the voice of beloved people might help coma patients. However. I'll leave you now so that you have some time for yourself. Do call me if you need anything", Dr Flinch said. He put back the paper chart which he had taken out when entering the room some minutes ago. When passing Moira he firmly touched her on her shoulder, looked her in the eyes for one more minute and then left the room.

Moira didn't have the slightest idea how long she was standing there in front of Kate's bed, without thinking, speaking or doing anything. It could have been seconds, minutes or even half an hour. But who cares anyway. Then, slowly, she began to move. She came closer towards Kate, touching her daughter's head tenderly. Tears were running down her face, but strangely, she didn't feel anything. She felt as if she was dead, being desperate, frustrated and left alone.

It started to rain outside. Raindrops were hitting the window which was darkened because of the blinders. The first drops came tentatively but soon it was raining like cats and dogs.

The funeral was only shortly after Kate's death. She had died that night when her mother had been with her. As if she had waited for her so not to be alone. Strange, but Moira had known that the story would end like that. She had known it the moment Dr Flinch had opened the door of room 2B.

* E * N * D *

Task 2   Comprehension

Answer the questions about Moira in full and correct English sentences.

1. When was Moira informed about her daughter's accident and which state was she (Moira) in at that time?

_____

2. Why do the Puma sneakers have a special meaning for Moira?

_____

3. Who did Moira see when entering the hospital?

_____

4. Why did Moira take the stairs to reach the Intensive Care Unit (ICU) on the third floor?

_____

Task 3 Sequencing

Find the summary of the story by putting the sentences into the correct order. Number them!

	Until she reached the hospital's information counter Moira had to run through some corridors.
	He briefly filled her in about the details of Kate's physical condition.
	Only a few minutes later she was fully dressed and on the verge of leaving home.
	At first Moira didn't understand what Dr Flinch was trying to tell her but then it suddenly hit her.
	Soon afterwards Moira arrived at the hospital where there was hardly anybody at that time.
	Eventually Kate died only shortly after her mother had arrived.
	In the early morning hours Moira was surprisingly woken up by a telephone call.
	There a nurse told her that the ICU was on the third floor and that it was better to take the elevator.
	But before she could actually drive off she had to search for the car's key, which she had dropped.
	When Moira finally reached the Intensive Care Unit she was presented with Dr Flinch, Kate's doctor.

Task 4 Note taking

Answer the questions in not more than FOUR words. Don't try to form sentences, just write key words.

1.	What do you know about Moira Pilkington? Give at least three details of her private life!	
2.	What is the relationship between Moira and her daughter Kate?	
3.	Why did Moira not look for another guy after she had been left by her husband?	
4.	What did room 2B at the Intensive Care Unit look like? Describe three aspects of it!	
5.	What happened to Kate and her body after she had taken the drugs?	
6.	What was the weather like while Moira was standing next to Kate's bed at the ICU?	

Task 5 Multiple choice

Tick the appropriate box so that your answer is correct according to the story.

1. When Moira first saw her daughter lying in the hospital bed in room 2B she had the impression ...
   - A that she was already dead. ❑
   - B that she looked innocent and happy. ❑
   - C that she had enormous pain to endure. ❑
   - D that she would never be able to speak again properly. ❑

2. What were Moira's thoughts when she drove to the hospital while being pregnant with Kate?
   - A That she wanted to have at least one more child in order to be really happy. ❑
   - B That she would have a happy little family and be satisfied for the rest of her life. ❑
   - C She thought about what name to give her baby daughter after birth. ❑
   - D She thought about what she would do if her husband left her. ❑

3. What was the atmosphere at the Intensive Care Unit like?
   - A It was silent and quiet despite the fact that some doctors were walking around. ❑
   - B Some nurses were doing their work but apart from that it was quiet. ❑
   - C The nurse was silently working at a rather old-fashioned computer. ❑
   - D It was very silent and quiet and apart from the nurse nobody could be seen. ❑

4. After being left by her husband, how did Moira behave towards other men?
   - A She withdrew from men as she was afraid to experience another disappointment. ❑
   - B She didn't want to risk another disappointment so she only dated colleagues. ❑
   - C Moira was absolutely happy and satisfied with not having a guy in her life. ❑
   - D It was hard for Moira to date men as she wasn't really attractive for them. ❑

5. Why was it possible that a 16-year old teenager suffered from a heart attack?
   - A The girl simply dehydrated because she hadn't drunk enough water. ❑
   - B The drugs, which Kate had taken, completely destroyed her liver. ❑
   - C Because of too much adrenaline the blood didn't sufficiently reach the heart. ❑
   - D The high amount of adrenaline in her body caused her to dehydrate. ❑

6. What did Dr Flinch do after he had led Moira into room 2B?
   - A He held Moira's hand to show sympathy and to support her. ❑
   - B He informed Moira about all the machines and their exact functions. ❑
   - C He left the room to consult another doctor who had more experience. ❑
   - D He left the room to give Moira the chance to be undisturbed with her daughter. ❑

7. Why should beloved people talk with coma patients? What's the use behind it?
   - A It might help coma patients if they hear a familiar voice. ❑
   - B Coma patients almost always wake up when hearing a familiar voice. ❑
   - C It's proven that coma patients feel better when hearing a familiar voice. ❑
   - D Hearing a familiar voice makes coma patients calm and more comfortable. ❑

8. In the end, what happened to Kate?
   - A Kate died because her inner organs had been completely destroyed by the drugs. ❑
   - B Kate died after having seen and talked to her mother one more time. ❑
   - C She died because of considerable brain damage created by the drugs. ❑
   - D She died after having spent many weeks at the Intensive Care Unit. ❑

WRITING

In deinem Übungsbuch DURCHSTARTEN für die 5. KLASSE hast du ja bereits die wichtigsten Textsorten kennengelernt. Nun heißt es: üben, üben, üben. Damit du dir noch einmal die wichtigsten Kriterien für jede einzelne Textsorte in Erinnerung rufen kannst, findest du auf den folgenden Seiten Checklisten, die dich an die wichtigsten Elemente eines jeden Texttyps erinnern. Bevor du also beispielsweise einen *opinion essay* verfasst, schnapp dir das Buch der 5. Klasse und lies dir noch einmal die Theorie dazu durch. Nachdem du deinen *essay* verfasst hast, überprüfe anhand der Checkliste, ob du auch wirklich an alles gedacht hast! Achte prinzipiell immer auf die genaue **Aufgabenstellung** sowie die **Wortangaben**. Gutes Gelingen!

INFORMAL (PERSONAL) LETTER

LAYOUT	
■ **Heading**: Adresse des Absenders, Datum	
■ **Salutation/Greeting** (Begrüßung): Hi Steve, Dear Christie, ...	
■ **Text** (introduction, body, conclusion: siehe unten)	
■ **Closing** (Verabschiedung): persönlich halten	
■ **Signature line** (Unterschrift): möglichst handschriftlich	
■ **Postscript** (Postskriptum): optional **PS**	

TEXT	
■ **Introduction** (Einleitung: Verweis auf das letzte Treffen, den letzten Brief, ...)	
■ **Body** (zusammenhängend, für den Leser nachvollziehbar, neue Idee: neuer Absatz)	
■ **Conclusion** (Freude auf Wiedersehen/Brief, Grund für Abschluss des Briefes)	

STYLE	
■ **Abkürzungen/Contractions** (What **I've** forgotten to tell you.)	
■ **Informelle Ausdrücke, Vokabeln, phrasal verbs** (What about the other **guys**?)	
■ **Satzfragmente** (Something I must tell you: Jack has asked me out.)	
■ **Direkte Fragen** (How are things going at school?)	
■ **Aktive Phrasen** (They closed our school for two weeks!)	
■ **Informelle *sentence linkers*** (**Well**, I was surprised to hear that ... **Anyway**, I have to ...)	
■ **Ausdrucksvolle Satzzeichen** (Rufzeichen, Doppelpunkte, Gedankenstriche)	

Fill in the words in the box on the lines provided on the next page.

text – postscriptum – conclusion – signature – closing – comma* – salutation/greeting – introduction – main body – return address – date – heading

---

* In einem persönlichen Brief darfst du auch ein Rufzeichen in der Anrede verwenden, um Nachdruck zu verleihen.

---

12 Holloway Circus
Birmingham B1,1

26 January 2011

Hi Jenna,

Thanks for your birthday card – I really love the CD you sent me. I'm listening to it right now! What's your favourite track? Mine is number 9 – it's so powerful.

Anyway, I'm writing to tell you that my parents want us to move. They've actually already bought a cute house in Brighton! The neighbourhood seems to be okay – loads of families with kids of my age. The house itself is fantastic! I'm finally going to have my own room – you know my little sister can be a real pest sometimes. Well, in the future I'll just shut the door if she gets too bad. Cool, isn't it? The garden is awesome too. We're going to have our own apples and raspberries. Yummy! The only thing that bothers me a bit is that I'll have to leave all my friends behind. But there are some cool youth clubs in Brighton – I guess I won't have troubles finding new friends. And there are still e-mails, letters and cell phones. At least, for us, nothing will change ☺.

That reminds me of Phil! He is fetching me in a minute to talk about the move … He wants us to keep a long-distance relationship – but I'm not sure if this will work out. Well, I'll keep you in the loop on that matter in the next letter.

Hugs and kisses, *Anna*

PS: Give my love to your sister! A. P.

Formal or informal style

Natürlich wirst du nicht nur Briefe an Freunde und Bekannte verfassen, sondern auch an dir unbekannte Personen. Bei formellen Schreiben musst du ganz besonders auf ein korrektes Layout und einen adäquaten Schreibstil achten.

Exercise 2

Find the formal expression.

INFORMAL	FORMAL	INFORMAL	FORMAL
Hi Sophie!		See ya on Monday.	
Thanks (Thx) for your letter!		Best wishes,	
Sorry (Sry) for not answering your last letter.		There are some things that really annoy me!	

FORMAL (BUSINESS) LETTER

LAYOUT	
■ **Heading:** Adresse des Absenders (rechts) Datum (rechts oder links): 15 February 2011 (st/nd/rd/th entfällt) reference line (links) (optional statt subject line) Name und Adresse des Empfängers (links)	
■ **Salutation/Greeting** (Begrüßung): Dear Mr. Smith, Dear Sir/Madam, ... (Komma!)	
■ **Subject line** (Betreff): unter der Anrede (optional statt reference line)	
■ **Text** (Aufbau: siehe unten): einzeilig, leere Zeile nach Absatz, nicht einrücken	
■ **Closing** (Verabschiedung): Yours faithfully,/Yours sincerely, (Komma!)	
■ **Unterschrift** (signature line): den Namen rechtsbündig ein paar Leerzeilen unter der Verabschiedung tippen, darüber handschriftlich unterschreiben	
TEXT	
■ **Opening/Beginning:** Erwähne den Zweck des Briefes (ein Absatz – Leerzeile vor:)	
■ **The main message:** Erkläre den Zweck des Briefes im Detail (ein Absatz – Zwischenabsätze: neue Zeile – Leerzeile vor:)	
■ **The close:** Beziehe dich auf einen zukünftigen Kontakt/ein zukünftiges Treffen (ein Absatz)	
STYLE	
■ **Keine Abkürzungen/Contractions** (I would be pleased to inform you that ...)	
■ Formelle Ausdrücke, Phrasen	
■ Vollständige Sätze	
■ **Sparsame Satzzeichen** (keine Ausrufezeichen, Gedankenstriche)	
■ logische Übergänge der Ideen	
■ **Formelle** *sentence linkers* (Firstly .../Secondly .../However, .../What is more ..., ...)	
■ Präzise Angaben, kurze, prägnante Sätze	

Exercise 1

Match the salutations with the purposes.

1. Dear Sir or Madam
2. Dear Sir
3. Dear Madam
4. Dear Mr. Smith
5. Dear Ms Smith
6. To whom it may concern

A to a man whose name you know

B to a woman if you do not know her name

C to a woman whose name you know

D you do not know the person you are writing to

E to a man if you do not know his name

1.	
2.	
3.	
4.	
5.	
6.	

Exercise 2

Fill in the words in the box on the lines provided on the next page.

opening – date – main message – closing phrase – subject line – signature – return address –
recipient's name and address – greeting/salutation – close

286 Wisteria Lane
Portland, OR 97205

_____

_____

Mr. Michael Kelzo   24 March 2011   _____
Colorful Inc.
476 Strong Road
Springfield, OR 97477

_____   Dear Mr. Kelzo,

_____   Subject: Request for fabric sample

_____   I am writing to enquire about the new set of fabric samples as
                   advertised in your leaflet sent out in February.

                   We are a manufacturer of high-quality upholstery, operating
                   in 10 states of the U.S.A. As we are interested in expanding
_____   our product range, we are currently looking for trendy fabrics.
                   Accordingly, your advertisement has caught our attention.
                   We would be grateful if you could send us a sample of your
                   collection.

_____   We are looking forward to hearing from you.

_____   Yours sincerely,

                                                     Jonathan Frazer   _____
                                                     Jonathan Frazer
                                                     Product Manager

Exercise 3

Match the phrases with the different purposes. Write the letters in the boxes provided.

A	We are writing in connection with/to enquire about …	**F**	I hope that this information will help you.
B	We are interested in … and we would like to know …	**G**	Your prompt reply will be appreciated …
C	We very much look forward to doing business with you.	**H**	Further to our conversation this morning …
D	Thank you for your letter (of + date) asking if/ concerning …	**I**	I look forward to receiving your reply/order/to hearing from you.
E	We appreciate the continued confidence you have placed in our company and assure you that we are happy to serve you well.	**J**	Please do not hesitate to contact us if you need any further information.

OPENING (beginning a letter)	REFERRING (expressing reference)	CLOSE (ending a letter)

E-MAIL

E-Mails folgen ähnlichen Kriterien wie Briefe. Anrede, Verabschiedung, Inhalt und Sprachstil hängen, wie bei Briefen, von der Aufgabenstellung ab (vgl. *informal/formal letter*). Praktisch ist jedoch, dass der Kopfteil (*heading*) bereits vorgedruckt ist und du diesen nur ausfüllen musst.

Exercise 1

Maria Musso has read the following advertisement on a website. She then wrote the following e-mail. Is there something she forgot to mention?

SAVE A TURTLE	
We are looking for volunteers to join our sea turtle conservation project on the west coast of South Thailand, 150 kilometres north of Phuket.	As we are working in an international team, a good knowledge of English would be essential.
Members will help to restore mangroves by planting trees, to survey and to clean coral reefs as well as to monitor, observe and protect sea turtle nests and juvenile turtles.	The next season will start in December 2010 and end in April 2011. If you are willing to support us, a unique experience of face-to-face contact with one of the most fascinating reptiles in our world will await you.
Participation requires experience in teamwork as well as good swimming and hiking skills.	To apply or send a query, click on the link below. INFO@SAVE-A-TURTLE

To:	INFO@SAVE-A-TURTLE
From:	MARIA MUSSO
Subject:	SAVE-A-TURTLE-HOLIDAYS IN THAILAND

Dear Sir or Madam,

I recently saw your advertisement requesting volunteers for your sea turtle project in Thailand, and I should very much like to become a part of your team for the following season.

Although I hold no academic qualifications in biology or ecology, I have already gained some experience in participating in projects designed to protect our nature. In 2008, I supported our school eco-team in cleaning and restoring the creek in my hometown, and I even initiated a waste-recycling project in my neighbourhood last year. Consequently, I have acquired a good knowledge of the processes of such projects. I consider myself to be a good team player and I am also eager to work hard and to face physical and mental challenges.

I have two queries about the project. Firstly, I would like to know for how long volunteers are expected to stay in Thailand. Secondly, could you give me some closer details on the accommodation available during the stay? I am used to camping, but if more comfortable facilities are available, I will happily make use of them.

I would be grateful if you could address these queries as soon as possible, as an eventual participation in the project would require some arrangements with my school for the following school year.

Thank you,

Maria Musso

TOOLBOXES FOR LETTERS AND E-MAILS

The following pages will provide you with toolboxes filled with vocabulary and phrases that might be helpful for writing various types of formal letters and e-mails.

Referring

Thank you for your letter of ...	I reply to your (request) ...
With reference to ...	Further to (our conversation this morning) ...
With regard to ...	I am writing in connection with ...
Thank you for your telephone call today, ...	

Offering help

I/We would be happy to ...	I/we are quite willing to ...
Would you like me/us to ...?	Our company would be pleased to ...

Giving good/bad news

I am/We are pleased to announce that ...	You will be pleased to learn that ...
I am delighted to inform you that ...	
After careful consideration we have decided (not) to ...	
We regret to inform you that ...	
Unfortunately we cannot/are unable to (comply with) ...	I am afraid it would not be possible to ...

Giving reasons

This is ... am Satzanfang

owing to ... (bad news)	as a result of ...
due to ...	because of ...

Requesting information

Polite requests

Could you kindly/possibly let me know ...?	Could I request/ask for some details about ...?
I'd be grateful if you could (tell me) ...	Could I have some details about ...?
I ... if you could inform me ...	Would it be possible to ...?
It would be helpful if you could ...	Could you possibly give me some information about ...?
I would appreciate if you could ...	In addition, I would like to (receive) ...
I am interested in (obtaining/receiving) ...	I would appreciate your immediate attention to this matter.
Could you please confirm ...	Please let me know what action you propose to take.

Expressing urgency

as soon as possible	without delay	immediately

Complaining

I am writing to express my dissatisfaction with ...

I am writing to complain about ...

Please note that the goods I/we ordered on ... have not arrived yet.

I/We regret to inform you that our order n° xy is now considerably overdue.

I would like to query (the transport charges) which seem unusually high.

Apologising

I am/We are sorry for (the delay in replying ... in complying with ...) ...

I regret the inconvenience caused (...)

I would like to apologise for (the delay/the inconvenience/...)

Once again, I apologise for any inconvenience.

Closing remarks

If I/we can be of any further assistance, please let me/us know.

If I can help in any way, please do not hesitate to contact me.

If you require any more information ...

For further details ...

Thank you for taking this into consideration.

Thank you for your help.

I/We hope you are happy with this arrangement.

I/We hope you can settle this matter to my/our satisfaction.

Enclosing documents

I am enclosing ...

Please find enclosed ...

You will find enclosed ...

Referring to future action/business/contact

We look forward to a successful working relationship in the future.

We would be (very) pleased to do business with your company.

I would be happy to have an opportunity to work with your firm.

I look forward to seeing you next week.

Looking forward to hearing from you, I ...

Looking forward to receiving your comments, I ...

I look forward to meeting on the (date).

I would appreciate a reply at your earliest convenience.

BLOG

Der Blog ist ein Text, der im Internet gepostet wird – entweder als unabhängiger Text oder als Antwort auf einen bereits vorhandenen Interneteintrag. Diese Textsorte kann entweder **persönlich** oder **beruflich** eingesetzt werden. Abhängig von der Angabe musst du **deine Meinung äußern**, **informieren**, **Erlebnisse und Erfahrungen mitteilen** oder beispielsweise **eine Firma im Internet präsentieren**.

LAYOUT	
■ **Title:** Does it inform on the blog's content? Does it catch the readers' interest?	
■ **User name:** Does the blog mention your username?	
■ **Date/Time:** Does the blog mention the date and time of publication?	
■ **Introduction:** Does the introduction either introduce the new topic of the blog or refer to a preceding blog?	
■ **Main body:** Is the content of the blog structured in paragraphs?	
■ **Conclusion:** Does it sum up the main idea of the blog? Does it call on the reader?	

STYLE – PERSONAL or NEUTRAL	
PERSONAL	
■ **Abkürzungen/Contractions**	
■ **Informelle Ausdrücke, Vokabel, phrasal verbs**	
■ **Satzfragmente**	
■ **Direkte Fragen**	
■ **Aktive Phrasen**	
■ **Informative Sprache, die Aufmerksamkeit erregt**	
■ **Anschauliche Darstellungen persönlicher Meinungen oder Erlebnisse**	
NEUTRAL	
■ **Keine Abkürzungen/Contractions**	
■ **Formelle Ausdrücke, Phrasen**	
■ **Vollständige Sätze**	
■ **Sparsame Satzzeichen (keine Ausrufezeichen, Gedankenstriche)**	
■ **logische Übergänge der Ideen**	
■ **Formelle sentence linkers (Firstly .../Secondly .../However, .../What is more ...)**	
■ **Präzise Angaben; kurze, prägnante Sätze**	

☺ **Writing a blog means that you are trying to reach a huge public with your ideas.** ☺

ARTICLE

Artikel haben ein primäres Ziel: die Leserinnen und Leser auf ein Thema aufmerksam zu machen und sie mit möglichst vielen Fakten und Hintergrundinformationen über dieses Thema zu versorgen.

Man unterscheidet *serious articles* (in *quality papers*) und *popular articles* (in *tabloids, gossip papers*). Der Schreibstil des Artikels hängt also primär von dem Medium ab, in dem er erscheint, und muss somit an die Leserinnen und Leser angepasst werden.

LAYOUT	
■ **Headline:** Introduces the subject/topic/problem AND catches the reader's interest.	
■ **Introduction:** Presents the basic facts (who, what, when, ...) in an interesting way.	
■ **Body:** Presents all the facts/aspects/arguments/solutions of the topic/problem/ ...	
■ **Conclusion:** Summarises the main aspects and calls for the reader to take action. Your last paragraph is the most important one: it has to address the reader.	
■ **Paragraphs:** Leave a line between the introduction and the body as well as between the body and the conclusion. Within the main body: Jump to the next line when you introduce a new aspect/argument.	

TEXT	
■ **Plan your article carefully:** Collect ideas, make a draft, revise and correct it.	
■ **Make a clear statement:** Your article must follow a line that combines all elements.	
■ **Be logical:** Your reader must be able to follow your line of reasoning: ▶ Organise your ideas in a logical order ▶ Find suitable transitional and linking devices	
■ **Keep a distance:** Avoid getting too personal and presenting your opinion too openly.	
■ **Be <u>interesting</u> and <u>relevant</u>:** ▶ Address your readers personally, ask them questions to involve them. ▶ Present facts, statistics, numbers: show all sides/aspects of the topic. ▶ Avoid generalisations, clichés, stereotypes – do not present rumours/assumptions as facts. ▶ When you quote statements, statistics etc. always mention the source. ▶ Surprise your readers: present something new. ▶ Do not repeat yourself – keep your article compact and precise.	
■ **Keep your readers in mind:** age, nationality, profession, level of education	
■ **Remember your aim:** Do you want to: convince/entertain/warn/give advice/inform ...?	
■ **Choose the correct style (language):** (formal: quality paper/adults – informal: school mag)	

☺ **Remember: Your article is interesting and informative** ☺

REPORT

Ein *report* kann mehreren Zwecken dienen, nämlich der sachlichen Beschreibung eines vergangenen Ereignisses/einer gegenwärtigen Situation oder eine Empfehlung für zukünftige Handlungen. Ziel eines *reports* ist es, die Leserinnen und Leser knapp und prägnant mit den wichtigsten Fakten zu dem Thema zu versorgen.

LAYOUT	
every part starts with a headline/always leave an empty line after a section	
■ **Introduction**: Presents shortly and precisely the aim/purpose of the report.	

■ **Body**: Lists all arguments/ideas/aspects.
      Needs a clear structure: every **section** has a **headline**
      (e.g.: Introduction – Positive Aspects – Negative Aspects – Conclusion)	

■ **Conclusion**: Summarises the most important arguments/ideas/aspects. Gives recommendations.	

TEXT AND STYLE	
■ **Plan your article carefully**: Collect ideas, make a draft, revise and correct it.	
■ **Use a formal style!**	
■ **Use appropriate linking words!**	
■ **Write clear and concise sentences!**	

Exercise 1

You have just returned from a study trip to Ireland with your class. You are now asked to write a report on the positive as well as on the *negative* aspects of your trip. You are also supposed to suggest *improvements*. Read the report and *find suitable headings* for the sections.

_____ The aim of this report is to assess the success of this year's study trip to Ireland and to recommend any improvements.	Irish lifestyle. I recommend that future trips should offer a larger variety of activities, like city trips, coach trips to the surrounding areas and evening entertainment, like cinema visits or theatre shows.
_____ Although the families that students stayed with were very hospitable, students sometimes did not feel integrated with the families. It would be preferable if host families had children of the students' age in order to propel interaction.	_____ While students got on very well with their teachers, students pointed out that the outline of their English classes did not meet their expectations. For future classes, it might be advisable to focus more on speaking than on writing activities.
_____ The programme concentrated highly on cultural activities and accordingly included many visits to museums. Students mentioned that they would have preferred seeing more of the countryside and learning more about	_____ To sum up, this year's trip was a great success, despite the reservations mentioned above. If the changes mentioned above can be put into effect, we will be looking forward to going on a further trip.

Exercise 2

Match the phrases with the different purposes.

A	This report is based on ...	**H**	This report describes/outlines/deals with ...
B	To sum up, ...	**I**	In conclusion, ...
C	It might be advisable to ...	**J**	It would be a good idea to ...
D	It would be preferable to ...	**K**	I suggest/propose/recommend that we should ...
E	The aim/purpose of this report is to ...	**L**	I have no hesitation in recommending ...
F	This report relates to ...	**M**	Summing up, I ...
G	I/we/... was/were highly enthusiastic about ...	**N**	I/we/... really appreciated ...

INTRODUCTIONS

POSITIVE ASPECTS

RECOMMENDATIONS AND SUGGESTIONS

CONCLUSIONS

PROPOSAL

Ein *Prosposal* – oder „Antrag" – ist ein Text, der auf die Unterstützung einer Idee oder eines Projektes durch Entscheidungsträgerinnen und Entscheidungsträger abzielt. Sinn und Zweck sind also, Personen – meist unbekannte – **von etwas zu überzeugen**. Mögliche Anlässe sind beispielsweise, **eine Idee/ein Projekt vorzuschlagen**, **um finanzielle und andere Unterstützung anzusuchen** oder **von den eigenen Fähigkeiten zu überzeugen**. Deine Leserschaft kann vielfältig sein: Institutionen, Behörden, Unternehmen, eine einzelne Person, welche Entscheidungsträger ist, oder eine Gruppe von eben solchen.

LAYOUT	
■ **Author**: Does the proposal mention your name?	
■ **Project title**: Does it inform on the proposal's main idea? Is it short and significant?	
■ **Introduction**: Is it short and to the point? Does the reader get the main idea of what you are proposing?	
■ **Main body**: Is the content of the proposal structured in paragraphs? Does every paragraph refer to a single idea of the proposal?	
■ **Conclusion**: Does it sum up the main idea of the proposal? Does it appeal on the reader?	
■ **Is there an empty line between every paragraph?**	
■ **Are there headings for every paragraph?**	

STYLE – NEUTRAL to FORMAL	
■ **Keine Abkürzungen/Contractions**	
■ **Formelle Ausdrücke, Phrasen**	
■ **Vollständige Sätze**	
■ **Sparsame Satzzeichen (keine Ausrufezeichen, Gedankenstriche)**	
■ **logische Übergänge der Ideen**	
■ **Formelle sentence linkers**	
■ **Präzise Angaben; kurze, prägnante Sätze**	
■ **Überzeugende Sprache**	
■ **Sachlich**	
■ **Präzise**	
■ **Nicht emotional**	

☺ **Ziel deines *Proposals* ist es, der Leserschaft dein Anliegen darzubringen und sie davon zu überzeugen!** ☺

LEAFLET

Ein *Leaflet* oder eine „Broschüre" – ist eine Form von Werbe- oder Informationsmaterial, das an eine genau definierte Zielgruppe verteilt beziehungsweise verschickt wird. Es dient primär dem Zweck, **Werbung** zu machen und die Leserschaft zu **informieren**. Die Leserschaft besteht aus möglichen Interessenten für ein bestimmtes Produkt, ein Projekt oder eine Idee.

LAYOUT	
▨ **Title**: Does it inform on the product/project the leaflet advertises?	
Does it catch the readers' interest?	
Is it striking enough to make the reader read on?	
▨ **Paragraphs**: Are there obvious paragraphs?	
Do the paragraphs have catchy headings?	
▨ **Numbers and key words**: Does your leaflet have clear and neat structuring?	
Does the reader feel informed at first sight?	
▨ **Is there an empty line between every paragraph?**	

STYLE – NEUTRAL	
▨ **Überzeugende Sprache, um den Inhalt informativ, interessant und ansprechend zu präsentieren**	
▨ **Leserinnen und Leser können direkt angesprochen werden**	
▨ **Abkürzungen sind erlaubt**	
▨ **Plakative Satzzeichensetzung**	
▨ **Präzise Angaben; kurze, prägnante Sätze**	
▨ **Überzeugende Sprache**	

☺ **Ziel deines *Leaflets* ist es, deiner Leserschaft ein Produkt oder eine Idee zu verkaufen.** ☺

OPINION ESSAY

Der sogenannte *opinion essay* ist sicher das Herzstück deiner schriftlichen Matura. Er umfasst ca. 400 Wörter und soll deine persönliche Meinung zu einem Thema wiedergeben. Natürlich bedeutet das einiges an Vorbereitung: Du musst dir möglichst viele inhaltliche Aspekte, Kriterien, Vor- und Nachteile des Themas überlegen, diese sammeln und dann logisch geordnet zu Papier bringen.

LAYOUT	
always leave a line after each part	
■ **Introduction:** Introduces the topic, your **thesis**, and catches the reader's interest.	
■ **Body:** Presents all aspects related to the topic (1 paragraph per statement!).	
■ **Summary:** Summarises the statements supporting your **opinion**.	

TEXT: PREPARATION	
■ **Step 1: Brainstorming:** Collect ideas – do research.	
■ **Step 2: Thesis statement:** Note down one sentence that summarises YOUR OPINION.	
■ **Step 3: Supporting statements:** Summarise all your ideas/aspects/arguments in 1 sentence each.	
■ **Step 4: Statement outline:** Arrange your statements in a logical order.	

TEXT: WRITING	
Step 0: Find a catchy title (this might be the last step in writing your essay)	
■ **Step 1: Introduction:** Grabs your reader's attention, sets up the issue, leads to your thesis.	
■ **Step 2: Paragraphs:** ▶ Every statement requires its own paragraph. ▶ Explain your statement in logical, coherent sentences. ▶ Emphasise your statements with examples. ▶ The statements supporting your opinion are stressed. ▶ Statements speaking against your opinion can be mentioned, but must be outweighed. ▶ All paragraphs must be linked in a logical way (on the level of content as well as on the level of language: linkers). ▶ The strongest argument, supporting your opinion best, is the final paragraph.	
■ **Step 3: Conclusion:** Summarises the best statements supporting your opinion AND leaves an impression on your reader (calls for action, makes him/her think ...).	

STYLE	
■ **Use formal style:** No contractions, use formal phrases.	
■ **Support your opinion:** Give examples, but mind the word limit.	
■ **Be interesting:** Address your reader: rhetoric questions.	

☺ **Your essay convinces the reader of your opinion on the topic!** ☺

TOOLBOXES FOR ESSAYS

Developing the argument

Central to this topic is ...	Let us start by considering the fact that ...
The first aspect to point out is that ...	To start with, ...
First, ...	To begin with ...
Firstly, ...	First of all ...
It must be/has to be stated/pointed out/mentioned that ...	
One argument speaking in support of/speaking against ...	
We must distinguish between ...	
First of all, let us try to analyse ...	

Ordering elements

Firstly, ... Secondly, ... Finally, ...
As a final point, ...
There are at least xyz points to highlight.

Adding elements

In addition (to ...), ...	What is more ...
Moreover, ...	It is important to add that ...
Furthermore, one should not forget that ...	Apart from that ...
Not only ..., ... but also	

Presenting the other side of the argument

However, it might be argued that ...
Of course, it has to be stated that ...
Equally relevant to the issue are the questions of ...
One should, nevertheless, consider the problem from another angle.

Personal opinion

I believe that ...	It is my contention that ...
My own point of view is that ...	I am convinced that ...
Furthermore, one should not forget that ...	My own opinion is that ...
As I see it ...	To my mind ...

Giving examples

for example	for instance	such as	like	To illustrate this point ...

Emphasising

This/The last example highlights the fact that ...	
No only ... but also ...	(!Not only **does** this mean that ...)
I would even go so far as to say that ...	

Other's opinion

Some people believe that ...	According to ...
It is claimed that ...	It is said (that) ...

Critics are convinced that ...	... argue that ...
... suggest that ...	... point out that ...
... emphasise that ...	... contend that ...
... go as far as to say that ...	... say that ...
... mention that ...	... add that ...

Consequences

For this reason, ...	Because of this, ...
Therefore, ...	Thus, ...
As a result ...	From these facts, one may conclude that ...
That is why ...	

Comparison

Some critics suggest ..., whereas others ...	Compared to ...
On the one hand (there is the firm believe that) ... On the other hand, (many people are convinced that ...)	

Contrasting

however	but
though	even though
despite	although
in spite of	nevertheless

Concluding

To conclude, ...	To sum up, ...
In summary, ...	Summing up, ...
In conclusion, ...	... (I am convinced that/I believe that)
What conclusions can be drawn from all this?	... (we have to accept that)
The most satisfactory conclusion that we can come to is ...	

Useful verbs

to analyse	to explain
to argue	to highlight
to claim	to maintain
to display	to point out
to demonstrate	to prove
to disagree	to reason
to examine	to reveal
to exemplify	to state

MODEL TASKS

Task 1 Formal letter/e-mail

> **Camp-for-kids**
>
> Spend 4 weeks sharing your passion for outdoors with a group as a coach of 8-to-14-year-olds on a summer camp in Canada. Camp-for-kids needs sporty and adventurous young people who have already gained some experience in working with kids. Earn $ 900 while having fun in the wilderness. Food and accommodation included.
>
> Write to: info@camp-for-kids

In order to get the job, you write an e-mail in which you

- give reasons why you want the job
- explain how you will prepare
- convince them that you are the most suitable candidate
- request further information

Write 200 words.

Task 2 Formal letter

You have just watched the final episode of "Britain's next top model". Write a letter to Living TV, complaining about the way women are treated and the way in which young girls may be negatively influenced by the show.

Write 250 words.

Task 3 Personal letter

You have just returned from the most horrible party you have ever been to. Write your pen friend about it, telling him/her what went wrong.

Write 250 words.

Task 4 Personal e-mail

You have just received this e-mail from one of your friends.

> Dear Jolene,
> I have just learned that my best friend is on Meth! You can't imagine how I feel at the moment. What can I do? Please help me.
>
> Yours, Mona

Answer this e-mail, giving Mona emotional support as well as informing her on

- what is Meth/what does it mean to be addicted to drugs
- which actions should be taken to help Mona's friend

Write 230 words.

Task 5 Blog

You have just returned from the summer camp in Task 1. Now, you comment in your blog on your experiences and whether you would recommend others going there too.

Write 250 words.

Task 6   Article

You have just returned from your 4-weeks-stay in the TV reality show "The 19th century house". You had to live in an old Victorian house without electricity and running water, following the daily routines of people living in the 1850s. Inform your readers on how you experienced that completely different lifestyle and whether you would recommend the project, or not.

Write 320 words.

Task 7   Article

As you and your class have just returned from your language trip, your school mag wants everyone of you to write an article on your experiences. The best article will be published in the next volume.

Write 220 words.

Task 8   Report

The city or town you live in wants to know how satisfied young people are with the following aspects:

- safety
- shopping
- sports areas
- nightlife

Write a report on those aspects, pointing out the positive as well as the negative sides and give recommendations for the future.

Write 200 words.

Task 9   Report

Last year, your school launched a project in your class: All schoolbooks were replaced by an e-reader and e-books. After one year, you are now asked to write a report on the success of this experiment. Point out the positive as well as the negative aspects and give recommendations for the future.

Write 200 words.

Task 10   Leaflet

You have decided to start a private tutoring club at your school where older students help younger ones with their school work. Now, you want to design a leaflet recruiting tutors as well as 'clients'. In your text of your leaflet you should

- explain how you want to organise the tutoring club,
- outline the positive consequences on the school climate,
- persuade older and younger students of the advantages.

Write 250 words.

Task 11   Opinion essay

Write an opinion essay discussing the question whether teenage alcohol abuse could be stopped by raising the age of buying and consuming alcohol to 21.

Write 300 words.

Task 12   Opinion essay

We should be happy to live in a multicultural society.
Discuss this statement in an essay presenting your opinion.

Write 320 words.

Task 13   Opinion essay

Are today's teenagers negatively influenced by the amount of sex portrayed on TV?
Discuss this question in an essay presenting your opinion.

Write 320 words.

GRAMMAR

MIXED TENSES

Fill in the correct tense. If you need some help, check the chart on the next two pages.

Hi Mark,

Sorry that I _____ (not can) to write earlier, but things _____ (be)

quite crazy recently. You know, the first four weeks of my holidays _____ (turn out) to be

quite rushed because I _____ (must) work in my father's company. However, in August, I

_____ (have) the most amazing time in my life. But, let me tell you from the start.

On my last Friday afternoon at work, I _____ (sit) in front of my computer,

_____ (key) in some receipts for my father, when he suddenly _____ (appear)

in my room. After he _____ (praise) me for my excellent work he _____

(show) me two tickets for Ibiza! I _____ (not can – believe) my ears

when he _____ (tell) me that those tickets _____ (are) for my best friend

Dave and me. The following Monday at nine, Dave and I _____ (sit) on the plane,

_____ (talk) about our plans for the following week. We _____ (relax)

on the beach, meet some cute girls and party all night long. Sounds good, ey? The first two days, we really

_____ (whoop) it up! One party after the other, lazy afternoons on the beach, the hot sun shining

down on us: HEAVEN. On the third day, Dave and I _____ (lie) in the sun, nearly dozing

off, when I _____ (feel) an ice-cold hand on my back. I _____

__ (not know) what was going on, so I screamed, "Dave, what _____

(you – do)?" But ... that _____ (not be) Dave! When I _____ (look up) I

saw that the most beautiful girl I _____ (ever – see) _____ (look

down) at me. I remembered that I _____ (meet) Amy the night before, but I thought that

she had a crush on Dave. Amy said, "Hi Ben! I _____ (think) about you all day

long. I _____ (lose) your numbers, but now that I _____ (find) you,

I _____ (not let) you go!" Quite bold, isn't she? You bet – I _____

(not mind) her talking so frankly. Anyway, Amy and I _____ (spend) a wonderful time in Ibiza ... and

who knows? She only _____ (live) twenty minutes from my house ...

Sorry, but I have to stop writing now. Mum _____ (call) me for dinner.

See ya, Ben

ZEITENÜBERSICHT

Zeit	Bildung und Formen		Verwendung
Present simple I play/he plays	**1. Form, he/she/it + s**		■ allgemeine Regeln ■ Gewohnheiten ■ regelmäßige Aktivitäten ■ Zustände
	I play	we play	
	you play	you play	
	he plays	they play	
Present progressive* I am playing	**to be (am/is/are) + verb-ing**		■ etwas passiert jetzt gerade ■ etwas passiert in einem eingeschränkten Zeitraum inklusive „jetzt"
	I am playing	we are playing	
	you are playing	you are playing	
	he is playing	they are playing	
Past simple I played	**2. Form: verb + -ed, irregular verbs**		■ abgeschlossene Handlungen in der Vght – kurz, aufeinanderfolgend ■ Was war dann? Handlungsstränge einer Geschichte
	I played	we played	
	you played	you played	
	he played	they played	
Past progressive* I was playing	**to be (was/were) + verb-ing**		■ längere Handlungen, die in der Vergangenheit ▶ parallel verlaufen ▶ von kurzen Handlungen unterbrochen werden ■ Beschreibungen
	I was playing	we were playing	
	you were playing	you were playing	
	he was playing	they were playing	
Present perfect simple I have played	**to have (have/has) + 3. Form**		■ eine Handlung in der Vergangenheit hat eine **Auswirkung** auf die Gegenwart
	I have played	we have played	
	you have played	you have played	
	he has played	they have played	
Present perfect progressive* I have been playing	**have/has been + verb-ing**		■ eine Handlung dauert von der Vergangenheit bis jetzt ■ Betonung der **Dauer** der Handlung
	I have been playing	we have been playing	
	you have been playing	you have been playing	
	he has been playing	they have been playing	
Past perfect simple I had played	**had + 3. Form**		■ Vorvergangenheit ■ eine Handlung passiert **vor** der Vergangenheit
	I had played	we had played	
	you had played	you had played	
	he had played	they had played	
Past perfect progressive* I had been playing	**had been + verb-ing**		■ längere Handlungen vor der Vergangenheit ■ Betonung der Dauer
	I had been playing	we had been playing	
	you had been playing	you had been playing	
	he had been playing	they had been playing	
Will-future I will play	**will + Nennform**		■ unsichere, spontane Zukunft ■ Entscheidungen aus dem Moment heraus
	I will play	we will play	
	you will play	you will play	
	he will play	they will play	
Going-to future I am going to play	**am/is/are + going to + Nennform**		■ geplante Zukunft ■ persönliche Absicht, etwas zu tun
	I am going to play	we are going to play	
	you are going to play	you are going to play	
	he is going to play	they are going to play	
Present progressive* mit "future meaning"	**to be (am/is/are) + verb-ing**		■ sichere Zukunft
	I am playing	we are playing	
	you are playing	you are playing	
	he is playing	they are playing	
Present simple mit "future meaning"	**1. Form, he/she/it + s**		■ fixe zukünftige Ereignisse ■ Fahrpläne ■ fixe Daten
	I play	we play	
	you play	you play	
	he plays	they play	

* progressive = continuous

ZEITENÜBERSICHT

Signalwörter	Beispiele	Frage und Verneinung
always, never, usually, often, sometimes, occasionally, … every Sunday	I **love** marshmallows, but I **hate** cupcakes. The sun **rises** in the east. I **play** tennis. = Ich kann es, es ist mein Hobby.	**Do** you play golf? **Does** he play tennis? I **don't** like coffee. She **doesn't** like tea.
Look! Listen! at the moment, currently, now, here	Look! It**'s snowing**. I **am playing** tennis. = Ich spiele jetzt gerade Tennis. This semester, I **am doing** a yoga course.	**Is** he **playing** tennis? No, he **isn't playing** tennis. **Are** you **talking** to Phil? No, **I'm not talking** to Phil.
yesterday, in 1998, last summer, suddenly, then, three years ago	Yesterday, I **got** up. Then I **washed** my hair and **brushed** my teeth. Suddenly I **remembered** that it **was** Sunday! So I **went** back to bed.	**Did** you **play** tennis? No, I **didn't play** tennis. **Did** Jeff **see** Kate yesterday? No, he **didn't see** Kate.
while	While mum **was reading**, dad **was cleaning** the kitchen. I **was having** a shower when the bell **rang**. When I **woke** up, the sun **was shining** and the birds **were singing**.	What **were** you **doing** yesterday at ten? I **wasn't doing** anything special.
ever, never, yet, not yet, already, just, so far, for, since, this year	I **have lost** my key. I can't get in now. He **has broken** his leg. It still hurts. She **hasn't eaten** anything all day long. She's extremely hungry.	**Have** you **done** your homework? No, I **haven't done** it yet.
for hours for a long time How long?	It **has been raining** for ten days now. Jane **has been waiting** for you for three hours!	**Have** you **been working** all day long? No, I **haven't been working**.
	I couldn't get in because I **had lost** my key. When I arrived at the bus stop I realized that the bus **had** already **left**.	**Had** Fiona **forgotten** to buy cheese? No, she **had not forgotten** …
	It **had been snowing** heavily in the past weeks. So, we could enjoy a great winter holiday.	**Had** the sun **been shining** all day long? No, it **hadn't been shining**.
perhaps, maybe, I hope, I think, I'm not sure, I'm afraid, I doubt	Oh – wait! I **will open** the door for you. I think I **will buy** this dress. I'm afraid I **won't** come.	**Will** you **join** me? No, I think I **won't join** you.
	This summer, I **am going to fly** to Greece. Finn **is going to see** Mary that weekend.	**Are** you **going to buy** that car you are interested in? No, **I'm not going to buy** it.
	We **are having** a party on the tenth of June. It would be great if you could come.	**Are** you **playing** a match on Monday? No, we **aren't playing** …
	The train **leaves** at six next Monday. The party **starts** at nine and **ends** in the morning.	**Does** the match **start** at ten? No, it **doesn't start** at ten. It **starts** at nine.

Exercise 2

Margo: Jimmy, how _____ (be) you? I really _____ (not/see) you

for ages! What _____ (you/do) within the last few months? I'm curious so

tell me please!

Jimmy: Hey Margo! It's nice to see you! You _____ (look) good. Well, there's a lot to tell you.

Did you know that I _____ (lose) my job two months ago?

Margo: No, I _____ (not/hear) about that! Why? What _____ (go) wrong

if I may ask?

Jimmy: Oh, the company _____ (go) bankrupt and so I _____ (must) look for

another job.

Margo: And _____ (you/already/find) something new?

Jimmy: Luckily yes! Actually it was much easier than I _____ (expect). At first I

_____ (think) I would have to write hundreds of letters of applications but in fact I

immediately _____ (find) something new.

Margo: Oh that's great! So where _____ (you/work) right now?

Jimmy: I _____ (be) responsible for online marketing at a German company for outdoor sports. I

really _____ (enjoy) doing that because, you know, I _____

(always/be) keen on doing sports myself. Actually I _____ (be) surprised that I _____

(get) this job so easily and quickly because after I _____ (send) my CV, they

immediately _____ (invite) me for a personal conversation and about six weeks later I

_____ (have) my first working day.

Margo: That's super, Jimmy! Congratulations! And what exactly _____ (you/must/do)

at that job? Can you explain that to me?

Jimmy: Well, at the moment I _____ (work) on improving the online Internet presentation

of the company. And one of my next projects _____ (be) to facilitate online

shopping possibilities for the customers. But it _____ (take) some time until I can work

on that one.

Margo: Sounds like a real challenge! Hey Jimmy, what about meeting for a cup of coffee next week?

Jimmy: Definitely! If you _____ (give) me your number, I _____ (call) you at

the weekend. I really look forward to _____ (see) you more often.

Margo: Great! Here is my card. Just let me know when you have time! Bye Jimmy!

Modal verbs

Fill in the verbs in brackets. Mind modal verbs, perfect modal verbs and multi-part verbs and the tenses.

Tricia: Hi Marla! Nice to see you. I'm sorry that I _____ (not can – go) to the cinema with

you yesterday. I _____ (must – help) my mum.

Marla: What _____ (you – must – do)?

Tricia: First, I _____ (must) iron tons of clothes and then I _____

(should – clean) my room. But when I was ironing one of my shirts, I burnt my finger. So, I _____

_____ (not can – go on).

Marla: Poor you. You know you have to be careful when you iron things. You _____

(might – get) badly hurt.

Tricia: I know, I know. I'm glad that nothing really bad happened. I simply _____

(should – pay) more attention to what I was doing. The next time I iron shirts I _____

(must – be) more careful. That's it.

Marla: I'm glad I _____ (not must – do) much housework recently. Two weeks

ago, my mum _____ (can – convince) Ms Jennings, our cleaning lady, to work for us

every day. Since then, all of us _____ (can – relax). You know, before

Ms Jennings came, my father, my brother and I _____ (must – work)

at least an hour a day to help our mum. That was quite hard.

Tricia: I remember! So, now that you have enough time, I guess that you _____

(can – come) to my party next Saturday?

Marla: I'm not sure. I think that I _____ (must – look after) my little brother

because my parents want to visit some friends.

Tricia: Oh Marla. You _____ (should – talk) to your parents again and tell them that you

need some time for your friends. Remind them that you _____ (not may –

go) to Lucy's party last week because you _____ (should – study) for

your Maths test.

Marla: I know, Tricia, I know. But I think that my parents were quite right last week. I really _____

_____ (can – study) more before the weekend. But I didn't. So, I _____

_____ (must – face) the consequences and stay at home.

Tricia: You sound like your own mother, Marla. Come on. You are fifteen years old. Give it a try.

Marla: You're right. By the way – do you know where Rick is? He _____ (should – join)

us an hour ago. He said that he wanted to do some homework, but he _____

(must – finish) by now.

Tricia: Right. I don't know. Let's call him …

CONDITIONALS/IF-SENTENCES

Conditionals oder *if-sentences* sind Bedingungssätze.
Sie haben zwei Teile: die Bedingung (*if* ... = wenn, falls ...) und die Folge (dann ...).

Bedingung	Folge
If you forget to feed your cat,	it is hungry and angry.
If you feed our dog Muesli now,	he will be happy.
If you spent more time with your girlfriend,	she would not complain all the time.
If you had listened to the teacher,	you would know the answer now.
If you had studied more,	you wouldn't have failed the test.

Im Deutschen verwendet man für die Folge im Bedingungsgefüge (Konditionalgefüge) den Konjunktiv. Da dieser Modus im Englischen nicht existiert, verwendet man anstatt des Konjunktivs *will*, *would* und spezielle Zeiten-kombinationen. Je nachdem, wie wahrscheinlich eine Bedingung eintritt, unterscheidet man zwischen *Conditional 0*, *1*, *2* und *3*.

Conditional 0

Bildung		Verwendung
Bedingung: If + present simple	**Folge:** present simple	Das *conditional 0* verwendest du für allgemeine Aussagen, Tatsachen und Naturgesetze sowie neutrale Bitten.
If you drop a glass,	it breaks.	
Folge: present simple	**Bedingung:** if + present simple	
A glass breaks	if you drop it.	Die Bedingung ist erfüllbar.

Exercise 1 Comma

Wie dir in den Beispielen oben sicher aufgefallen ist, kann die Bedingung, also der *if*-Teil, sowohl am Anfang als auch in der Mitte des Satzes stehen. Kreuze an, welche Aussage zutrifft:

1. Wenn die Folge zu Beginn steht, werden Folge und Bedingung durch einen Beistrich getrennt. ☐

2. Bedingung und Folge bzw. Folge und Bedingung werden immer durch einen Beistrich getrennt. ☐

3. Wenn das *if* am Anfang steht, werden Bedingung und Folge durch einen Beistrich getrennt. ☐

Exercise 2 Conditional 0

Translate the following sentences. Mind the commas!

1. Wenn du Schnee erwärmst, schmilzt er. _____ ☐

2. Wenn ich fröhlich bin, höre ich Musik. _____ ☐

3. Bitte frage, wenn du etwas wissen willst. _____ ☐

4. Wenn man schnell läuft, schwitzt man. _____ ☐

5. Wenn das Baby hungrig ist, schreit es. _____ ☐

Exercise 3 Conditional 0: Verwendung

Re-read the sentences above and match them with the following meanings. Write the letters in the boxes.

A allgemeine Aussage   **B** Naturgesetz   **C** neutrale Bitte, Aufforderung

Conditional 1

Bildung		Verwendung
Bedingung: If + present simple	**Folge:** will + Nennform	Das *conditional 1* verwendest du für spezielle Situationen in der Gegenwart. Es ist wahrscheinlich, dass die Bedingung eintritt.
If you drop this glass,	it will break.	
Folge: will + Nennform	**Bedingung:** if + present simple	
This glass will break	if you drop it.	

! Statt **will** kann auch ein anderes *modal verb* verwendet werden: **can, may, must, mustn't**.

Exercise 4 **Conditional 1**

Translate the following sentences.

1. Wenn du wieder auf den Geburtstag deiner Freundin vergisst, wird sie dich nicht mehr sehen wollen.

_____

2. Ich werde dir nicht helfen können, wenn du mir nichts über dein Problem erzählst.

_____

3. Jane wird dir helfen, wenn du sie fragst. Ich bin mir ganz sicher.

_____

Conditional 2

Bildung		Verwendung
Bedingung: If + past simple	**Folge:** would + Nennform	Das *conditional 2* verwendest du für spezielle Situationen in der Gegenwart. Es ist unwahrscheinlich, dass die Bedingung eintritt.
If you dropped this glass,	it would break.	
Folge: would + Nennform	**Bedingung:** if + past simple	
This glass would break	if you dropped it.	

! Statt **would** kann auch ein anderes *modal verb* verwendet werden: **could, might**.

Exercise 5 **Conditional 2**

Translate the following sentences.

1. Ich würde sie heute nicht anrufen, wenn ich du wäre.

_____

2. Wenn ich eine Million Euro gewinnen würde, könnte ich endlich eine Weltreise machen.

_____

3. Wenn Eric Zeit hätte, würde er mit dir ins Kino gehen. Er muss aber leider arbeiten.

_____

Conditional 3a: Auswirkung auf die Gegenwart

Bildung		Verwendung
Bedingung: If + past perfect	**Folge:** would + Nennform	Das *conditional 3a* verwendest du für eine Bedingung in der Vergangenheit, die eine Folge in der **Gegenwart** auslöst. Die Bedingung ist unmöglich.
If you had dropped this glass,	you would have to tell mum.	
Folge: would + Nennform	**Bedingung:** if + past perfect	
You would have to tell mum	if you had dropped the glass.	

! Statt *would* kannst du auch *could* oder *might* verwenden.

Exercise 6 Conditional 3a

Translate the following sentences.

1. Wenn ich mein Zimmer gestern geputzt hätte, könnte ich jetzt mit euch schwimmen gehen.

_____

2. Peter würde jetzt in einer erfolgreichen Band spielen, wenn er nicht aufgehörte hätte, Schlagzeug zu üben.

_____

3. Jake und Angie wären jetzt verheiratet, wenn sie ihn nicht betrogen hätte.

_____

Conditional 3b: Auswirkung auf die Vergangenheit

Bildung		Verwendung
Bedingung: If + past perfect	**Folge:** would + have + 3rd form	Das *conditional 3b* verwendest du für eine Bedingung in der Vergangenheit, die eine Folge in der **Vergangenheit** auslöst. Die Bedingung ist unmöglich.
If you had dropped this glass,	you would have broken it.	
Folge: would + have + 3rd form	**Bedingung:** if + past perfect	
You would have broken this glass	if you had dropped it.	

! Statt *would* kannst du auch *might* oder *could* verwenden.

Exercise 7 Conditional 3b

Translate the following sentences.

1. Jim hätte seinen Schlüssel nicht verloren, wenn er ihn in die Lade gegeben hätte.

_____

2. Wenn ich Alicia die Wahrheit gesagt hätte, hätte sie mich nicht angeschrien.

_____

3. Wir hätten den Bus noch erwischt, wenn du nicht so lange zum Anziehen gebraucht hättest.

_____

Mixed conditionals

Make conditional sentences out of the following situations.

1. **If**: I: have a plane   **Folge**: fly to Paris every Sunday   **Situation**: I don't have one.

2. **If**: we: catch the 11:30 train   **Folge**: arrive on time   **Situation**: It's very likely we'll catch it.

3. **If**: I: not break my leg   **Folge**: go skiing this weekend   **Situation**: My leg is broken.

4. **If**: my mum: wake me before 11 on Sundays   **Folge**: I: tell her to go away   **Situation**: She does that nearly every Sunday.

5. **If**: I: have an older brother   **Folge**: I: ask him to do my homework   **Situation**: I don't have one.

6. **If**: Trisha: ask Pete   **Folge**: he: invite her to the party   **Situation**: she didn't ask – he didn't invite her

7. **If**: put salt in water   **Folge**: it: not freeze at 0 degrees   **Situation**: natural law

8. **If**: Kim: not hand in her essay today   **Folge**: get an F   **Situation**: She hasn't finished it yet.

9. **If**: I: not think of buying cream   **Folge**: I: not can mix those great cocktails   **Situation**: I thought of buying cream and could mix the cocktails.

10. **If**: Jim: not forget his calculator   **Folge**: he: can do his homework now   **Situation**: he forgot it

11. **If**: I: be better at playing poker   **Folge**: join your game   **Situation**: I'm very bad at poker.

12. **If**: it: rain   **Folge**: I: not go swimming   **Situation**: There are thick clouds in the sky.

13. **If**: I: close the window   **Folge**: wind: not blown away my essay   **Situation**: I didn't close the window, the essay is gone.

14. **If**: you go shopping   **Folge**: not forget to buy strawberries   **Situation**: neutrale Bitte

15. **If**: my cat catch a mouse   **Folge**: I: try to save the mouse   **Situation**: My cat rarely catches mice.

REPORTED SPEECH

Aussage

Die indirekte Rede oder *reported speech* wird verwendet, um Gesprochenes indirekt wiederzugeben.

DIRECT SPEECH:	Mark says, "I always have coffee for breakfast."
INDIRECT SPEECH:	Mark says that he always has coffee for breakfast.

Wenn eine Rede indirekt wiedergegeben wird, musst du auf folgende Punkte achten:

- Welches ist das passende *reporting verb*? Mark **says** that he always has coffee. (Siehe Seite 97).
- Habe ich alle Pronomen an das Subjekt angepasst? <u>Mark</u> says that **he** always has coffee for breakfast.
- In welcher Zeit steht das *reporting verb*? **says:** present simple

! Wenn das *reporting verb* in *present tense, present perfect tense* oder *future tense* steht, bleibt die Zeit im Satz der indirekten Rede gleich wie im Satz der direkten Rede.

(reporting verb) TENSE	DIRECT SPEECH	INDIRECT SPEECH
present tense	Kim **says**, "I *played* tennis yesterday."	Kim **says** that she *played* tennis yesterday.
present perfect	Pit **has** just **answered**, "I *play* the keys."	Pit **has** just **answered** that he *plays* the keys.
future	She **will say**, "I *don't like* that colour."	She **will say** that she *doesn't like* the colour.

! Wenn das *reporting verb* in *past tense* steht, musst du in der indirekten Rede einen Zeitensprung machen.

DIRECT SPEECH	INDIRECT SPEECH
present simple	**past simple**
Mona said, "I **love** café latte."	Mona said that she **loved** café latte.
present progressive/continuous	**past progressive/continuous**
Leni cried, "There **is** a spider **sitting** over there!"	Leni cried that there **was** a spider **sitting** over there.
present perfect simple	**past perfect simple**
Tracy shouted, "I **have lost** my key!"	Tracy shouted that she **had lost** her key.
present perfect progressive/continuous	**past perfect progressive/continuous**
Max explained, "I **have been waiting** for an hour."	Max explained that he **had been waiting** for an hour.
past simple	**past perfect simple**
Sue answered, "We **went** to the movies."	Sue answered that they **had gone** to the movies.
past progressive/continuous	**past perfect progressive/continuous**
Cal said, "Tina **was playing** tennis at ten."	Cal said that Tina **had been playing** tennis at ten.
will/can/may	**would/could/might**
Mia said, "Perhaps I **will** give Frank a call."	Mia said that she **would** perhaps give Frank a call.
Fiona answered, "I **can't** help you."	Fiona answered that she **couldn't** help me.
Tony said, "I **may** visit my aunt."	Tony said that he **might** visit his aunt.

Exercise 1

Underline the reporting verbs. Decide whether you have to change the tense of the reported speech sentence or not.

1. Mum suggested, "You can take the car. I don't need it."

_____

2. Sabrina remarked, "I was reading my favourite magazine when I suddenly felt cold."

_____

3. Dad has just said, "I don't want to drive to town. I think we should take our bikes."

_____

4. Barbara will say, "I'm sure that it is going to be sunny."

_____

5. Greg replied, "I haven't seen Melissa for a year. You don't have to worry."

_____

6. My girlfriend always complains, "You spend too much time with your friends."

_____

7. Melissa mentioned, "It's sunny! We may go to the beach."

_____

! Wenn das _reporting verb_ in der _past tense_ steht, musst du auch noch einige andere Veränderungen beachten.

DIRECT SPEECH	INDIRECT SPEECH
pronouns (I, we, you, me, her, our, ...)	
here	there
now	then
this/these	that/those
today	that day
yesterday	the day before
tomorrow	the next day
last week/month/year	the previous week/month/year
a year ago	the previous year/a year before
next week/month/year	the following week/month/year

! Folgende Verben bleiben normalerweise unverändert; _could_ und _must_ können umschrieben werden.

would	ought to	might	could ► could oder: was/were/had been/would be able to
should	mustn't	had better	must ► must oder: had to, would have to

Frage

Bei der indirekten Fragestellung musst du zwei Arten unterscheiden:

1. Entscheidungsfrage: Frage ohne Fragewort   **2. Ergänzungsfrage: Frage mit Fragewort**

1. Frage ohne Fragewort: Entscheidungsfrage

DIRECT SPEECH	INDIRECT SPEECH
Dora said, "Does the train leave at ten?"	Dora asked **if** the train left at ten.
Trina said, "Didn't you read this book?"	Trina asked **whether** I hadn't read that book.
Michael says, "Is the water warm enough to swim?"	Michael asks **if** the water is warm enough to swim.

Bei der Frage ohne Fragewort musst du folgende Punkte beachten:

- In welcher Zeit steht das *reporting verb*? Regeln siehe „Aussage", Seite 94.
- Verwendest du ein passendes *reporting verb*? Liste siehe Seite 97.
- Leite die indirekte Frage mit *if* oder *whether* ein!
- Achte darauf, aus dem Fragesatz der direkten Rede in der indirekten Rede einen Aussagesatz zu machen!

2. Frage mit Fragewort: Ergänzungsfrage

DIRECT SPEECH	INDIRECT SPEECH
Veronica said, "Where did you buy this dress?"	Veronica asked **where** I had bought that dress.
Kirsten said, "Where is Cornflake?"	Kirsten asked **where** Cornflake was.
The teacher says, "Who is absent?"	The teacher asks **who** is absent.

Exercise 2

Lies dir noch einmal aufmerksam die Punkte durch, die es zu beachten gilt, wenn Entscheidungsfragen in der indirekten Rede wiedergegeben werden sollen. Einen Punkt musst du ändern, um diese Regeln für die Ergänzungsfrage umzuformulieren. Wie lautet dieser?

_____

_____

Exercise 3

Write down the correct indirect questions.

1. He said to me, "Did you call me at ten?"

_____

2. Douglas will say to Sally, "Where do you want to go on holiday?"

_____

3. Mum said to us, "Have you forgotten to lock the door?"

_____

Bitte und Befehl

Bei indirekten Bitten und Befehlen musst du besonders auf die Wahl eines passenden *reporting verbs* achten. Der sogenannte „Zeitensprung" entfällt, weil indirekte Bitten und Befehle mit der Nennform (*to-infinitive*) gebildet werden. Es gibt vier Formen:

1. Höfliche Bitte: ask, beg, invite, implore, ... + object pronoun + to + Nennform

Thomas said to me, "Open the window, <u>please</u>."	
Thomas **asked me to open** the window.	Thomas **implored me to open** the window.
Thomas **begged me to open** the window.	Thomas **said politely that I should open** the window.
Thomas said that I **should be so kind as to** open the window.	

2. Neutraler Befehl: tell, advise, recommend, suggest, ... + object pronoun + to + Nennform

Mum said to us, "Open the window."	
Mum **told us to open** the window.	Mum **advised us to open** the window.
Mum **reminded us to open** the window.	Mum **wanted us to open** the window.
Mum **said that we should/ought to** open the window.	Mum **suggested opening** the window.

3. Strenger Befehl: shout at, scream at, urge, command, order + object pronoun + to + Nennform

She shouted at me, "Tell me the truth!"	
She **shouted at me to tell** her the truth.	She **urged me to tell** her the truth.
She **screamed at me to tell** her the truth.	She **commanded me to tell** her the truth.
She **ordered me** to tell her the truth.	

4. Verneinter Befehl: tell, order, advise, warn, suggest, ... + object pronoun + not to + Nennform

Ginger said to Connor, "Don't forget my birthday."	
Ginger told Connor not to forget her birthday.	Ginger ordered Connor not to forget her birthday.
Ginger warned Connor not to forget her birthday.	Ginger advised Connor not to forget her birthday.
Ginger commanded Connor not to forget her birthday.	

Ausrufe

Help!	She called for help.	No!	We refused.
Thank you!	He thanked me.	Yes!	I agreed.
Good morning!	Pat wished me a good morning.	Yes, I'll come.	He agreed to come.
Congratulations!	They congratulated me.	Hello!	She greeted him.
Fool!	Angie called me a fool!	How cute!	I said that it was cute.

Reporting verbs

add	claim	deny	insist on	order	remark	think	... astonished
admire	complain	enquire	know	promise	reply	urge	... conscious of
admit	confess	expect	mention	protest	state	to be ...	... indifferent
agree	consider	explain	note	refuse	suggest	... afraid	... interested in
ask	continue	hope	observe	regret	suppose	... amazed	... sure

Mixed exercises

Exercise 4

Kim, who has had a crush on Brian for a while, is sitting in the school cafeteria with one of her friends, Jane. Suddenly Brian addresses Jane. Read their conversation and then do the task below.

Brian: Hi Kim! How are you?

Kim: Great!

Brian: May I take the seat next to you?

Kim: Go ahead. *(silence)* So, Brian, have you already done your Maths homework?

Brian: I tried it yesterday, but I couldn't do some of the exercises.

Kim: Do you want me to help you?

Brian: No, thank you. But ... Kim, what I am trying to ask you is ...

Kim: Yes?

Jane: *(interrupts Brian and Kim)* Brian – pass me the salt, please.

Kim: Here Jane. Yes Brian – what do you want to ask me?

Jane: *(interrupts Brian and Kim again)* Pass me the mustard, please.

Kim: *(passes Jane the mustard impatiently)* Jane – don't interrupt us constantly!

Brian: So – do you want to go to the movies with me, this evening?

Kim: *(smiles happily)* I'm so glad you finally asked.

Brian: Cool! When do you want to go?

Kim: Let's go tonight. Have you already seen *Inception* with Leonardo DiCaprio?

Brian: No, I haven't. I will fetch you at seven, okay?

Kim: Fine! See you at seven.

Brian: Bye!

Jane: *(shouts)* Kim! What have you done? Didn't you know that Brian has been dating Veronica for three weeks?

Kim: Stop shouting! What are you talking about?

Jane: Brian asked her out after the school dance. They've been seeing each other quite a lot since then. I can't believe he asked you out! Brian is one of the most awful cheaters at school. Don't trust him.

Kim: I don't believe you! Don't talk that badly about Brian, I beg you. I've been looking forward to this moment for months.

Jane: I just want to warn you. I just don't want to be blamed in case Brian disappoints you.

Kim: Thanks, but I will see Brian anyway.

Jane: That's up to you.

The next evening, Kim writes an e-mail to her best friend, telling her about the conservation. Write the e-mail.

Dear Adrienne,
Imagine what happened yesterday! I was sitting in the school cafeteria, when I suddenly saw Brian standing next to me.

_____

_____

_____

_____

_____

_____

_____

_____

_____

_____

_____

_____

_____

_____

_____

_____

_____

_____

_____

_____

_____

_____

_____

Of course I asked Brian about Veronica. He informed me that Jane hadn't told me the truth. He only saw Veronica once, but they didn't get on.

I will keep you in the loop.   *Love, Kim*

Exercise 5

Write reported speech sentences. Find the most suitable reporting verb.

admit – greet – regret – promise – implore – urge – deny – call – observe – admire – suggest – complain – advise – claim

1. Alan said, "Gerry hasn't washed his car for a while."

_____

2. My mum said to my father, "Buy the bigger car!"

_____

3. My sister said, "I didn't take your blouse."

_____

4. Mathew said, "I copied my homework from Tina."

_____

5. Roland said to Vanessa, "My darling".

_____

6. Lilly said, "Patrick and Hannah are dancing so beautifully."

_____

7. Emma said to her boyfriend, "Don't leave me! I can't live without you."

_____

8. Stephen said to Ralph, "Take the stronger car."

_____

9. I said, "I couldn't join the party yesterday. I really wanted to."

_____

10. Anthony said, "My motorbike is much faster than yours."

_____

11. Mike said to Jennifer, "This will be the best day in your life."

_____

12. Samantha said to Bianca, "Hello."

_____

13. Georgiana said, "I won't be able to see you all summer if you work in Spain!"

_____

14. Cynthia said, "Let's go swimming."

_____

PASSIVE VOICE

ACTIVE	PASSIVE
The landlady **serves** breakfast from 7 to 10.	Breakfast **is served** from 7 to 10 (by the landlady).
They **are repairing** the old bridge.	The old bridge **is being repaired**.
The estate agent **sold** the house.	The house **was sold** (by the estate agent).
Someone **has stolen** my bike.	My bike **has been stolen**.
The painters **will paint** the wall.	The wall **will be painted** (by the painters).

Exercise 1

Unterstreiche das Subjekt in rot und das Objekt in blau in dem Kästchen der Sätze im Aktiv. Dann unterstreiche diese in der Spalte des Passivs. Was fällt dir auf?

_____

_____

Exercise 2

Vervollständige die Regeln zur Bildung des Passivs.

BILDUNG	**to be (in der entsprechenden Zeit) + past participle** Subjekt wird zum _____ Objekt wird zum _____

Das Passiv wird verwendet, um die Handlung zu betonen. Derjenige, der die Handlung ausübt, also der Handlungsträger (_doer, by-agent_) tritt dabei in den Hintergrund. Das Passiv wird oft verwendet, wenn der Handlungsausübende unbekannt, unwichtig oder offensichtlich ist. Es kann auch als Mittel zur Verschleierung der Akteure verwendet werden.

Exercise 3

Vervollständige die Zeitentabelle.

TENSE	ACTIVE	PASSIVE
Present simple	The gardener mows the lawn twice a week.	
		Our car is being repaired (by the mechanic).
Past simple		The house was built in 1756 (by them).
Past cont.	Someone was following us.	
Present perfect		The cat hasn't been fed today (by me).
	They had closed the restaurant.	
Will-future		The album will be released next month.
	They are going to release the film in April.	
	They would invite Sally.	

Exercise 4

Put into passive voice:

1. I have fed the dog twice today.

   _____

2. You must clean Tweety's cage more carefully.

   _____

3. The maid should have served dinner at eight.

   _____

4. They are going to shoot the film in Mexico.

   _____

5. You ought to learn the poem by heart.

   _____

6. The scientists have been observing the birds for two months now.

   _____

7. Someone had stolen my keys.

   _____

8. They will build a new skyscraper.

   _____

9. The reporter was interviewing me when someone hit me with a tomato!

   _____

10. They couldn't turn off the water.

    _____

11. Someone has found my lost dog.

    _____

12. You cannot see the baby elephant today.

    _____

13. He didn't sell the car yesterday.

    _____

14. They would have caught the bear if they had taken better traps.

    _____

15. They don't close the zoo before seven.

    _____

Exercise 5

Fill in the correct active or passive form of the verbs. Mind the tenses.

Steve: Hi Donna. How _____ (things – go)?

Donna: Great!

Steve: Why _____ (not – be) Claire at the last training session?

Donna: Haven't you heard? She _____ (throw) out for stealing.

Steve: No! When _____ (that – happen)?

Donna: Yesterday evening. She _____ (see) taking money from someone's bag

in the changing room.

Steve: Who by?

Donna: The sports club manager. She _____ (check) the changing rooms when

she _____ (find) Claire there with Karen's bag.

Steve: Oh no! What _____ (do) about Claire then?

Donna: When Claire _____ (interview) she said she _____

_____ (ask) to fetch some money for Karen. However, after Karen _____

_____ (question) it became clear that the sports club manager _____

_____ (not tell) the truth. Karen _____ (not say) a word

to Claire about fetching the money.

Steve: That's a terrible story. But I think that Karen _____ (not should – leave)

her money in the locker!

Donna: Sure. She _____ (just – tell) the same by the manager.

Now, Claire promised that she _____ (definitely – not do)

such a stupid thing again.

Steve: Who knows. What do you think Claire _____ (do) now?

Donna: I really don't know. This is the second club she _____ (must – leave)

so far, isn't it?

Steve: Yes, as far as I know. I wonder what _____ (can – do) to help a

person like her.

Donna: Maybe she _____ (should – send) to a psychologist. I hope she

_____ (not arrest) for something worse one day.

Steve: Yes, I'm afraid she _____ (not can – change) all on her own.

ADJECTIVES AND ADVERBS

Adjective or adverb?

ADJECTIVE	ADVERB
■ describes nouns My father is a *careful* **driver**. Nach: feel, smell, taste, sound, look, be, seem, become, turn, grow, get, remain	■ describes verbs (adverb of manner) My father **drives** *carefully*. ■ describes adjectives (adverbs of degree) My father is an *extremely* **careful** driver. ■ describes adverbs (adverbs of degree) My father drives *extremely* **carefully**.

Ausnahmen: good – well, long – long, fast – fast, low – low, straight – straight, doubtless – doubtless, friendly – in a friendly way

unregelmäßige Formen:
hard – hard (hardly: *kaum*), high – high (highly: *höchst*), near – near (nearly: *beinahe*), fair – fair (fairly: *ziemlich*), late – late (lately: *vor Kurzem*), direct – direct (directly: *sofort*), close – close (closely: ressemble – *sehr ähnlich sein*/watch – *genau beobachten*), deep – deep (deeply: *zutiefst*), free – free (freely: *ungezwungen*), pretty – pretty: *ziemlich* (prettily: *hübsch*)

! look: She looks angry. (*aussehen*: Adjektiv)	She looks at me angrily. (*ansehen*: Adverb)
! taste: The cake tastes good. (*schmecken*: Adjektiv)	I taste the cake carefully. (*kosten*: Adverb)

Exercise 1

Fill in the correct forms.

1. That bird over there sings _____ (*schön*).

2. Our team played _____ (*schlecht*) today.

3. Shannon looks _____ (*fantastisch*) in her new dress and she smiles so

   _____ (*glücklich*).

4. Those shoes are _____ (*ziemlich*) expensive!

5. Taste the cake _____ (*vorsichtig*). It's hot!

6. Marina speaks Spanish very _____ (*gut*), but her French is not very

   _____ (*gut*).

7. My father works very _____ (*viel, hart*) and he _____ (*kaum*) ever

   goes on holiday.

8. Go _____ (*geradeaus*) and then turn _____ (*rechts*).

9. She walked into the room _____ (*leise, ruhig*) so as not to disturb the dogs.

10. Have you seen Alex _____ (*vor Kurzem*)?

11. I was _____ (*zutiefst*) shocked when I heard the news.

12. The cat watched me _____ (*genau*) while I was eating the cake.

Comparisons

ADJECTIVES 1-silbig	ADJECTIVES 2-silbig, Endung: -y, -er, -le, -ow	ADJECTIVES restliche 2-silbig mehrsilbig	ADVERBS Endung: -ly
-er/-est	-er/-est	more/most	more/most
slow – slower – the slowest big – bigger – the biggest hot – hotter – the hottest	happy – happier – the happiest clever – cleverer – the cleverest simple – simpler – the simplest	beautiful – more beautiful – most beautiful	angrily – more angrily – most angrily Adverbs ohne -ly: -er/-est high – higher – the highest

Ausnahmen

ADJECTIVES		
good	better	best
bad	worse	worst
little	less	least
much/many/some	more	most
far	further	furthest

ADVERBS		
well	better	best
badly	worse	worst
much/many	more	most
little	less	least

Exercise 2

Fill in the correct forms of adjectives and adverbs.

1. You should drive _____ (vorsichtiger) here! It's dangerous.

2. Your computer works _____ (viel schneller) than mine.

3. You didn't help me! Quite on the contrary, you made it even _____ (schlechter).

4. My cat can jump _____ (viel höher) than my dog.

5. This is an _____ (extrem interessant) story.

6. James Cameron's _____ (jüngste) film is _____ (weniger aufregend) than his _____ (letzte) before.

7. I can ride my board _____ (schneller) than you! But I guess Tim is _____ _____ (der Schnellste).

8. Have you ever seen her dancing _____ (fröhlicher)?

9. My dad is a really _____ (schlecht) cook, but my mum cooks even _____ (schlechter).

10. Don't do that! I thought you were _____ (intelligenter) than that!

11. I think I will buy two _____ (weitere) T-shirts.

12. If you work _____ (härter) you will get _____ (bessere) marks.

13. I have never seen a _____ (traurig) face than yours after the party!

14. This is _____ (grauenhafteste) mistake you have ever made.

15. If it snows _____ (stärker) today, we won't be able to go skiing.

Word order of adjectives

OPINION	DESCRIPTIVE							
	number	size	shape	age	colour	origin	material	purpose/type
fantastic	countless	small	round	new	green	Australian	leather	jazz

Find the correct order of the adjectives.

1. Yesterday I bought a *leather / dark blue / marvellous* jacket.

_____

2. When I was lying in the warm grass, a swarm of *tiny / numerous / black* beetles surrounded me.

_____

3. Look at that *Victorian / coffee / horrible / mahogany / 150-year-old /* table.

_____

4. There must be *Belgium / ice-cold / some / cherry-flavoured / delicious* beers in the fridge.

_____

5. Take off those *muddy / boat-shaped / basketball / disgusting / old* shoes.

_____

Compound adjectives

With which other words do the following adjectives collocate so as their meaning is intensified?

jet – wide – dead – pitch – stone – fool – crystal – stark – dog – skin – flat

1. I'll go to bed immediately. I'm _____-tired.

2. Jump in! The water is _____ clear.

3. This train is a pest! It's _____-slow and overcrowded!

4. Jumping into the lake with your bike is quite a _____hardy thing to do.

5. I really envy you for your _____-black hair.

6. I can't see a thing in that _____ dark room.

7. My gramps *(Opa)* is _____-deaf! He doesn't hear a word I'm saying.

8. These _____-tight jeans look great on you.

9. I'm sorry, I can't pay for the pizza. I'm _____ broke.

10. I can't sleep! I'm _____ awake!

11. Yuck! Do you see that old man lying _____ naked in the sun?

RELATIVE CLAUSES

Relativpronomen ersetzen Nomen in einem Relativsatz und dienen dazu, zwei Sätze zu verbinden.

MAIN CLAUSE	MAIN CLAUSE	MAIN CLAUSE and RELATIVE CLAUSE
A man has hit my car.	He is standing over there.	The man **who** has hit my car is standing over there.
I wanted to buy a flat.	It was sold yesterday.	The flat **which** I wanted to buy was sold yesterday.

Relative pronouns

	PERSONS	THINGS and ANIMALS
nominative	**who/that**	**which/that**
	The boy who/that lives next door is so cute!	This is the cat that/which stole my steak.
genitive	**whose**	**whose/of which**
	This is the girl whose bike was stolen.	The bike whose/of which the tyre is punctured is mine.
dative/ accusative	**who/whom/that**	**which/that**
	The girl who(m)/that Jeff married is a real beauty.	The photo which/that you took of me is awful!
after prepositions	**to/for/with … whom (kein that!)**	**to/for/with … which (kein that!)**
	My friend for whom I had planned the surprise party was overjoyed.	The key for which you are looking is on the table.
Other relative pronouns:	**when:** The day (when) I married you was the best day in my life.	
	where: This is the place where your dad and I had our first date.	
! Genaue Regeln zur Verwendung von who, which und that: siehe defining/non-defining relative clauses.		

In folgenden Situationen darf nur THAT, nicht who und which, verwendet werden:		
NACH all, everything, everybody, something, somebody, someone, anything, anybody, anyone, nothing, nobody, no one, much, little, few, the only …	NACH Superlativen That's the best book (that) I have ever read.	Wenn man über eine Person UND ein Tier zur selben Zeit redet: The girl and the dog (that) you see over there live next to me.

, which (!Komma!)	what
Kann sich auch auf einen ganzen Satz beziehen. She finally found the answer, **which** surprised us.	Kann am Satzanfang für „the thing(s) that" stehen. The things that/**What** we saw frightened us.

Defining/Non-defining relative clauses

DEFINING	NON-DEFINING
Jane's brother *who lives in London* is married. KEIN KOMMA Der Relativsatz gibt WICHTIGE Informationen.	Mary's brother, *who lives in London*, is married. KOMMA Der Relativsatz gibt unwichtige Zusatzinformationen.
that kann verwendet werden.	**that** darf NICHT verwendet werden.
that/who/which kann als Objekt entfallen: This is the boy (that/who) I met yesterday.	**that/who/which** darf nicht entfallen: This boy, who is seventeen, is so cute.

Exercise 1

Read the information box about defining and non-defining relative clauses. Who has got more than one brother, Jane or Mary?

Exercise 2

Write one sentence. Mind the commas and put the relative pronouns that can be omitted in brackets.

1. The River Thames flows through London. Its name is derived from the Celtic name *Tamesas*.

_____

2. Malcolm kept on talking for hours. That annoyed us a lot.

_____

3. My cousin teaches in a school. The school offers twenty different sports clubs.

The school _____

4. I danced with a girl at prom night. She asked me for a date.

_____

5. My sister's husband plays in a rock band. He often takes me to cool concerts.

_____

6. The coach and the dolphin always do a great show. You can see them on this picture.

_____

7. I went to see the doctor. He told me to stay in bed for a week.

_____

8. There are some phrases in this text. They are very difficult to translate.

_____

9. My father bought an apartment. He never wants to spend a lot of money. The apartment is too small.

_____

Exercise 3

Tick the correct sentences. Underline the mistakes and correct them.

1. Boris always orders the most expensive steak which costs him a lot of money. _____

2. The bike what I saw in the shop costs 3000 dollars. _____

3. Lenny showed me a photo of his dog, that he loves very much. _____

4. The girl and her pony that are riding over there have already won many prices. _____

5. My mother who has just left the house will call you back. _____

6. My cat Scratchy, that is sleeping in my lap, is digging her claws in my thigh. _____

7. Pluto which is the second largest dwarf-planet in the Solar System is a member of the Kuiper belt. _____

8. You are all what I need. _____

GERUND

Bildung

	ACTIVE	PASSIVE
PRESENT	seeing	being seen
PERFECT	having seen	having been seen

Verwendung

verbal noun (hauptwörtlich gebrauchtes Zeitwort)	after possessive adjectives and accusative personal pronouns	after possessive cases
Dancing is my favourite hobby. The keeping of cats is forbidden. No skating!	Do you mind my singing? (F. E.) Do you mind me singing? (I. E.)	I love Peter's smiling at me. (F. E.) I love Peter smiling at me. (I. E.)
F. E. = formal, written English	**I. E.** = informal, spoken English	

Verben, die das *Gerund* verlangen					
admit	zugeben	**fail**	scheitern	**need***	brauchen
advise*	(be)raten	**fancy**	gern mögen	**pardon**	entschuldigen
allow*	erlauben	**finish**	beenden	**permit***	erlauben
anticipate	erwarten	**forbid**	verbieten	**postpone**	verschieben
appreciate	wertschätzen	**forget***	vergessen	**practise**	üben
avoid	vermeiden	**forgive**	vergeben	**prefer***	bevorzugen
begin*	beginnen	**hate***	hassen	**recollect**	erinnern
can't help	nicht anders können	**imagine**	vorstellen	**regret**	bedauern
consider	in Betracht ziehen	**intend***	beabsichtigen	**remember***	erinnern
continue*	fortsetzen	**involve**	beinhalten	**resent**	übel nehmen
delay	verzögern	**justify**	rechtfertigen	**resist**	widerstehen
deny	leugnen	**keep**	weitermachen	**risk**	riskieren
detest*	hassen	**like***	mögen	**start***	anfangen
dislike*	nicht mögen	**love***	lieben	**stop*/quit**	beenden
dread	fürchten	**mention**	erwähnen	**suggest**	vorschlagen
enjoy	genießen	**mean***	meinen	**try***	versuchen
escape	entkommen	**mind**	kümmern	**understand**	verstehen
excuse	entschuldigen	**miss**	vermissen	**want***	wollen

* see pages 113 ff.

Exercise 1

Which of the verbs in the list above can also be followed by a "that" clause?

Verben mit Präpositionen, die das *Gerund* verlangen					
accuse of	beschuldigen	**consist of**	bestehen aus	**object to**	protestieren
adjust to	anpassen an	**cope with**	fertig werden mit	**prevent from**	hindern
agree with	zustimmen	**count on**	darauf zählen	**put off**	aufschieben
aim at	abzielen auf	**decide against**	entscheiden gegen	**refrain from**	unterlassen
apologise for	entschuldigen für	**decide for/on**	entscheiden für	**rely on**	verlassen auf
approve of	dafür sein	**delight in**	erfreuen an	**save from**	bewahren
ask about	erkundigen	**depend on**	abhängen von	**see about**	kümmern
ask for	fragen nach	**despair of**	verzweifeln an	**speak about**	sprechen über
be against	dagegen sein	**devote to**	widmen	**speak of**	sprechen von
be for	dafür sein	**die of**	sterben an	**specialise in**	spezialisieren
begin by	beginnen mit	**disapprove of**	dagegen sein	**spend on**	ausgeben für
believe in	glauben an	**dream of**	träumen von	**stop from**	abhalten von
benefit from	profitieren von	**escape from**	entkommen	**succeed in**	Erfolg haben
blame for	tadeln für	**forget about**	vergessen	**suspect of**	verdächtigen
boast of	prahlen mit	**forgive for**	verzeihen	**take to**	beginnen
brag about	angeben mit	**give up**	aufhören	**take part in**	teilnehmen
care for	kümmern um	**go on**	weitermachen	**talk about**	sprechen über
carry on	weitermachen	**insist on**	bestehen auf	**talk into**	überreden
charge with	vorwerfen	**keep on**	weitermachen	**thank for**	danken für
complain of	beklagen	**leave off**	aufhören	**think of**	denken an
concentrate on	konzentrieren auf	**look forward to**	freuen auf	**vote against**	dagegen stimmen
confess to	zugeben	**nag about**	nörgeln über	**warn against**	davor warnen
congratulate on	gratulieren zu	**negotiate about**	verhandeln über	**worry about**	Sorgen machen

Exercise 2

Translate the following sentences using gerund forms.

1. Ich gebe zu, das Auto genommen zu haben, ohne dich vorher zu fragen.

_____

2. Wir freuen uns darauf, euch nächstes Wochenende zu sehen.

_____

3. Ich konnte einfach nicht widerstehen, den Schokokuchen zu essen.

_____

4. Du solltest wirklich aufhören zu rauchen.

_____

5. Ich schätze es sehr, dass du den Traum meiner Schwester, Schauspielerin zu werden, unterstützt.

_____

Adjektive mit Präpositionen, die das *Gerund* verlangen					
accustomed to	gewohnt sein	**excited about**	aufgeregt	**pleased at/about**	erfreut über
afraid of	fürchten vor	**famous for**	berühmt sein für	**proud of**	stolz auf
alarmed at	beängstigt	**far from**	weit entfernt von	**ready for**	bereit für
angry at/about	zornig	**fed up with**	es satt haben/ leid sein	**right in/about**	recht haben
annoyed at/ about	verärgert/ genervt	**fined for**	Geldstrafe bekommen	**sad about/at**	traurig über
appropriate for	geeignet für	**fond of**	begeistert sein	**shocked about/at**	schockiert
astonished at	erstaunt	**free from**	frei sein	**sick of**	es satt haben
bad at/in	schlecht bei	**get used to**	gewöhnen an	**sorry for/about**	leidtun
capable of	fähig sein	**glad at/about**	froh sein über	**sure about**	sicher wegen
certain of	sicher sein	**good at**	gut sein bei	**surprised at**	erstaunt
charged with	angeklagt	**happy at**	glücklich über	**tired from**	müde von
clever at	geschickt sein	**impressed by**	beeindruckt von	**tired of**	es satt haben
crazy about	verrückt nach	**interested in**	interessiert an	**thankful for**	dankbar für
conscious of	bewusst	**involved in**	verstrickt sein	**used for**	verwendet für
disappointed at	enttäuscht sein	**keen on**	begeistert von	**worried about**	Sorgen machen
		notorious for	berüchtigt für	**wrong in**	falschliegen

Exercise 3

Translate the following sentences using gerund forms.

1. Ich glaube nicht, dass Marco fähig ist, so etwas Grausames zu tun.

_____

2. Dein Mann ist genervt von deinem ständigen Jammern.

_____

3. Sandra ist enttäuscht darüber, nicht gewonnen zu haben.

_____

4. Du liegst falsch, wenn du denkst, dass ich dich nicht liebe.

_____

5. Er ist berüchtigt dafür, nie aufzugeben.

_____

6. Elias ist nicht begeistert davon, mit uns Schifahren zu gehen.

_____

7. Ich bin es leid/Ich habe es satt, ständig deine Fehler ausbügeln zu müssen.

_____

Nomen mit Präpositionen, die das *Gerund* verlangen					
advantage of	Vorteil	**difficulty (in)**	Schwierigkeit	**no point (in)**	sich nicht auszahlen/ keinen Sinn haben
alternative of	Alternative	**doubt about**	Zweifel an	**reason for**	Grund für
art to/in/of	Kunst	**experience in**	Erfahrung in	**take an interest in**	Interesse haben
aversion to	Abneigung	**gift of**	Begabung für	**trouble with**	Schwierigkeiten
chance of	Gelegenheit	**idea of**	Idee, Plan	**way of**	Art und Weise
choice between	Wahl zwischen	**opportunity of**	Gelegenheit zu	**freedom of**	(Wahl)Freiheit
danger of	Gefahr	**the point (of)**	Zweck, Sinn		

Bestimmte Ausdrücke, die das *Gerund* verlangen					
can't stand/bear	nicht ertragen	**it's no use**	es nützt nichts	**There is no ...**	Man ... nicht ...
can't help	nicht anders können	**it's a waste of**	es ist eine Verschwendung	**this is ...**	das heißt
it's worth	wert sein	**to waste (one's) time/money**	Zeit/Geld verschwenden	**to be busy**	beschäftigt sein
it's fun	Spaß machen	**How about ...?**	Wie wär's mit?	**to feel like**	zumute sein nach
it's no good	es ist sinnlos	**What about ...?**	Wie wär's mit?	**Thank you for**	Danke für

Exercise 4

Translate the following sentences. Use gerund forms.

1. Ich kann es nicht ertragen, in einem Raum mit geschlossenem Fenster zu schlafen.

_____

2. Bella kann nicht anders, als Edward anzustarren.

_____

3. Es hat keinen Sinn, mich zu beschuldigen.

_____

4. Wie wär's mit Eisessen im Park?

_____

5. Es ist Zeitverschwendung, nach Lucky zu suchen. Er wird schon nach Hause kommen.

_____

6. Es hat keinen Sinn, ihn anzusprechen. Er ist beschäftigt, mit Jessica zu flirten.

_____

7. Mir ist nach einem Spaziergang zumute.

_____

8. Der Film ist sehenswert.

_____

Gerund or infinitive?

Es gibt einige Verben, die sowohl *Gerund* als auch Infinitivformen verlangen. Es kann dabei jedoch zu Bedeutungsunterschieden kommen.

love – like – dislike – detest – hate – can't bear – prefer – allow – permit – forbid – advise

Exercise 1

Read the following examples.

GERUND	INFINITIVE
I always hate waiting for Emma.	I hate to wait for Emma today because it's cold.
He prefers taking the bus on schooldays.	He prefers to walk this time.
I can't bear seeing sad people. I always feel like having to cheer them up.	I can't bear to see you so sad! How can I cheer you up?
The headmaster doesn't permit skating on the school premises.	Would you please permit me to see Ally today?
Fluffy loves romping around in our garden.	Look! Fluffy apparently loves to dig up your flowers.
I detest eating cauliflower! It always stinks.	I detest to see Mike flirting with Nina over there!
I generally advise taking the steps. The elevator is extremely slow.	I advise to take the steps. The elevator is currently out of order.

Now tick the correct rules:

1. Das *Gerund* wird hier verwendet, um über eine spezielle Situation zu sprechen. ☐
2. Das *Gerund* wird hier verwendet, um die Bedeutung des Verbs (love, ...) zu verstärken. ☐
3. Der Infinitiv wird hier für spezielle Situationen verwendet. ☐
4. Der Infinitiv schwächt die Bedeutung des Verbs (love, ...) ab. ☐
5. Das *Gerund* wird hier für eine allgemeine Situation bzw. eine generelle Aussage verwendet. ☐

remember – forget – regret

Read the following examples.

GERUND	INFINITIVE
I remember buying milk. Look, it's in the fridge.	I must remember to buy some milk in the afternoon.
I'll never forget seeing you in your wedding gown.	Don't forget to order the flowers! We are going to need them this Saturday.
Do you regret not telling her the truth?	I regret to tell you that Mia is not here at the moment.
Do you remember feeding the cat? It looks quite hungry to me.	You must remember to feed the cat. If you don't, it will catch some disgusting mice.

Exercise 2

Now tick the correct rules.

1. Das *Gerund* drückt in diesen Beispielen einen Zwang aus. ❏

2. In diesen Beispielen drückt das *Gerund* eine Handlung in der Vergangenheit aus. ❏

3. Der Infinitiv mit *remember*, *forget* und *regret* bezieht sich auf vergangene Aktivitäten. ❏

4. In diesen Beispielen drückt das *Gerund* eine zukünftige Aktivität aus. ❏

5. Der Infinitiv mit *remember*, *forget* und *regret* bezieht sich auf aktuelle und zukünftige Aktivitäten. ❏

---

stop – start

Exercise 3

Match the English sentences with the correct meanings they convey.

	SENTENCE		MEANING
1	Pamela stopped to smoke.	A	He/She started to go/leave in order to do something.
2	Christopher finally started talking.	B	He/She stopped with the action itself.
3	Anthony started to catch the train.	C	He/She stopped walking/driving in order to do something.
4	Franceska stopped smoking.	D	He/She started with the action itself.

1	2	3	4

---

mean – go on – try

Exercise 4

Match the English sentence with the correct meanings they convey.

	SENTENCE		MEANING
1	Your coming late means having to go without dinner.	A	mit einer Handlung weitermachen
2	I have never ment to hurt you.	B	ausprobieren, den Versuch machen
3	We went on working on our project the whole night.	C	beabsichtigen, wollen
4	After I had told them about the wedding dress I went on to tell them about the cake.	D	versuchen, sich bemühen
5	Have you ever tried eating Soletti with chocolate?	E	und dann, als Nächstes
6	I tried to cook lasagne, but I failed.	F	bedeuten

1	2	3	4	5	6

Exercise 5

Translate the following sentences. Use gerund or infinitive forms.

1. Er hielt an, um die Katze über die Straße gehen zu lassen.

   _____

2. Ich konnte es nicht vermeiden, das Glas fallen zu lassen.

   _____

3. Deine schlechte Note bedeutet mehr Lernen.

   _____

4. Er nahm ihr ihr Lügen übel.

   _____

5. Wir entschuldigten uns dafür, vergessen zu haben, die Blumen zu gießen.

   _____

6. Er hörte einfach nicht auf, mich anzustarren.

   _____

7. Alan überredet Maria, mit ihm ins Kino zu gehen.

   _____

8. Ich werde nie vergessen, Julie unter den Palmen geküsst zu haben.

   _____

9. Wir dürfen nicht vergessen, die Türe abzuschließen.

   _____

10. Danke, dass du mir mit der Mathe-Hausübung geholfen hast.

    _____

11. Ich habe versucht, dir die Wahrheit zu sagen, aber du hast mir nicht zugehört.

    _____

12. Man kann nicht wissen, was sie als Nächstes tun wird.

    _____

13. Ich habe nie beabsichtigt, Nadja von uns zu erzählen.

    _____

14. Es macht Joan nichts aus, eine Uniform zu tragen.

    _____

15. Denk bitte daran, uns eine Karte aus deinem Urlaub zu schreiben.

    _____

16. Lass uns anfangen, um rechtzeitig fertig zu werden.

    _____

LANGUAGE IN USE

TESTFORMATE

MULTIPLE GAP TEXT

Es geht darum, einen Lückentext zu vervollständigen. Pro Lücke hast du jeweils vier Möglichkeiten vorgegeben und du musst entscheiden, welches das richtige Wort ist. *Study the example*:

The number of illegal immigrants in the United States **(1)** ... to 10.8 million in January 2009, that's a drop of **(2)** ... one million since the peak in 2007. Researchers noted that the decline goes hand in hand with the current recession even though immigrant workers would urgently be **(3)** ... in times of crisis.

1	A	stagnated	B	increased	C	doubled	D	**declined**
2	A	although	B	**almost**	C	already	D	alone
3	A	**needed**	B	need	C	needing	D	needs

GAPPED TEXT

Auch hier soll ein Lückentext mit vorgegebenen Wörtern vervollständigt werden. Aber Achtung: Es gibt meistens zwei Wörter mehr, als du brauchst! *Study the example*:

Everybody knows the famous "HOLLYWOOD" sign in Los Angeles. A week ago the letters were covered by **(1)** ... and now read "SAVE THE PEAK". Why? Well, because the government is thinking about building luxury homes on the peak of the hill and a group of **(2)** ... is trying to stop the project.

A	opponents	B	pictures	C	banners	D	friends

The correct answers are: 1C, 2A

OPEN GAP TEXT

Ein Text soll vervollständigt werden, allerdings ohne dass du etwas zur Wahl vorgegeben hast. Du musst also eigenständig erkennen, welche Art von Wort in die Lücke eingefüllt werden muss. *Study the example*:

According to the British police, there is no such thing **(1)** ... road rage. Drivers **(2)** ... harass or attack other drivers are breaking the law. However, British motoring organisations **(3)** ... believe in road rage.
Lösungen: 1 as; 2 who; 3 do

EDITING

Ein Text soll dahingehend korrigiert werden, dass jene Wörter, die zu viel sind, herausgeschrieben werden sollen. Bedenke aber, dass nicht in jedem Satz ein Fehler ist. *Study the example*:

Australian scientists **all** have developed a revolutionary tracking system that	*all* 1
automatically sends a text message to the authorities whenever a killer shark nears one	*OK* 2
of **the** America's tourist beaches.	*the* 3

WORD FORMATION

Bei einem Lückentext sollen die vorgegebenen Wörter in die jeweils richtige Form gebracht werden (also zum Beispiel Nomen ▶ Verb). *Study the example*:

In times of **(1)** ... **(significance)** environmental problems more and more European countries unite in order to rebuild a renewable energy supergrid. It would make use of wind turbines, solar panels and the power of waves. By autumn the nine governments **(2)** ... **(involvement)**, hope to have a plan to begin building.

1   *significant*   2   *involved*

Task 1 Multiple gap text: Shoot up the school

You are going to read a text about a shooting in a US High School. Some words are missing from the text. Choose the correct answer (A, B, C or D) for each gap (1–10) in the text. Write your answers in the boxes provided. The first one (0) has been done for you.

Shoot up the school

November 21st, 2010 was a **(0)** ... day for the Red Lake High School in Minnesota, USA. What happened? The story is very simple: 16-year-old Jeremy Crux first shot and killed both his grandparents, then went off to the school he **(1)** ... and wounded seven fellow students. But that was not enough. He **(2)** ... killing one security guard who tried to stop him, one of the teachers, five classmates and finally himself by shooting his head.

Teachers, parents and the headmaster now ask themselves whether there were any **(3)** ... of warnings and if that massacre could have been **(4)** ... . A question that is quite difficult to answer. What is sure, though, is the fact that Crux was a complete outsider. He was frequently **(5)** ... by his classmates because of his appearance: he was six feet tall (1,8 meters) and weighed about 250 pounds (113 kilos). Besides he always wore black clothing and he had a horn-shaped hairstyle. At school he spent most of the breaks sitting in the corner of the classroom and creating **(6)** ... and gory drawings that he posted on the Internet afterwards. Fellow students used to describe him as not very communicative, rather unfriendly and introvert. So it's actually no wonder that Crux was not very popular and didn't have many friends.

A check of Crux' notebook further revealed shocking information about the teenager. It was completely **(7)** ... with Nazi and Hitler stickers and the boy regularly posted neo-Nazi messages on the web. He also **(8)** ... e-mails about shootings and brutal massacres with other students and brought a video of the Columbine shooting murders to a friend's house some weeks ago. Most shocking, however, is the statement Crux gave only two days before the shooting. Some students **(9)** ... that he had said it would be cool to shoot up the school. Well, seems as if he turned his plan into reality.

The sad truth is that so far this has by no means been the only shooting in an American High School. Unfortunately **(10)** ... like the one just described happen repeatedly and in most cases it's extremely difficult, if not to say impossible, to predict or in best case prevent them. What most of them have in common, however, are fanatic teenagers that are usually loners, outsiders and outcasts. Being probably inspired by the Internet and/or TV, they fanatically plan their killings in every detail. Mostly they also commit suicide afterwards and see their own killings as climax of the whole story.

0	A	grey	B	dark	C	**black**	D	bright
1	A	attended	B	visited	C	joined	D	participated
2	A	convicted	B	confessed	C	conquered	D	continued
3	A	sighs	B	sights	C	signs	D	symbols
4	A	preferred	B	prearranged	C	prevented	D	preserved
5	A	ridiculed	B	ridiculous	C	resembled	D	remained
6	A	violating	B	violate	C	violence	D	violent
7	A	cover	B	covered	C	coloured	D	coded
8	A	exchanged	B	explained	C	extended	D	exampled
9	A	combined	B	cancelled	C	claimed	D	caused
10	A	insignificances	B	incidents	C	imbalances	D	intrigues

0	1	2	3	4	5	6	7	8	9	10
C										

Task 2 Gapped text: Too violent to play

You are going to read a text about the effects of playing violent video games. Some words are missing from the text. Choose from the list (A–P) the correct part for each gap (1–13) in the text. There are two extra words that you should not use. Write your answers in the boxes provided. The first one (0) has been done for you.

Too violent to play

Ever heard about Grand Theft Auto: San Andreas? Some time ago it was the biggest-selling video game of all time. It sold 1 million **(0)** ... in only nine days in the UK and some 32 million copies worldwide. These sales figures have only been reached by very few other video games so its success must really be taken seriously. The game presents a **(1)** ... world in which the players become gangsters cruising around the ghettos in California. They can **(2)** ... stores, beat up women, get tatoos, **(3)** ... drugs, shoot cops, hijack cars and do all the other things people in real life are never ever allowed to do. Therefore it has an M (mature) rating which means that only players **(4)** ... than 18 are allowed to play it.

So far so good. But where's the problem? The problem is that shortly after the **(5)** ... of GTA (Grand Theft Auto) two 16-year-old teenage boys from Miami shot at vehicles on the interstate with a 22 calibre **(6)** ... . One man was killed and two women were **(7)** ... . When being questioned why they had committed that crime, they simply answered that they had been **(8)** ... the GTA video game. The question that comes up is relatively straight forward: can playing a violent video game really change your **(9)** ... ? And even worse: can it cause you to kill somebody? The arguments as well as export's opinions are diverse.

Those who think that violent video games do not change your behaviour say that the **(10)** ... for cruel acts belongs to those who commit them. The people who behave violently exactly know what they are doing, no matter if they have played a violent game before or not. Besides, all video games must have a rating, indicating the minimum **(11)** ... of players. If children don't respect this rating, or respectively, if parents don't care about which video games their children play, nobody else can be blamed. Finally, reliable research proving that watching violent scenes, no matter if on TV or in video games, desensitises children, does not exist. If there was a connection between children's behaviour and watching violent content, children should also not be allowed to watch the news.

Opponents, however, say that violent video games do change the way children perceive real life and the real world. Permanently seeing deaths and shoot-outs on computer screens can mean that kids become **(12)** ... to the horror and reality of death. They simply don't understand that, if carrying out a violent act in real life, there are enormous consequences related to that behaviour. In addition, certain parts in your brain (the so-called front lobe to be more accurate) are not fully developed and grown until you are about 20. The problematic aspect now is that the front lobe is **(13)** ... for our behaviour. Playing (violent) video games too excessively can hinder the development of this front lobe and consequently change our behaviour to the negative.

A	rifle	B	smoke	C	responsibility	D	responsible
E	rob	F	immune	G	**copies**	H	injured
I	behaviour	J	killed	K	copying	L	publication
M	older	N	age	O	younger	P	virtual

0	1	2	3	4	5	6	7	8	9	10	11	12	13
G													

Task 3 **Editing: Obama's policy turned from "Yes, we can" to "Yes, we did"**

You are going to read a text about one of the most important successes of president Barack Obama. In most lines of the text there is an unnecessary word that should not be there. Spot it and write it in the space provided after each line. Some lines are correct. Indicate these with an OK. There are two examples at the beginning.

Obama's policy turned from "Yes, we can" to "Yes, we did"

The **current** summer of 2010 was characterised for US president Barack Obama	*current*	1
with an enormous victory. It was a victory he had been fighting for desperately	*OK*	2
and a victory hardly anybody had believed to be really happen. It was the victory		3
in the all health care debate, which was also a personal triumph for Obama as no		4
other American president who had ever reached that goal before. But what exactly		5
does that mean in the detail?		6
It will help millions of some Americans to find affordable health insurance for the		7
first time. Up to that point every inhabitant of the United States who was		8
responsible himself/herself for having a sufficient health insurance. This, of		9
course, was a problem for those who did not have enough money. Quite often		10
they were not insured at all and when they had to visit a physician, the same		11
trouble started. The summer 2010, however, changed it everything. Yet it also		12
divided as of never before a nation that still today teaches its children that		13
America was built on self-reliance and suspicion of a strong government.		14
Americans who were simply not used to relying on the government as they have		15
always tried to come to terms with their own affairs. When the White House press		16
secretary announced of the changes related to health care he even did that with the		17
words, "Freedom dies a little bit today". For yet sure, Europeans cannot		18
understand about how health insurance benefits can be seen as a limitation of		19
personal freedom. But then, people in the Europe have never had a system		20
comparable with the one in the United States.		21
As is always the case when a fight is won, not everybody is not happy with the		22
new regulation. Obama critics announced that the president would have to pay a		23
high price for your reforms that force Americans for the first time to buy health		24
insurance or else pay a fine. And also the Democrats were not reluctant with their		25
criticism. According to them Obama will be punished by the voters for expanding		26
the state rather than being reward him for this achievement. In any case, the		27
public does remains sceptical.		28
The impact of the Obama's health reforms will be felt by the American society for		29
decades. Within the first six months new rules outlawing the worst insurance		30
company abuses which were set up and within the next four years benefits and tax		31
credits should not reach poor and indigent families.		32

Task 4   Word formation: Barack Obama – what the US president stands for

You are going to read a text about Barack Obama and the goals he wants to achieve during his presidency. Some words are missing from the text. Use the words in brackets to complete each gap (1–12) in the text in the correct form. Write your answers in the spaces provided at the end of the text. The first one (0) has been done for you.

Barack Obama – what the US president stands for

What exactly do you know about the president of the United States of America? And have you ever asked yourself which plans Barack Obama has for his presidency? Here comes the answer.

Economy and especially **(0) ... (improvement)** American economy stands on top of Obama's agenda. His plan to re-energise the economy is multifaceted and includes reinvestment, a smart health care reform, smarter government budgets and spending more. But it also **(1) ... (involvement)** addressing issues like credit card problems and making too many debts.

As far as the **(2) ... (environmental)** is concerned Obama plans to end US **(3) ... (dependant)** on foreign oil and dirty energy. In times of constant environmental problems this aspect should definitely be given a high level of priority. Furthermore Obama wants to ensure an adequat supply of affordable energy which should, at the same time, also **(4) ... (creation)** new jobs in newly-developed industries. Unfortunately the environmental subject **(5) ... (suffering)** a lot in summer 2010 when BP didn't manage to seal the leak in its oil pipeline. The amount of oil **(6) ... (flood)** the Gulf of Mexcio was incredible and it took several months until the leak was finally sealed.

Family is another important issue Obama **(7) ... (concern)** with. He created the so-called Middle Class Initiative in order to raise the living standards of middle class and working class families. The main goals of this plan are to **(8) ... (expansion)** education and offer lifelong training opportunities, to improve work and family balance, to **(9) ... (restoration)** labour standards – including workplace **(10) ... (safe)** and to protect retirement security. The topic of education should also not be excluded as the president wants to revitalise the American education system from preschool to college. In this context, however, he also calls on parents' **(11) ... (responsible)** to always support and help their children.

Finally, Obama **(12) ... (intention)** to rebuild American relationships abroad, thereby building up a new era of American diplomacy. He is working to enhance US relationships with their Latin American neighbours as well as trying to bring the leaders of the Middle East together in peace. Especially as far as foreign affairs are concerned Barack Obama really has some ambitious aims to achieve.

0   *improving*

1   _____

2   _____

3   _____

4   _____

5   _____

6   _____

7   _____

8   _____

9   _____

10 _____

11 _____

12 _____

Task 5   Multiple gap text: How "teenspeak" leaves a generation lost for words

You are going to read a text about how writing text messages changes the speaking behaviour of teenagers. Some words are missing from the text. Choose the correct answer (A, B, C or D) for each gap (1–10) in the text. Write your answers in the boxes provided. The first one (0) has been done for you.

How "teenspeak" leaves a generation lost for words

Do the following abbreviations **(0)** ... a bell or have you never heard them before: *it's a gr8 plc* (it's a great place), *brb* (be right back), *2g2bt* (too good to be true) or *kpc* (keeping parents clueless)? These are only some of the most common phrases and expressions used by teenagers to make their communication via Internet or SMS easier and shorter.

But **(1)** ... it's fun for the teens to have their own "language" and their own codes, it's actually a quite dangerous **(2)** ... . "What we have to face is a generation of teenagers who are highly endangered of not finding a **(3)** ... job after school", says Joshua Neill from the department of youth unemployment in Bradford, Yorkshire. Today an **(4)** ... teenager's daily vocabulary only consists of about 800 words which is a relatively shocking number. Recent surveys showed that they are **(5)** ... to know about 40,000 words but favour a "teenspeak" used in short messages and on social networking sites like *Facebook* or *My Space*. Experts now try to make the public more **(6)** ... towards this topic, informing them that the narrow range of vocabulary teenagers use these days, will harm their chances of getting a job later on.

As a consequence a nationwide campaign is started next year to ensure that children and teenagers use their full linguistic **(7)** ... and are not at a disadvantage at school, or later on, the workplace. The source of this problem, however, will continue to exist as kids simply spend more time communicating **(8)** ... electronic media and SMS. What is necessary to be done is to help the young generation understand the difference between their textspeak and the formal language they need to have in order to **(9)** ... in their lives. And 800 words are definitely not going to be enough for a good job and a decent career.

Experts further discovered that the language teenagers speak starts to differ significantly from the one older generations speak. Words and expressions have come up that did not exist a decade ago and are entirely **(10)** ... to adults. An example would be the word *chenzed* for "tired/drunk". An honorary professor for linguistics at Harvard University also pointed out that the real problem is parents' objection to their kids having a good vocabulary for hip hop and other teen-related matters but not for politics and social affairs. "We simply have to accept this change which is to a certain degree also normal", he points out. "Different generations have always had their different issues, topics and focuses. That's nothing to worry about."

0	A	rule	B	rise	C	raise	D	**ring**
1	A	when	B	while	C	whereas	D	whatever
2	A	fact	B	phenomenal	C	force	D	phenomenon
3	A	professional	B	part-time	C	proper	D	prefered
4	A	average	B	avenge	C	available	D	averse
5	A	suppressed	B	supplied	C	supposed	D	supported
6	A	sensible	B	sensitive	C	sensual	D	sensuous
7	A	performance	B	potential	C	profession	D	powder
8	A	on	B	by	C	threw	D	through
9	A	succeed	B	success	C	succeeding	D	successful
10	A	funny	B	understandable	C	alien	D	harmful

0	1	2	3	4	5	6	7	8	9	10
D										

Task 6 **Gapped text: SMS – catching your partner when being unfaithful**

You are going to read a text about how mobiles and SMS more and more often reveal unfaithful partners. Some words are missing from the text. Choose from the list (A–P) the correct part for each gap (1–13) in the text. There are two extra words that you should not use. Write your answers in the boxes provided. The first one (0) has been done for you.

SMS – catching your partner when being unfaithful

No doubt, mobile phones are useful and necessary. They have become an **(0)** ... part of our lives and many of us cannot imagine a life without them. We usually have a **(1)** ... personal connection to our cellphones because we keep contact lists and family photos. But within the last few years one aspect related to writing text messages has become more prominent and more important: SMS have become the digital lipstic on your **(2)** ... if you cheat your spouse or partner. Text messages nowadays can be the **(3)** ... of a cheat, an affair or another delict because every message we send leaves a digital footprint.

This became painfully **(4)** ... some time ago when a woman who claimed to have had an affair with golf star Tiger Woods told the newspapers that he had sent her flirty text messages. After checking her statement it turned out that everything was just **(5)** ... and the woman was lucky enough for not being sued because of libel and slander. It goes without saying that cases like the one just described are not seldom these days.

Coming back to unfaithful relationships among partners things have changed as well. In earlier times companions were only **(6)** ... to be disloyal but very often one could not do anything but wait until explicit proof was found. Nowadays text messages do provide proof and evidence. Therefore it's no wonder that divorce lawyers say they have seen an enormous increase in cases where text messages are used to document the partner's wrongdoing and **(7)** ... . An American association for lawyers reacted to that whole topic immediately and started to offer seminars on how to use electronic evidence (that means text messages, browsing history and social networks) in proving a case.

Usually e-mails are **(8)** ... likely to reveal the secret of a cheat. By now e-mail users have come to understand that messages remain on their computers even if deleted. For text messages the situation is different. Many people believe that once the "send" button has been **(9)** ..., the message is gone and never seen again. But that's not the case as communication companies are forced to **(10)** ... messages for a certain period of time, ranging from days to a few weeks. So always keep in mind that the evidence is still there ...

(11) ... we must never forget that sending mails, texting messages or posting news on platforms is not private even though we might think so. It's one thing to write a personal note to somebody who shares it with some friends. It's a completely different thing to express your **(12)** ... for your partner on a social network where the information is, in the end, public. What feels intimate and anonymous at the time, perhaps, really isn't. It can be shared widely. In that context an American company called "Life Project" carried out a survey which revealed that one quarter of the people questioned **(13)** ... having posted and shared information online. And that number clearly speaks for itself.

A	regretted	B	hit	C	obvious	D	dislike
E	fake	F	confirmation	G	like	H	store
I	eventually	J	**integral**	K	suspected	L	deeply
M	more	N	guilt	O	collar	P	less

0	1	2	3	4	5	6	7	8	9	10	11	12	13
J													

Task 7 **Open gap text: Stalking: intrusive, abusive and deadly**

You are going to read a text about stalking, a particularly creepy crime. Some words are missing from the text. Figure them out and write them in the space provided at the end. The first one (0) has been done for you.

Stalking: intrusive, abusive and deadly

Lots of women dream of a romantic guy **(0)** ... permanently observes and watches every step they take and every move they make. They dream of a loyal and trustworthy man who is ready to wait for the love of his life for almost an eternity. But acknowledged love and passion can soon turn **(1)** ... something else: a phenomenon that is known as stalking. This term is commonly used to describe unwanted and obsessive attention by individuals (mostly men) to others (mostly women). Stalking behaviours are often related **(2)** ... harassment and intimidation.

It's a particularly intimidating crime, often scarier **(3)** ... violence overtly carried out because it acts in a small gap between unfulfilled love and perverse desire. It is bound to important human emotions such **(4)** ... trust, courtesy and kindness and turns something normal (love) into a form of persecution. In most cases it therefore ranges from the intrusive to the abusive to the deadly.

The lives of those people who are stalked are almost always completely destroyed. They are under permanent observance and the stalker is near **(5)** ... all the time. Margaret Miller, a mother of three, once declared that the guy who had been stalking her had been a former school colleague. The nasty thing was that he was constantly around her, intruding and invading her private life. She once saw him jogging in front of her house **(6)** ... Christmas Day and on another day he turned up at her workplace. He phoned her late at nights, sent her Valentine cards and once he even changed his identity to gain access to her child's nursery. After she had found out that he had googled her **(7)** ... than 40,000 times, she went to the police straightway. He was sent to prison at once where he currently has to stay for another half a year.

It might be interesting to note that stalking is a relatively new and modern phenomenon. Its meaning was not coined until 1991 and the number of reported cases has risen dramatically within the last decade. A stalker can be a fanatic fan, an ex-partner, a rejected lover, a patient, a student, an employee or a stranger. Their work has been made much easier **(8)** ... new technologies like the Internet and social networks such as Facebook. All techniques available today can **(9)** ... used to track down a person, record her, watch photos of her, get into her home and finally under her skin. Scary, isn't it? In the end one also has to point out that, to a certain extent, it's people's fault as we more and more live our lives publicly.

0 _____ *who* _____

1 _____

2 _____

3 _____

4 _____

5 _____

6 _____

7 _____

8 _____

9 _____

Task 8 Multiple gap text: Organic farmers should approve GM food

You are going to read a text about organic food related to genetically modified food. Some words are missing from the text. Choose the correct answer (A, B, C or D) for each gap (1–10) in the text. Write your anwers in the boxes provided. The first one (0) has been done for you.

Organic farmers should approve GM food

As is commonly known, the organic movement is strictly against genetically modified food and crops. But in fact they should overcome their **(0)** ... because then the rapidly growing population could be fed better and the environment would be **(1)** ... . It's time to see and accept the positive contribution GM crops have on **(2)** ... and to embrace and welcome the new opportunities they offer.

So far organic farmers have been among the hard-fighting **(3)** ... of genetic engineering, not being ready to label any GM food as organic. They clearly **(4)** ... themselves from this movement. But according to Professor Gilbert Epson from the Standford University genetic engineering should be accepted and considered as fully legitimate. Furthermore he says that farmers should use the best aspects of organic methods and **(5)** ... them with the most promising features of GM technology. By doing so it can be ensured to maximise the output and to limit the damage and harm done to our ecosystem. But unfortunately reality presents another picture as it is still impossible to mix GM technology and organic approaches. "If people got over the **(6)** ... that GM is somehow not organic", he says, "great benefits for all parties involved could be achieved." Furthermore Professor Epson explains that GM crops are perfectly compatible with the organic movement's goal of making farming more sustainable and long lasting. "People simply have to overcome the limitation concerning their personal views. They **(7)** ... everything nature produces as good and everything humanity creates as bad. But it's not always that clear-cut and things are not always only black or white", he goes on. "In the end genetic engineering can create and produce crops with significant and essential advantages."

In the meantime, however, **(8)** ... start to increase pressure as far as the use of GM crops is concerned. A greater use of genetically modified crops would easily ensure food security for a global population. And one must bear in mind that we are talking about a population that is predicted to have reached nine billion by 2050. It's actually unacceptable that the world goes on **(9)** ... the potential of genetic engineering in order to improve agriculture.

What else is there left to say? Well, people will probably end up in a very interesting hybrid world in which suitable and fitting technologies are chosen **(10)** ... to their needs. But we will see anyway.

0	A	hangover	B	helplessness	C	**hostility**	D	hospitality
1	A	damaged	B	protected	C	ruined	D	helped
2	A	humanity	B	human	C	men	D	peoples
3	A	opponents	B	opportunities	C	opposition	D	opinion
4	A	disguised	B	distinguished	C	developed	D	distanced
5	A	contain	B	confirm	C	combine	D	confront
6	A	nation	B	notion	C	opinion	D	view
7	A	consider	B	consideration	C	contextualise	D	context
8	A	scientist	B	science	C	scientific	D	scientists
9	A	reducing	B	handling	C	ignoring	D	facing
10	A	addressing	B	absorbing	C	affording	D	according

0	1	2	3	4	5	6	7	8	9	10
C										

VOCABULARY WORK

EINLEITUNG

Das englische Vokabular zu beherrschen und damit entsprechend umgehen zu können, ist beim Spracherwerb (und in Folge natürlich auch beim Verfassen von Texten) extrem wichtig. Im Laufe der letzten fünf Jahre hast du sicherlich bereits herausgefunden, dass es unerlässlich ist, ein gewisses Grundvokabular zu haben und dieses sicher und fehlerfrei anwenden zu können. Nun gilt es, einen Schritt weiterzugehen, das vorhandene Wissen aufzustocken und zu perfektionieren. Das vorliegende Kapitel soll dir dabei helfen, denn es hat seinen Schwerpunkt auf verschiedenen sprachlichen Phänomenen, die allesamt sehr nützlich und hilfreich für dich sind. Die einzelnen Aspekte werden nun in den folgenden Abschnitten erklärt und erarbeitet.

SYNONYME

Synonyme sind unterschiedliche Wörter mit der gleichen Bedeutung. Es gibt sie nicht nur im Englischen, sondern auch in der deutschen Sprache. Ein Beispiel dafür wäre das Wortpaar „hübsch – schön". Auch wenn die Wörter unterschiedlich sind, so haben sie doch die gleiche Grundbedeutung. Es ist immer gut und wichtig, Synonyme zu kennen (egal in welcher Sprache), denn sie ermöglichen dir eine unglaubliche Flexibilität in deinem Ausdruck (sowohl schriftlich als auch mündlich). Die folgende Tabelle stellt nun einen kleinen Ausschnitt einiger Synonyme dar. Bitte beachte, dass dies keinesfalls eine vollständige Aufstellung ist, da es weit mehr Wörter gibt, als du hier finden wirst. Für den Anfang sollte diese Darstellung aber reichen. Im Anschluss daran findest du Übungen zum Thema Synonyme. Fange aber erst damit an, wenn du dir die Synonyme in der Übersicht ein wenig eingeprägt hast.

List of selected English synonyms

ENGLISH WORD	SYNONYM	GERMAN TRANSLATION
about	approximately	ungefähr
to accomplish	to achieve	etwas erreichen
to admit	to confess	zugeben, gestehen
almost	nearly	fast, beinahe
to annoy	to irritate, to bother	nerven, belästigen
to answer	to reply	(be)antworten
anyway	besides	außerdem
to appear	to seem	scheinen, den Anschein haben
to arrive	to reach	ankommen, erreichen
attractive	appealing	ansprechend
awful	terrible	schrecklich
bad	poor, naughty	schlecht, schlimm
to begin	to start	starten, anfangen
to behave	to act	sich benehmen
believable	plausible	glaubwürdig
belly	stomach	Bauch
beneficiant	generous	großzügig
bizarre	weird	seltsam, komisch
blameless	innocent	unschuldig
brave	courageous	mutig
to bring sb. up	to raise sb.	jem. aufziehen, großziehen
busy	engaged	besetzt (Telefon)
candy	sweet	Süßigkeit

ENGLISH WORD	SYNONYM	GERMAN TRANSLATION
to categorize (AE)/to categorise (BE)	to classify	klassifizieren
chiefly	mainly	hauptsächlich
to chop	to cut	schneiden
clever	intelligent	intelligent
to close	to shut	schließen
to collapse	to break down	zusammenbrechen
to collect	to gather	sammeln
completely	totally	total
conflict	clash	Konflikt
to confuse	to mix up	verwirren
to connect	to put through	verbinden (Telefon)
considerate	thoughtful	überlegt
contemporary	modern	zeitgenössisch
contrary	opposite, counterpart	Gegenteil
to cope	to manage	zurechtkommen, schaffen
correct	right	richtig
couch	sofa	Sofa
cube	dice	Würfel
curative	healing	heilend
deceptive	misleading	missverständlich
defective	faulty	fehlerhaft, defekt
deliberately	intentionally, planned	planmäßig, absichtlich
deserted	abandoned	verlassen
destiny	fate	Schicksal
to differentiate	to distinguish	unterscheiden
to diminish	to decrease	vermindern
to disappear	to vanish	verschwinden
disaster	catastrophe	Katastrophe
discount	reduction	Nachlass (Preis)
disgrace	shame	Schande, Scham
dubious	doubtful	zweifelhaft
dull	stupid	dumm (Person)
earth	soil	Erde
economic	profitable	rentabel
egocentric	selfish	egoistisch
to emphasize (AE)/to emphasise (BE)	to stress, to point out	betonen
enormous	huge, immense	riesig
to enquire (AE)/to inquire (BE)	to investigate	ermitteln, befragen
especially	particularly	besonders
to establish	to set up	gründen

Vocabulary work

ENGLISH WORD	SYNONYM	GERMAN TRANSLATION
exactly	precisely	genau, exakt
except	apart from	außer, abgesehen von
extra	additional	zusätzlich
fantastic	great, brilliant	fantastisch
to float	to drift	treiben (zB am Wasser)
foolish	silly	blöd, dumm
to foretell	to predict	vorhersagen
fortunate	lucky	glücklich
fragrance	perfume	Duft, Parfum
to function	to operate	funktionieren
garbage	rubbish	Müll, Mist
grasping	greedy	gierig
gratis	free of charge, for free	gratis
to hand sth. out	to distribute sth.	etwas verteilen, austeilen
handsome	good-looking	gut aussehend (Männer)
hard	tough	hart, rauh
hint	trace, tip	Hinweis, Tipp
home	domestic	Heim, Haus(halts) ...
homicide	murder	Mord
housebreaking	burglary	Einbruch
hunger	starvation	das Verhungern
to hurry	to rush	beeilen
if	whether	ob
to ignore	to disregard	ignorieren
to illuminate	to clarify, to light up	aufklären
to illustrate	to demonstrate	illustrieren, zeigen
to imagine	to suppose, to assume	etwas annehmen, sich vorstellen
to imitate	to mimic	imitieren, nachmachen
immediate	instant, at once	sofort
immobile	motionless	unbeweglich
to impact	to affect	sich auswirken
impolite	rude	unhöflich
infantile	childish	kindisch
to infect	to contaminate	verschmutzen, kontaminieren
infrequent	rare, seldom	selten
to inspect	to examine	untersuchen
instructions	directions	Instruktionen
insufficient	inadequate	unzureichend
to intend	to mean	meinen
to intensify	to heighten	intensivieren

ENGLISH WORD	SYNONYM	GERMAN TRANSLATION
isolated	lonely	einsam
jealous	envious	eifersüchtig, neidisch
joy	delight	Freude
knowingly	deliberately	wissentlich, absichtlich
lacking	missing	fehlend
to learn	to memorize	lernen
lethal	deadly	tödlich
wild	furious	wild
loopy	crazy	verrückt
lousy	awful	schrecklich
madness	insanity	Wahnsinn
to maintain	to preserve	behalten, (auf)bewahren
manmade	artificial	künstlich
matters	things	Angelegenheiten
maybe	perhaps, possibly	vielleicht
in the meantime	meanwhile	in der Zwischenzeit
merciless	cruel	gnadenlos, grausam
mild	gentle	sanft, höflich
to mimic	to imitate	nachmachen, imitieren
mindless	senseless	gedankenlos
to mirror	to reflect	(wider)spiegeln
to misconceive	to misunderstand	falsch verstehen
miserable	depressed	unglücklich, bedrückt
misread	misinterpret	falsch interpretieren
missing	lost	vermisst
mistrust	distrust	Misstrauen
moderate	reasonable	vernünftig
modern	contemporary	zeitgemäß
more and more	increasingly	zunehmend, ansteigend
moreover	in addition	weiters, außerdem
movie	film	Film
murderer	assassin	Mörder
naked	bare	nackt
nameless	anonymous	namenlos

Vocabulary work

ENGLISH WORD	SYNONYM	GERMAN TRANSLATION
napkin	serviette	Serviette
narrative	story	Geschichte
native	local	einheimisch, ansässig
to near	to approach	sich nähern
necessary	essential	wichtig
to nominate	to appoint	nominieren
nonstop	continuous	durchgehend
noon	midday	Mittag
to notify	to inform	zur Kenntnis nehmen
numerous	many	viele, zahlreiche
obligatory	compulsory	verpflichtend
out of season	low season	Nebensaison
to operate	to function	funktionieren
organic	biological	biologisch
outside	external	außerhalb
to overtake sb.	to outrun sb.	jem. überholen
overseas	abroad	im Ausland
to oversee	to supervise	beaufsichtigen
painting	portray	Gemälde
particular	specific	speziell, besonders
poisonous	toxic	giftig
possibility	opportunity	Möglichkeit
pressing	urgent	dringend
previous	preceding	vorhergehend
to provide	to supply	versorgen, bereitstellen
provided	if	vorausgesetzt
to put sth. back	to postpone	verschieben
quite	fairly	ziemlich
reasonable price	fair price	fair, gerecht (günstiger, gerechter Preis)
to receive	to get, to obtain	erhalten
religious	devout	religiös
remark	comment	Bemerkung
to respond	to reply, to answer	antworten

ENGLISH WORD	SYNONYM	GERMAN TRANSLATION
rubbish	nonsense	Unsinn
to rue	to regret	bereuen
to select	to choose	auswählen
selection	choice	Auswahl
self-assured	self-confident	selbstsicher, selbstbewusst
significant	essential	essentiell, bedeutend
sincere	honest	ernsthaft, ehrlich
spotlight	highlight	Höhepunkt
steady	regular	regelmäßig
suggest	propose	vorschlagen
sundown	sunset	Sonnenuntergang
sunrise	dawn	Sonnenaufgang
sure	certain	bestimmt, sicher
surroundings	environment	Umwelt, Umfeld
to survive	to outlive	überleben
tailored	tailor-made	maßgeschneidert
temper	mood	Laune, Stimmung
today	nowadays	heutzutage
trustworthy	reliable	verlässlich
uncared for	neglected	vernachlässigt
uncommon	unusual	ungewöhnlich
uncooked	raw	roh
understandable	comprehensible	verständlich
unforeseen	unexpected	unvorhersehbar
unfortunate	unlucky	unglücklich, ohne Glück
unlawful	illegal	illegal
unmarried	single	unverheiratet
unstated	unspoken	unausgesprochen
unusual	strange, uncommon	ungewöhnlich, seltsam, komisch
unvoiced	voiceless	stimmlos
usually	generally, normally	normalerweise
vacancy	emptiness	die Leere
to vacuum	to hoover	staubsaugen
in vain	useless	vergebens, sinnlos
valueless	worthless	wertlos
to vary	to differ	sich unterscheiden
vast	huge	riesig, enorm
warranty	guarantee	Garantie
well mannered	well-behaved, polite	wohlerzogen, höflich

Task 1 **Sentence completion**

Complete the sentences with a suitable word from the box. Mind that there are more words than you need.

numerous – home – unmarried – stupid – nonsense – misread – behave – disaster – generous – unusual – hoover – rude – obligatory – rush – respond – plausible

1. Lucy is never _____. In fact she's one of the nicest and friendliest people I know.

2. Mum always instructs me to _____ my room but somehow I never do it.

3. I can tell you, my little brother Joseph tells so much _____ when the day is long.

4. Yesterday I really had to _____ not to miss the bus to school. That would have been a

   complete _____ and the teacher would have been angry with me.

5. Caroline's best friend Melissa has never had a husband so consequently she is _____.

6. Unfortunately doing home-exercises for school is _____ for children and teens.

7. Peter completely _____ his girlfriend's behaviour and so she was angry.

8. When I have to write an English exam I usually make _____ stupid mistakes.

9. In the film I have watched recently Leonardo DiCaprio played a _____ rich guy.

10. Mark's excuse was absolutely _____ so Sue forgave him his strange behaviour.

Task 2 **Find the correct synonym.**

The following words are taken from the grey box above. Complete the grid with the correct synonyms.

ENGLISH WORD	SYNONYM
numerous	
home	
unmarried	
stupid	
nonsense	
misread	
behave	
disaster	
generous	
unusual	
hoover	
rude	
obligatory	
rush	
respond	
plausible	

Task 3 **Find the missing word.**

Read through the definitions given and try to find out the correct word. The first one has been done for you.

annoying	if your younger brothers and/or sisters permanently go on your nerves
	the moment the sun starts shining in the morning
	if you don't die but go on living
	feeling sorry for something you have done or said to somebody
	if you are uncertain whether to do something or not, being hesitant
	you can do it with any food and afterwards you have small pieces
	if you don't have any artificial substances or additives in food
	if something is absolutely clear to everybody
	if something is not said, not expressed, not articulated with words
	being completely on your own and not having any friends or family
	to present an idea to somebody, to make a suggestion
	if you do something with full knowledge and intention

HOMONYME

Homonyme sind Wörter, die (zur Gänze oder zumindest fast) gleich klingen, aber eine komplett andere Bedeutung haben. Als Beispiel soll hier das Wortpaar *through – threw* genannt werden. Weder von der Art, wie sie geschrieben werden, noch von ihrer Bedeutung haben diese beiden Wörter irgendetwas gemeinsam. Trotzdem verwechselt man sie (vor allem in der Hitze des Gefechtes einer Schularbeit) sehr leicht und ärgert sich dann meist über einen unnötigen Vokabelfehler. Wie gesagt, phonetisch (also von der Art, wie das Wort klingt und ausgesprochen wird) ist zwischen dem Wortpaar kein Unterschied feststellbar. Deshalb macht dieses Phänomen in der gesprochenen Sprache auch keine Probleme. Schwierig wird es also nur bei der Textproduktion und hier hilft letztendlich nur das bewusste Lernen solcher Wortpaare. Die folgende Übersicht über (einige) dieser Homonyme soll dir das Leben ein wenig erleichtern. Studiere sie aufmerksam, um dann die darauffolgenden Übungen problemlos meistern zu können.

List of selected English homonyms

AFFECT	EFFECT
verb: to change or influence sth. or sb.	noun: the result of a change or influence

AISLE	ISLE
noun: the walkway through a supermarket	noun: island

ALLOWED	ALOUD
past tense of allow, to permit	adverb: using your voice, not silent

ATE	EIGHT
past tense of eat	number: the number eight (8)

BEAR	BARE
verb: to stand something *(aushalten)* noun: animal living in the wood	adjective: naked, without clothes

Vocabulary work

BLEW	BLUE
past tense of verb blow	adjective: colour blue

BOARD	BORED
noun: a plan of wood	adjective: not interested

BREAK	BRAKE
verb: to damage/ruin something	noun: stopping device on a (motor)bike, car

BUY	BY
verb: to purchase something	preposition: often indicating passive voice

CELL	SELL
noun: small room usually in a prison	verb: to provide for sale

SCENT	SENT
noun: an aroma, the way something smells	past tense of send

CLOSE	CLOTHES
verb: to shut, opposite of open	noun: garments, clothing you put on

DAYS	DAZE
noun: plural of day	noun: a confused state of mind

DEAR	DEER
adjective: beloved, beginning of a letter	noun: an animal (dt.: *Wild*)

FAIRY	FERRY
noun: a magic person or being	noun: a boat to transport cars and people

FLOUR	FLOWER
noun: powdered substance you need for cooking	noun: blooming part of a plant

FOR	FOUR
preposition	number: the number four (4)

FORWORD	FORWARD
noun: introduction to a book/an article	adjective: advancing

HEAR	HERE
verb: to listen to something	adverb: at this place

HOARSE	HORSE
adjective: rough voice (dt.: *heiser*)	noun: animal

HOLE	WHOLE
noun: round opening	adjective: entire, all

Vocabulary work

HOUR	OUR
noun: sixty minutes	possessive adjective: sth. belongs to us

KNIGHT	NIGHT
noun: warrior from the Middle Ages	noun: time span between evening and morning

KNOW	NO
verb: to have knowledge of someting	adverb: to express refusal

MADE	MAID
past tense of verb make	noun: domestic help

MAIL	MALE
noun: electronic post	adjective: opposite of female; related to men

MARRY	MERRY
verb: to join as husband and wife	adjective: happy (Merry Christmas)

MEAT	MEET
noun: animal flesh (chicken, beef, ...)	verb: to see/date somebody

MISSED	MIST
past tense of verb miss	noun: light fog

MORNING	MOURNING
noun: after getting up	noun: remembering dead people

ONE	WON
number: the number one (1)	past tense of verb win

PEAR	PAIR
noun: a type of fruit, usually yellow	noun: two pieces of something

PATIENCE	PATIENTS
noun: to be ready to wait	noun: persons treated in hospital or seeing the doctor

PIECE	PEACE
noun: the part of something	noun: the opposite of war

PLAIN	PLANE
adjective: not fancy, rather simple	noun: short form of airplane

WHICH	WITCH
question word: indicating for example choice	noun: magic woman appearing in fairy tales

WOOD	WOULD
noun: material coming from trees	modal verb: indicating for example a request

PRACTICE	PRACTISE
noun: the period of training	verb: to train for something

ROAD	RODE
noun: street	past tense of verb ride

SAIL	SALE
verb: to go by sailing boat	noun: selling at reduced prices

SCENE	SEEN
noun: visual location, part of a film	past participle (3rd form) of verb see

SEA	SEE
noun: large area of salty water	verb: to visualise

SOLE	SOUL
adjective: the only one	noun: important part of a person

STAIR	STARE
noun: step	verb: to look at somebody intensively

STEAL	STEEL
verb: to take something illegally	noun: metal

THEIR	THERE
possessive adjective: belonging to them	adverb: indicating a location, at or in a place

THREW	THROUGH
past tense of verb throw	preposition: moving from one place to another

TO	TOO
preposition: towards (but there are many uses!)	adverb: also

VARY	VERY
verb: to change	adverb: to a high degree

WAIST	WASTE
noun: body part between ribs and hips	verb: to not use well

WAIT	WEIGHT
verb: to remain ready for someone/something	noun: the amount of heaviness

WEAR	WHERE
verb: garments you put on your body	question word: asking for a place/direction

WEAK	WEEK
adjective: opposite of strong, without power	noun: seven days

WEATHER	WHETHER
noun: the meteorological condition	conjunction: if (stating a condition)

Task 1   **Sentence completion**

Fill in the words from the box to get meaningful sentences. Mind that there are three extra words.

whether – practice – aisles – meet – weight – missed – isle – through – weather – waist – meat – threw – waste – mist – through

1. I think tomorrow's _____ will be very bad: lots of rain and thunderstorm.

2. Pat has really grown strong. She must have put on a lot of _____.

3. Marcus is really keen on fish but he can't stand _____. Not even chicken.

4. If you want to go to the London Eye, you have to go _____ Hyde Park.

5. I was walking through the supermarket's _____ for 10 minutes before I found what I was

   looking for. That was really a _____ of time.

6. Apart from a really pretty face top models need to have a slim _____.

7. Gilian never knows _____ to put on blue jeans or black ones.

8. Paula and Lory have a *Jour fixe*. This means they always _____ on Monday evening.

9. When David _____ the ball to Jason he unfortunately hit the window and broke it.

10. Yesterday morning Melanie overslept and so she almost _____ the bus.

11. I'm not very good at English so I usually need a lot of _____ and training.

12. When I was in Ireland I was surprised that there was always _____ in the morning.

Task 2   **Choose the right word.**

Spot the correct word for every sentence and cross out the one that is wrong.

1. *Patience/Patients* is not my strong point because it always drives me crazy when I have to wait.

2. My English teacher permanently tells me how important regular *practice/practise* is.

3. Yesterday evening dad had played tennis with his colleague before he *eight/ate* his dinner.

4. "And will you *marry/merry* him?", Juliana asked her best friend Beth.

5. At the end of every season it's good to go shopping because most shops have a special *sail/sale*.

6. Joanna is shocked when she hears that her little sister *road/rode* on a horse in the summer holidays.

7. "Your new perfume really has an interesting *scent/sent*", Paul said to his girlfriend Pandora.

8. My dad always keeps telling me that if I don't have enough money I must *sell/cell* some of my stuff.

9. Some years ago we learned about King Arthur, the Round Table and his famous *nights/knights*.

10. "*Wear/Where* were you yesterday at nine p.m. and what were you doing?", mum wanted to know.

11. My likings for music constantly *very/vary* and it's impossible to say which my favourite song is.

12. I have to confess that so far I have never travelled to the *see/sea* but some day I will go to Greece.

13. Christine, can you please tell me *witch/which* book is better and more exciting?

14. I don't have a lot of contact with my neighbours but I like *their/there* dog and often play with it.

Task 3 Sentence translation

Translate the German sentences into good English, taking care to use the correct homonym.

1. Irgendwie fühle ich mich heute sehr schwach und müde.

_____

2. Ich habe auch die Englisch-Aufgabe nicht gemacht.

_____

3. Es ist sehr unhöflich, jemanden anzustarren. Bitte hör damit auf!

_____

4. Ich mochte die Szene am meisten, in der sie ihm den Kuchen ins Gesicht geworfen hat.

_____

5. Ich hoffe, dass eines Tages auf der ganzen Erde Friede sein wird.

_____

6. Bitte ziehe deine Schuhe an und warte vor der Türe auf mich.

_____

7. Wenn ich reich wäre, würde ich ein Hausmädchen haben.

_____

8. Drew las den Text laut vor, so dass jeder ihn hören konnte.

_____

COLLOCATIONS

Collocations sind Kombinationen aus Wörtern. Es gibt eigene Bücher (zB _LTP Dictionary_), voll mit solchen _selected collocations_, die dir sagen, welches Adjektiv oder Verb mit welchem Nomen zusammenpasst.

Betrachte folgendes Beispiel:

Es ist gutes Englisch zu sagen _to construct a road_, allerdings wäre die Phrase _to design a road_ völlig falsch und unenglisch.

Es ist ein langwieriger Prozess, solche Wortkombinationen zu erlernen. Am besten schnappt man sie beim Lesen englischer Bücher oder beim Anschauen englischer Filme auf. Man lernt sie kaum bewusst, sondern bekommt – durch möglichst viel Kontakt mit der englischen Sprache – mit den Jahren ein gutes Gefühl dafür, welche Kombinationen gut und welche weniger gut sind.

Da es wenig zielführend wäre, hier eine Liste möglicher _collocations_ zu geben, beginnen wir gleich mit den Übungen. Schau einfach, wie viele Wortkombinationen dir schon geläufig sind, und versuche dein Wissen zu erweitern.

Task 1 **Find the odd one out.**

Look at the nouns and find out the one verb it cannot be combined with. Mark the odd one with a cross.

1. an ADVANTAGE
- [ ] to offer
- [ ] to see
- [ ] to break
- [ ] to present

2. an ASPECT
- [ ] to neglect
- [ ] to ignore
- [ ] to survey
- [ ] to postpone

3. a thrilling BOOK
- [ ] to digest
- [ ] to purchase
- [ ] to promote
- [ ] to reduce

4. a high BUILDING
- [ ] to save
- [ ] to blow up
- [ ] to construct
- [ ] to refurbish

5. a CAREER
- [ ] to abandon
- [ ] to change
- [ ] to ruin
- [ ] to release

6. a DESCRIPTION
- [ ] to match
- [ ] to describe
- [ ] to provide
- [ ] to fit in with

7. your EDUCATION
- [ ] to forget
- [ ] to prioritise
- [ ] to put money into
- [ ] to neglect

8. a good and safe EMPLOYMENT
- [ ] to find
- [ ] to guarantee
- [ ] to reload
- [ ] to seek

9. your own FAULT
- [ ] to discover
- [ ] to draw attention to
- [ ] to deny
- [ ] to correct

10. some tasty FOOD
- [ ] to swallow
- [ ] to process
- [ ] to offer
- [ ] to abandon

11. general GUIDELINES
- [ ] to follow
- [ ] to destroy
- [ ] to keep to
- [ ] to violate

12. a HABIT
- [ ] to adopt
- [ ] to take up
- [ ] to forget
- [ ] to grow out of

13. a good IDEA
- [ ] to find
- [ ] to have
- [ ] to propose
- [ ] to reject

14. IMPORTANCE
- [ ] to deny
- [ ] to gain
- [ ] to grow
- [ ] to lose

15. an interesting JOB
- [ ] to quit
- [ ] to work on
- [ ] to work up
- [ ] to put off

16. a KISS
- [ ] to withdraw
- [ ] to steal
- [ ] to give somebody
- [ ] to have

17. good and profound KNOWLEDGE
- [ ] to absorb
- [ ] to soak up
- [ ] to possess
- [ ] to perform

18. your knowledge of the English LANGUAGE

☐ to brush up   ☐ to share   ☐ to enrich   ☐ to cancel

19. your LIFE

☐ to commit   ☐ to ruin   ☐ to enjoy   ☐ to lead

20. a romantic MARRIAGE

☐ to announce   ☐ to break up   ☐ to enter into   ☐ to refuse

21. a nasty MISTAKE

☐ to clear up   ☐ to provide   ☐ to forgive   ☐ to admit

22. your NAME

☐ to omit   ☐ to fill in   ☐ to deserve   ☐ to put down

23. your own OPINION

☐ to ignore   ☐ to impose   ☐ to change   ☐ to convey

24. a fantastic PARTY

☐ to throw   ☐ to arrange   ☐ to fix   ☐ to go to

25. PEACE all over the world

☐ to discover   ☐ to bring about   ☐ to achieve   ☐ to guarantee

26. many QUESTIONS

☐ to formulate   ☐ to pose   ☐ to respond to   ☐ to resist to

27. strict REGULATIONS

☐ to apply   ☐ to introduce   ☐ to ensure   ☐ to maintain

28. High SCHOOL

☐ to finish   ☐ to attend   ☐ to drop out of   ☐ to go in

29. a difficult SITUATION

☐ to handle   ☐ to make the worst of   ☐ to avoid   ☐ to land in

30. a nasty English TEST

☐ to take   ☐ to drop   ☐ to get through   ☐ to score

31. UNEMPLOYMENT

☐ to cope with   ☐ to lead to   ☐ to combat   ☐ to demand

32. your personal VIEWS

☐ to exchange   ☐ to spell out   ☐ to extract   ☐ to express

33. drinking WATER

☐ to refresh   ☐ to boil   ☐ to contaminate   ☐ to sip

34. eternal and everlasting YOUTH

☐ to buy   ☐ to look back at   ☐ to waste   ☐ to pass

35. a ZONE

☐ to approach   ☐ to extend   ☐ to review   ☐ to patrol

ADJEKTIVE

Adjectives (Eigenschaftswörter) sind wie das Salz in der Suppe – sie entscheiden darüber, ob ein von dir verfasster Text spannend und lesenswert und eine Unterhaltung mit dir interessant und lebhaft ist. Verwende Adjektive so oft wie möglich und versuche beim Lernen auch gleich das Gegenteil mitzulernen, denn dadurch erweiterst du deinen Sprachwortschatz enorm. Schau dir die folgende Übung an und versuche so viel wie möglich davon zu profitieren.

Task 1 Find the opposite.

Complete the following grid with the opposite forms of the adjectives given.

ADJECTIVE	OPPOSITE	ADJECTIVE	OPPOSITE
active		innocent	
afraid		interested	
after		keen	
alike		kind	
alive		lazy	
apart		less	
asleep		loud	
awful		major	
bad		many	
best		narrow	
beautiful		native	
calm		occasionally	
cheap		occupied	
clean		pleasant	
dangerous		polite	
desperate		poor	
early		quick	
easy		rough	
elementary		rude	
false		similar	
far		serious	
fat		solid	
generous		tight	
guilty		trivial	
healthy		urban	
heavy		voluntary	

IDIOMS

Englische *idioms* (*idiomatic expressions*) sind feststehende Redewendungen, die hauptsächlich von *native speakers*, also von Menschen mit Englisch als Muttersprache, verwendet werden. Es gibt unzählige davon und auch hier existieren bereits ganze Bücher voll mit Redewendungen zu den unterschiedlichsten Aspekten und Themen. Es ist klar, dass – wenn überhaupt – du nur ein paar wenige dieser *idioms* lernen und aktiv anwenden kannst. Es ist aber auch klar, dass sich dadurch dein Ausdruck signifikant verbessert. Schau dir die folgende Liste von Redewendungen durch und versuche dir so viele wie möglich einzuprägen.

List of selected English idioms

ENGLISH IDIOM	MEANING
Variety is the spice of life.	If you often change what you do, your life is more interesting.
to spill the beans	To tell people secret information you are not supposed to pass on.
That's the way the cookie crumbles.	Said to show that things don't always work the way you've planned them. It means that's the way things happen.
to go bananas	This means that you become very angry.
walk on egg shells	Like in German it indicates that you are careful and cautious.
bring home the bacon	This refers to the person who earns the money for a family to live on.
to get in (to) a jam	You have to face a difficult situation.
get out of jam	You get out of a bad situation.
to separate the wheat from the chaff	It means that you devide important from unimportant things.
to eat one's words	If you have said something that you now regret, you take it back.
to feel blue	This means that you feel sad, depressed or uncomfortable.
to be the black sheep	This refers to the disreputable member of a family or group.
out of the blue	If something happens out of the blue, it is completely unexpected.
whiter than white	You use this expression if you never do anything wrong.
to be in the pink	It indicates that you are in very good health.
sth. is a race against time	This means you have to finish something within a limited time.
in a split second	If something happens in a split second, it happens in just an instant.
to call it a day	This phrase indicates that you stop working for that day.
a man/woman of few words	It describes a person that doesn't usually say a lot.
to pay lip service	That's what you say if you agree with somebody but don't support and help this person.
to make a clean breast of sth.	This idiom means that you confess something to somebody.
to be a pain in the neck	It refers to a person/a thing that highly annoys you.
in the blink of an eye	If something happens in the blink of an eye, it happens very quickly.

TEST 1

RC: I took drugs but I'm clean now!

Read this inner monologue of 18-year-old Benjamin whose life was almost destroyed by taking drugs.

No, I never wanted it to happen that way. Of course not. And, I have to confess, at some point I simply no longer had control over it. What? Well ... my drug problem. Or should I rather say my drug addiction? Today I can talk about it quite openly as I seem to have the hardest part behind me. Or at least I hope so. I've gone through so much crap that things can't get any worse right now ...

Well. I must have been some 16 years old when I first got in touch with that stuff. I remember it clearly. My best buddy invited our whole gang to celebrate his driving license with him. So off we went. First to a pub and then to a disco. After we had drunk our third beer Luca pulled a little bag out of the pocket of his jeans jacket. There were small pills in it and all of them had different colours. I was too naïve to realise it at first. And too much worried about what my mates would say later on ...

Without hesitating, all the guys took one pill. I was the last one. And I didn't even think about not giving it a try. I was curious. The guys were there with me. We had fun. I simply did it. I picked a little pink pill and washed it off with the rest of my beer ...

I only have blurred visions of the rest of the evening. But that doesn't matter anyway. What matters far more is the fact that I got addicted to that stuff. And that it almost killed me. I really got hooked on this feeling of being high, forgetting all my problems and simply feeling free and independent. But I pushed too hard, didn't know when to stop and finally ended up in a detox institute where I had to stay for eight months ...

Never, in all my life, has anything required so much will, power and strength like the fight back into life. I wanted to live. And I was not ready to give up and die so young. It was the hardest time in my life, for sure, and I paid an incredibly high price for my own stupidity ...

Benjamin, 18 years old

Task Sequencing

Find the summary! Put the sentences into the correct order by numbering them.

	Suddenly Benjamin was faced with the decision of taking the small colourful pills or not.
	But unexpectedly an invitation of his best friend clearly changed Benjamin's life.
	Eventually Benjamin could not get rid of his addiction without professional help.
	Benjamin soon got addicted because he loved to forget his problems and to feel free.
	First he was afraid of what his friends would say and that they might call him a coward.
	They went to different locations and drank some bottles of beer.
	Actually Benjamin had never intended to get in touch with drugs.
	But as he basically felt comfortable in his friends' company he quickly took one of the pills.
	Consequently Benjamin and some friends went out at night to go dancing.

1 Punkt pro richtiger Antwort [   ] / 9

Language in Use: Fitness instead of fatness

You are going to read a text about how little exercise children make these days. Some words are missing from the text. Use the words in brackets to complete each gap (1–12) in the text. Write your answers in the spaces provided at the end of the text. The first one (0) has been done for you.

Fitness instead of fatness

No, not **(0) ... (obese)** is the topic of that article but being fit and doing, at least, some exercise every day. A nationwide study carried out in the United Kingdom in 2010 **(1) ... (revelation)** that too little exercise is the number one health issue for children. The figures are self-explanatory: nowadays every third child has a lifestyle necessary to **(2) ... (consideration)** as too lazy. Most kids don't go out to spend their freetime in the nature or to regularly ride their bikes. A full generation has turned into couch potatoes, only spending their time watching TV and playing video or computer games. It's actually needless to talk about the **(3) ... (disaster)** results of such a lifestyle but still, not talking about it would even be **(4) ... (bad)**.

Child fitness **(5) ... (decline)** by about nine percent within the last decade and in this context UK's chief medical officer warned that being **(6) ... (inactivity)** and lazy is even more dangerous than being obese. Children of normal weight who are unfit face greater health risks than those who are fat but fit. The human body simply needs exercise and training. It **(7) ... (condition)** to moving around and being active for hundreds of decades and if we stop doing that now, we make it almost impossible for our organism to function and work the way we want and **(8) ... (expectation)** to.

The perfect dosage of exercise would be some thirty minutes five times a week. This is the average of what our bodies need. What they get, however, runs up to almost zero. "The **(9) ... (irony)** thing is that exercise would boost the nation's health", says David Simpton from the national health association. Today inactivity affects more people in England than the **(10) ... (combination)** total of those who smoke, misuse alcohol or are obese. That's incredible as being physically fit is crucial to good health. Fitness decreases during childhood, possibly due to a decreased emphasis on physical fitness in older age groups. And that's no wonder as 70% of Britain's adults **(11) ... (failure)** to meet the minimum fitness level mentioned above.

In the end it's probably all about bad role models. If parents exercised more, their kids would probably also do so. And if the nation's health were better, the outbreaks of the six most prominent chronic diseases would **(12) ... (limitation)**. These are heart disease, stroke, diabetes, breast cancer, colon cancer and osteoporosis. Finally, also the health system would profit, resulting in a win-win situation for everybody.

0 _____*obesity*_____

1 _____

2 _____

3 _____

4 _____

5 _____

6 _____

7 _____

8 _____

9 _____

10 _____

11 _____

12 _____

1 Punkt pro richtiger Antwort ☐ / 12

Grammar

Task 1 Conditionals

Write matching conditional sentences to the following situations.

1. If: Pete: drive more carefully   **Folge**: I: go with him   **Situation**: He drives dangerously.

_____

2. If: we: not forget to invite Sady   **Folge**: she: not be angry   **Situation**: we forgot, Sady is angry

_____

3. If: you: tell me your secret   **Folge**: I: not say a word   **Situation**: it's likely you tell me

_____

4. If: you: drop a stone into water   **Folge**: it: sink   **Situation**: general rule

_____

5. If: Sue: pay more attention   **Folge**: she: not break her arm   **Situation**: Sue didn't pay attention.

_____

6. If: Dana not sell her car   **Folge**: we can drive to Italy   **Situation**: Dana sold her car.

_____

Task 2 Reported speech

Put the sentences into reported speech. Remember to use a suitable reporting verb!

1. Simon said to me, "<u>Please</u> don't tell dad about the car."

_____

2. Sharon said to Anthony, "Did you go to Spain last summer?"

_____

3. My sister said to me, "Could I borrow your blue dress tonight?"

_____

4. Robby said to Anna, "Take the bus, it's faster than the train."

_____

5. My neighbour said to his dog, "Get the stick!"

_____

6. My brother said to me, "Are you going to visit granny this weekend?"

_____

7. Miranda said to Joe, "Do you hear the noise? What do you think is it? You'd better go and see."

_____

1 Punkt pro richtiger Antwort ☐ / 13

LC: Computers are becoming Cupid's best weapon

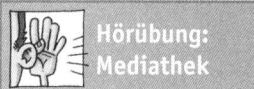
Hörübung:
Mediathek

Task   **Answering questions (key words)**

0.	Before the rise of the Internet, which event has made a deep impact on the dating scene?	*invention of the telephone*
1.	According to Prof. Rosenfeld, what is new about people connecting online?	
2.	Which practical aspect of online dating does Nicole Adams appreciate?	
3.	Apparently, the Internet is especially important for people who look for someone special. 61% of which group of people meet online?	
4.	How can the typical "online dater" be described?	
5.	In how far do successful couples have an impact on the fact that Web-dating will grow?	
6.	Why did people use to prefer saying they met their partner in a bar, rather than on the Internet?	
7.	What are the third most likely places for couples to meet?	

Gesamtpunkte ☐

2 Punkte pro richtiger Antwort ☐ / 14

Note	Punkte
Sehr gut	44–48
Gut	38–43
Befriedigend	32–37
Genügend	24–31
Nicht genügend	0–23

TEST 2

RC: LETHAL FUMES – SMOKING

Read the article about smoking and its dangers, ignoring the gaps for the headlines.

1_____

Smoking is one of the most controversial topics. While some people perceive it as a life-philosophy and wouldn't want to miss their cigarettes at any price, others are absolutely against it and fear about their health. There are only very few topics about which opinions are so divided and where it's so difficult – if not to say impossible – to come up with a compromise. But what actually makes smoking so attractive? Joana Heyworth has looked into the details why especially more and more teenagers and even kids start to smoke these days and which risks they take by doing so.

2_____

First of all, role models play a big role when it comes to smoking children. In a family where both parents are regular smokers, the kids are three times more likely to start smoking themselves compared to when growing up in a non-smoker family. "Kids almost always copy the behaviour of their parents, no matter if it's good or bad", says Howards Riffles from the Saint Mary Children Hospital in Wales. "Apart from the parents, also friends or older brothers and sisters may take over this function of the role model", he goes on explaining. So seen from this point of view kids grow up regarding smoking as completely normal. They often don't even think about possible health risks or dangerous long-term effects.

3_____

But also advertisements play a not insignificant role in the rising number of teenage smokers. Ads in magazines and on billboards seduce teens to try out cigarettes and to enjoy the feeling of freedom and coolness. TV spots feature relaxed young people enjoying themselves while smoking. As is always the case with advertisements, a completely wrong picture is presented which kids are often not able to distinguish from real life. A further interesting fact is that children tend to smoke the brands that are most advertised.

4_____

Clearly, the dangers related to regular smoking are countless and only a few should be mentioned here. Children who smoke are two to six times more susceptible to coughs and shortness of breath than those who don't smoke. This is particularly manifested when doing sports, for example. Besides, children who smoke are three times more likely to have time off school. Smoking reduces people's overall health and it weakens the immune system. That's why smokers (no matter if adult or child) frequently suffer from colds and often have to stay at home. Rather shocking 85% of regular teenage smokers (aged between 11 and 15) say that they would find it difficult not to smoke for one single week. 72% out of these think it would hardly be possible to give up smoking at all. Well, that sounds as if the number of teenage addicts is quite high, doesn't it?

5_____

The remaining question now is what can actually be done against these rising figures? The probably only way are campaigns that tell and show teenagers how dangerous smoking really is. Smokers must be made aware of the fact that once their health is ruined, they won't get a second chance. Lung cancer and other bad long-term effects are nothing to play around with and people must be careful and protective with their bodies.

Task ## Matching headlines

Find the correct headline but mind that there are two extra sentences.

A	The media and their influence	D	We only have one life – protect it!
B	Anti-smoking campaigns as solution for the future	E	Smokers versus non-smokers
C	Finding a compromise – mission failed	F	Media: showing real life
		G	Dangers, problems and risks – the world of smoking

2 Punkte pro richtiger Antwort ☐ / 10

Language in Use: Burger King under financial pressure (editing)

In most lines of the following text there is an unnecessary word. Spot it and write it in the space provided after each line. Some lines are correct. Indicate these with an OK. There are two examples at the beginning.

Burger King under financial pressure

Text	Answer	Line
Let's for a minute not talk about **the** Burger King's tasty hamburgers,	*the*	1
cheeseburgers and fries. Let's rather spend a minute thinking about the financial	*OK*	2
crisis the fast food company is all currently facing and trying to handle. While		3
only a few years ago the Miami-based chain which ranked worldwide second and		4
had a booming business, things have obviously changed and the single restaurants		5
and franchise partners now have to deal with a significant drop as in sales and		6
profits. The reasons for this phenomenon are numerous and to easy to explain.		7
To begin with, Burger King's rather narrow business philosophy has not changed		8
for quite of some time. Consequently the food they have on offer no longer		9
corresponds with the customers' wishes. Consider the following example: Burger		10
King's biggest rival at McDonalds has managed to enlarge and diversify its		11
product range, now also not including various salads, wraps, paninis and even		12
coffee shop areas. And this development is a good and necessary because due to an		13
extended understanding of healthy food and healthy eating habits like the current		14
market demands such changes and adoptions. Burger King, in contrast, still sticks		15
to traditional food only offering burgers, fries and fizzy drinks. It goes without		16
saying that if by doing so they lose a significant number of customers to		17
McDonalds, which is one main reason for the permanently decreasing profits.		18
This tendency which specially holds true for working class mothers who rather		19
drive their kids to the McDonalds after the soccer training than to Burger King		20
where the children are soon fed up with the small choice of products on available.		21
But Burger King's customers who have also changed due to the recession. Again,		22
prosperous families rather likely shift to McDonalds while the proportion of		23
blacks and Hispanics eating at Burger King restaurants constantly rises up. The		24
problem here is, that these two population groups were particularly and hard hit		25
by unemployment and have therefore only little money to spend it on food.		26
Sounds like the perfect vicious circle.		27
Burger King's full dilemma is manifested at the Wall Street. While fast food still		28
enjoys enormous popularity in the USA, the company has been losing a support		29
from various investors since a profit warning of a few months ago. And indeed,		30
sceptical investors really feel discontent and remain hesitant. As if it seems today,		31
McDonalds will enlarge its profits and become even more prominent and popular.		32

0,5 Punkte pro richtiger Antwort ☐ / 15

Grammar

Passive
Fill in the correct active or passive form of the verbs. Mind the tenses.

The history of the hot dog

The history of the hot dog _____ *(can – trace back)* to Ancient Greece and

_____ *(must – link)* to the creation of sausages in general. Accordingly,

the term "sausage" _____ *(mention)* in Homer's *Odyssey*, which

_____ *(write)* in the late eighth century B.C. The first cook of sausages,

however, _____ *(claim)* to have been the Roman Emperor Nero's cook who

_____ *(stuff)* a pig's intestines with meat and then _____ *(tie)* them

into separate sections. Thus, the "wiener" _____ *(bear)*. Several other

stories and myths _____ *(entwine)* around the creation of the hot dog

sausage. One of them says that the butcher's guild in Frankfurt _____ *(introduce)*

a spiced and smoked sausage in 1852. This thin sausage _____ *(call)* "Frankfurter"

after its hometown. As the sausage's shape _____ *(remind)* people of a "dachshund",

it _____ *(call)* the dachshund sausage. When German emigrants _____

(move) to the United States, the sausage and its name _____ *(take)* with them. In the

1860s, German immigrants then _____ *(start)* selling "frankfurters" and "wieners" in

milk rolls with sauerkraut on pushcarts. In 1867, Charles Feltman _____ *(found)*

the first Coney Island hot dog stand in Brooklyn. From that moment on, various forms of hot dogs

_____ *(spread)* all over the U.S.A. Today, the hot dog _____

(know) all over the world. Numerous variants _____ *(create)*, like the

famous chilli hot dog, or the corn dog. Hot dogs _____ *(appreciate)* as a

quick, delicious snack that _____ *(meet)* nearly everybody's taste. When you are

in LA drop in at "Pink's", the city's most famous hot dog stand. But don't come hungry – every hot dog

_____ *(prepare)* fresh and individually for you – and the queue always holds

a huge crowd. But it _____ *(be)* worth the wait – I promise.

0,5 Punkte pro richtiger Antwort ☐ / 12

LC: Hearing loss increases in U.S. teens

Hörübung: Mediathek

Multiple choice
Find the best answers to the questions. Tick the correct box.

1. **What do we know about the reasons why teens suffer from hearing loss?**

   A A survey shows that using earbuds causes hearing loss. ❏

   B Scientists do not have any actual suspicions about the reasons. ❏

   C High-frequency tones lead to hearing loss. ❏

   D It's likely that using earbuds can lead to hearing loss. ❏

2. **How many percent did teenage hearing loss increase in the last years?**

   A 15 ❏

   B 12 to 19 ❏

   C 30 ❏

   D 13 ❏

3. **Which consequences can going to a rock concert have?**

   A You may feel dizzy and disorientated. ❏

   B You may not be able to hear somebody's whispering. ❏

   C You may only suffer temporary damage to hearing. ❏

   D You may even suffer permanent hearing damage. ❏

4. **What are the physical consequences of listening to loud music with earbuds?**

   A The brain can no longer respond to particular pitches. ❏

   B Parts of the inner ear may get damaged. ❏

   C Sound may be transmitted more slowly to the brain. ❏

   D The sensitivity of tiny hairs that transmit sound can decrease. ❏

5. **Which recommendations does Dr. Grimes give for listening with earbuds?**

   A You should have annual hearing checkups. ❏

   B You should not listen to high volume. ❏

   C You should not listen longer than 10 or 15 minutes. ❏

   D You should take your earbuds out at intervals when listening to loud music. ❏

Gesamtpunkte ☐   2 Punkte pro richtiger Antwort ☐ / 10

Note	Punkte
Sehr gut	43–47
Gut	37–42
Befriedigend	31–36
Genügend	23–30
Nicht genügend	0–22

TEST 3

RC: Arranged marriages in the UK

Read through the following article dealing with arranged and forced marriages.

There are not many countries that have such an increasingly multi-cultural nature like Great Britain. Due to the rising number of immigrants, Britain has faced a rise in arranged marriages in the last few years. The stunning and almost unbelievable aspect, however, is that divorce rates for arranged marriages are lower than for "love marriages".

As the name already indicates, an arranged marriage is one where parents decide and arrange for their children who to marry. Arranged marriages therefore stand in contrast to love marriages where the children find their partners on their own and decide themselves who they want to share their lives with. Arranged marriages in Britain predominantly happen within the Asian community. The degree of contact between the future spouses varies. Sometimes they have never seen each other before, but more often a series of meetings precedes the actual marriage.

Arranged marriages actually don't exist among white Britons. In western society the general idea is to look for and find your dream partner on your own. The concept of marriage is, despite rising divorce rates, a life-long commitment and the decision to marry somebody ranges among the most difficult ones in your life. Marrying somebody who you hardly know and strictly speaking don't love, is unbelievable for the majority of us. For people having their origin in the Indian sub-continent, arranged marriages are anything but alien. Very often they are the only acceptable form of marriage because love marriages are seen to be celebrated due to primitive motives like lust. Young Asians living in Britain today face, however, the full dilemma as they are torn between these two diverse views and concepts of marriage.

The term "forced marriage" is related to arranged marriages and gives this idea a very negative touch. It is the case when parents not only arrange the marriage, but also force one or both of the partners involved to marry against their will. Quite often emotional and physical pressure is then carried out. It goes without saying that forced marriages violate human rights and are strictly forbidden. The motivation for parents to put so much pressure on their child is easy to explain: they want to preserve the family honour, desire to strengthen the family and prevent relationships that are considered unsuitable.

The basic idea of an arranged marriage is to ensure it's based on more important and long-lasting qualities than a love marriage. Unfortunately, quite frequently the opposite is the cases and the biggest problem is that when you don't know a lot about your future partner, you primarily judge him/ her on his/her looks. And this can definitely not be the long-lasting quality. Besides, how can you tell if you can live with someone for the rest of your life if you don't know this person's character? What is the basis for your decision then?

Whatever opponents say, arranged marriages do have their advantages as well. As mentioned above, they show a much lower divorce rate than love marriages. At that point we must not forget, however, that Asians regard divorce as absolutely unacceptable social behaviour. Those who are in favour of arranged marriages often argue that physical love is not the most important ingredient in a marriage and the future spouses learn to sympathise with each other. Finally, in cultures that practise arranged marriages, there is little or no risk of being left without a partner. It's like having a guarantee to marry sooner or later.

When it comes to an arranged marriage one must also not neglect the parents' role. Whether such a marriage will work or not, strongly depends on the motive of the parents. Do they just try to help find the right partner or do they want to prevent their child from sex outside marriage? Summarising it seems to be the fact that the most important factor in a successfully arranged marriage is to have understanding parents.

Note taking

Answer the questions in not more than FOUR words. Don't try to form sentences, just write key words.

1.	Why have there been more arranged marriages in Britain recently?	
2.	How exactly does an arranged marriage work and who decides about your spouse?	
3.	What's the concept of marriage for people from Great Britain?	
4.	Concerning marriage what's the problem young Asians have when living in the UK?	
5.	What is it that gives forced marriages such a negative image?	
6.	What are possible advantages of arranged marriages?	
7.	What are possible disadvantages of arranged marriages?	
8.	Why is the role of the parents in arranged marriages such an important one?	

1 Punkt pro richtiger Antwort ☐ / 8

Language in Use: The power of power napping

You are going to read a text about how relaxing an afternoon nap can be. Some words are missing from the text. Choose from the list (A–P) the correct word for each gap (1–13) in the text. There are three extra words that you should not use. Write your answers in the boxes provided. The first one (0) has been done for you.

The power of power napping

Do you sometimes feel a bit tired, sleepy and **(0)** ... in the afternoon? Do you then have the feeling that your work is completely unproductive and you only long for some rest? Well in that case a short nap might be the perfect **(1)** ... as it is a short period of sleep, usually during the daytime. Actually power napping is common for small children and elderly people but it has come to enjoy **(2)** ... also among adults. Today even top managers give themselves a short break in order to recharge their inner batteries.

Napping has been found to be very **(3)** ... . Napping for 20 minutes can help refresh the mind, improve overall alertness, change your mood to the better and consequently increase productivity. But that's not all as napping may also benefit the heart. In an eight-year study, researchers found that adults who took naps at least three times a week had a 37 percent **(4)** ... risk of heart-related death.

Scientists have been investigating the benefits of (power) napping for years and have found out that they are at least as **(5)** ... as a good night of sleep. Certain memory functions are positively influenced by these short naps and information overlap is **(6)** ... likely to occur. People can simply concentrate better after such a short rest. It's much easier for them to **(7)** ... and store information in their brains and to think more clearly. But it's eagerly important not to sleep too long as the short duration prevents nappers from entering the normal sleep cycle. This would rather be **(8)** ... as the sleeping cycle cannot be completed and people would be even more tired, groggy and disoriented afterwards. In fact they would be even more sleepy than before beginning the nap.

In order to stop yourself from fully falling asleep it's the best thing to **(9)** ... your sleeping time in advance. Make sure that you set your alarm clock or mobile phone to ring 18 to 25 minutes later, that's the time your body and mind need to switch off. People who regularly take these short naps may develop a good idea of the **(10)** ... that works best for them. Furthermore they will also soon find out about their right tools, environment, position and associated factors that help produce the best results. Some people might listen to slow and relaxing music while others need complete **(11)** ... . Some will prefer to simply lie down on the floor (probably on a gymnastic mat), whereas others are keen on lying down on the sofa. Different people have different preferences and likes of course. But in any case, power naps are highly effective, even when people have a full night's sleep. The one does not necessarily exclude or impede the other. It's only important to get the **(12)** ... of power napping into people's minds so that they no longer have the impression that short afternoon rests are similar to being lazy. Especially in America people fortunately slowly change their opinions concerning this topic and top managers in big companies often use their extended lunch breaks for their naps. People simply have to stop feeling **(13)** ... about taking this time for themselves.

A	higher	B	limit	C	popularity	D	more
E	guilty	F	silence	G	unproductive	H	lower
I	**drowsy**	J	significance	K	valuable	L	less
M	process	N	beneficial	O	duration	P	solution

0	1	2	3	4	5	6	7	8	9	10	11	12	13
I													

1 Punkt pro richtiger Antwort ☐ / 13

Grammar

Task 1 **Adjectives and adverbs**

Find as many adjectives/adverbs from the box for the numbers written in bold **(1)**, **(2)**, **...** . Use them only once.

black and white – boring – brand new – bright – cool – dreadful – final – good – incredible – long-desired – hard – overwhelming – peaceful – powerful – quick – simple – smooth – sparkelling – Swiss

My first day in the sky

On my 18th birthday, my parents surprised me with a/an **(1)** present: I was **(2)** allowed to do my pilot's licence! Of course, this meant **(3)** hours of studying the theory, but soon I got my **(4)** reward: The day I had my first flight lesson the sun was shining **(5)** and **(6)** sunbeams reflected on the plane! My plane: my **(7)** sailplane. I **(8)** climbed into the cockpit, eager to take off. We were hauled up **(9)**, but when I was supposed to take over control of the plane, I felt nervous. I could **(10)** keep my hands from trembling like mad. However, within seconds, a/an **(11)** feeling of peace and strength swept over me. We were gliding **(12)** through the air. I have never felt **(13)** before. Flying is **(14)** the most wonderful experience you can make.

1		8	
2		9	
3		10	
4		11	
5		12	
6		13	
7		14	

0,5 Punkte pro richtiger Antwort ☐ / 7

Task 2 **Relative clauses**

Make one sentence out of the following two or three phrases. Mind the correct pronouns and commas.

1. Benjamin called the police. His car was stolen. He had bought the car only two months ago.

_____

2. We put super glue in Emmet's shoes. He didn't find that funny.

_____

3. The girl was crying. Her dog had run away. She loved it like mad.

_____

4. The boy called me a minute ago. We met him yesterday at the party. You lost his number.

_____

5. My friend has just married. She lives in Australia. Her job is studying crocodiles.

_____

1 Punkt pro richtiger Antwort ☐ / 5

LC: 15 percent of teens with cells receive "sexts"

Hörübung:
Mediathek

Sentence completion (exact words)

Fill in the missing words or phrases.

0.	"Sexting" is a _____ word for a relatively new activity.	*provocative*
1.	Teens told us that this is something they have quite _____ with.	
2.	Alpert was prosecuted and _____ sending out child pornography.	
3.	Now the ACLU _____ the DA for violating the girls' First Amendment rights.	
4.	A few state legislatures are trying to make _____.	
5.	As DA Skumanick _____ in an earlier interview, sexting can be dangerous.	
6.	Getting teens to think before they act is a fight that's gone on for generations. Unfortunately, in this digital age, it may be taking on _____.	

Gesamtpunkte ☐   2 Punkte pro richtiger Antwort ☐ / 12

Note	Punkte
Sehr gut	41–45
Gut	36–40
Befriedigend	30–35
Genügend	23–29
Nicht genügend	0–22

TEST 4

RC: "Germany's Next Top Model" and other plagues

Read the text about beauty contests.

In times of perfect looks and appearance beauty contests boom. They are broadcasted on TV and made public for everybody. And the audience is wide, people enjoy watching the young and ambitious girls fighting to become top models. Nobody, however, is actually interested in the question whether this is really desirable.

Beauty contests have already existed for a very long time. They are neither new nor specially creative. The only aspect that has changed is their popularity. Because of shows like "Germany's Next Top Model by Heidi Klum" beauty contests have been opened up for a broad audience and the German TV Channel Pro 7 used to broadcast this show once a week. The number of viewer was enormous, mostly young girls and women of course. The idea behind the show is quite simple: a number of pretty young girls compete against each other and they have to solve several more or less difficult challenges and tasks. Every week one girl has to leave the show and in the end the winner girl becomes Germany's next top model and gets a contract with a modelling agency.

For the girls this would be the fulfilment of all their wishes and they are ready to give everything. They have their hair cut and dyed, undergo regular hard workouts and permanently have to overcome their personal fears by doing things they would never ever do if they were in their right mind. They experience the thrill of their first modelling jobs and they suffer from nervous breakdowns when they are expelled by Heidi Klum at the end of the week. So their lives are marked by permanent ups and downs.

"Beauty contest, no matter which form they finally take, are simply no longer up to date", says Mia Lidlow from the Institute of Science and Psyche in Boston. "Girls, or respectively women, no longer need to prove themselves through beauty and good looks. Thanks to emancipation and gender equality they have the same access to education and universities like men and they can follow any career they want. Their social standing and status is defined by what they have reached in their lives and not by how good-looking they are."

Task Multiple choice

Tick the appropriate box so that your answer is correct according to the text.

1. Beauty contest are ...

   A ... a relatively new phenomenon everybody is really interested in. ❏

   B ... an old phenomenon nobody is really interested in. ❏

   C ... not new but only young girls are interested in them nowadays. ❏

   D ... not really innovative but people are nevertheless interested in them. ❏

2. Who basically watched shows like Germany's Next Top Model?

   A Actually everybody with a special focus on young adult girls and women. ❏

   B Only Heidi Klum watched her series. ❏

   C Men and women equally liked watching these shows. ❏

   D Only adult women with teenage girls watched them. ❏

3. What was the idea behind Germany's Next Top Model?

   A To find as many top models as possible – the more the better. ❏

   B To put the young girls under so much pressure until they finally give up. ❏

   C To show them that being a top model is much harder than expected. ❏

   D To bring one girl to the top of Germany's modelling scene. ❏

4. During the show, what did the girls have to do?

   A Every girl had to lose at least 5 kilograms of weight. ❏

   B They only had to learn how to walk and move their bodies on a catwalk. ❏

   C They had to overcome fears and anxieties and improve their performance. ❏

   D All of them had to take part in a three-hour workout every day. ❏

5. What were they willing to do in order to become Germany's Next Top Model?

   A They were ready to give everything that was necessary. ❏

   B They were ready to cut their hair, even if it had been nice and long. ❏

   C They were ready to present themselves in underwear for a photo shooting. ❏

   D They were ready to forget about their biggest dream of becoming top model. ❏

6. What was one of Heidi Klum's roles in this series?

   A To decide which girl had to change her physical appearance. ❏

   B To decide which girl won't participate in the following week. ❏

   C To decide which girl had to do some extra workout. ❏

   D To decide which girl won't join a photo shooting the following week. ❏

7. According to Mia Lidlow, why are beauty contests no longer up to date?

   A Because they put too much pressure on young girls and women. ❏

   B Because they only reduce women to their appearances and looks. ❏

   C Because by nature women don't look perfect anyway. ❏

   D Because they cost too much money and are difficult to organise. ❏

8. How do women these days define themselves?

   A They define themselves by their children. ❏

   B They define themselves by their husbands and their social status. ❏

   C They define themselves by their education, their job, their actions and behaviour. ❏

   D They define themselves by their brainpower, their intellect and their looks. ❏

1 Punkt pro richtiger Antwort ☐ / 8

Language in Use: Unhealthy school lunches (open gap text)

You are going to read a text about what kids eat at school. Some words are missing. Figure them out and write your answers in the spaces provided at the end of the text. The first one (0) has been done for you.

Unhealthy school lunches

A survey, carried **(0)** ... only a few months ago, revealed that 99 out **(1)** ... 100 packed lunches eaten at elementary schools are unhealthy. Most of them contain, or rather exclusively consist of, chocolate, chips and any type of sugary drink. It goes without saying that due **(2)** ... this reason, most of them don't meet government's nutritional standards concerning school lunches. But that's the crux. In the UK these standards only hold true **(3)** ... meals and food offered by the schools, not for the food items kids bring in their lunch boxes. They are part of parents' responsibility. And the big majority of the parents ignores this responsibility. They basically pack their **(4)** ... lunch boxes with sugar, fat and salt, justifying their behaviour by stating that the kids would not eat **(5)** ... else. Over and over again they argue that if they put broccoli spears in their children's packed lunch, the kids would refuse eating it and would throw it into the bin. They would not even touch the food. So consequently parents provide their children with something they do eat which is, according to their opinion, better than nothing.

A voluntary inspection **(6)** ... school lunch boxes in an elementary school in Manchester showed that chocolate is all around. The first lunch box that **(7)** ... opened was found to be filled with a chocolate spread white sandwich, a pack of crisps and a bottle of Coke. Another one included a cheese pastry, a pack of chips and some chocolate biscuits. The boxes **(8)** ... followed weren't any different and things like mineral water, vegetables or wholemeal bread were not found at all. At least two out of twenty eight kids had apples and pears **(9)** ... them.

The inspection of these lunch boxes only shows what is happening all over England and probably also in **(10)** ... of other countries: just 1.1 percent of children's pre-packed lunch boxes meet the nutritional values and standards for school children. So it's actually no wonder that, paired with the combination of **(11)** ... doing any exercise, more and more kids have a disposition to become fat and/or obese. In order to find a way out of this vicious circle UK's School Food Trust currently runs a campaign trying to raise parents' awareness related **(12)** ... that topic. They also promote healthy eating and highlight the importance of a well-balanced school lunch and diet.

0 _____*out*_____

1 _____

2 _____

3 _____

4 _____

5 _____

6 _____

7 _____

8 _____

9 _____

10 _____

11 _____

12 _____

1 Punkt pro richtiger Antwort ☐ / 12

Grammar

Gerund or infinitive?

1. Ich entschuldige mich, nicht an deinen Geburtstag gedacht zu haben.

_____

2. Ich werde dein ständiges „Mich-Ignorieren" nicht länger entschuldigen.

_____

3. Wir haben vergessen, unsere Eltern zu bitten, uns von der Party abzuholen.

_____

4. Heute bevorzuge ich es, kein Dessert zu nehmen.

_____

5. Hat Serena wirklich aufgehört, Aden zu daten?

_____

6. Patience freut sich schon so, dir die Neuigkeiten zu erzählen.

_____

7. Ich bin es leid/Ich hab die Nase voll, darauf zu warten, dass er mich anruft.

_____

8. Die Vorteile von SMS können nicht geleugnet werden.

_____

9. Ich bereue es, Gina beim Ausmalen ihres Zimmer nicht geholfen zu haben.

_____

10. Wie wär's mit einem Film im Autokino?

_____

11. Ich bewundere sein Talent, immer einen Parkplatz zu finden.

_____

12. Es macht Spaß, hier zu sitzen und den Burschen beim Surfen zuzusehen.

_____

13. Ich habe eine Geldstrafe bekommen, weil ich hier geparkt habe.

_____

14. Wir werden uns nie daran gewöhnen, diese Uniformen zu tragen.

_____

1 Punkt pro richtiger Antwort ☐ / 14

Ms. SARAH ROSE (Author, "For All the Tea in China: How England Stole the World's Favourite Drink and Changed History"): (Reading) The task required a plant hunter, a gardener, a thief, a spy. The man Britain needed was named Robert Fortune.

RAZ: That's Sarah Rose, reading from her new book, "For All the Tea In China." It tells the story of what she calls the greatest single act of corporate espionage in history, the story of how Britain sent an agent to China to steal its tea and end that country's dominance of the tea trade. Sarah Rose is at NPR's New York studio. Welcome to the program.

Ms. ROSE: Thanks, Guy, for having me.

RAZ: So basically, you had this system where Britain was shipping opium to China. China was shipping tea back. Why did Britain feel like it had to get into the tea business?

Ms. ROSE: The Chinese emperor hated that opium was the medium of exchange because a nation of drug addicts was being created. So the emperor confiscated all the opium, destroyed it all. England sent warships. At the end of the day, they realized that if they were going to keep pace with the British tea consumption and not deal with the Chinese, they had to own it for themselves.

RAZ: This is where Robert Fortune comes in, and he is the one who sort of guides the narrative here. Tell us who Robert Fortune was.

Ms. ROSE: Robert Fortune was a botanist, a horticulturalist, at a time when botany and the natural sciences were on the ascent in Britain. A great deal of them had university educations and were trained as doctors.
Robert Fortune was Scottish but grew up quite poor, and so he kind of worked his way through the ranks of professional botany, learning with hands-on training instead of book training.

RAZ: And by the time he reaches his early 30s, he goes on a trip to China. This is around 1845. It's a two-year trip, just in search of plants. You talk about how he then publishes a travelogue of his adventures, where he sort of fights off pirates, and it kind of captures the imagination of Victorian society.

Ms. ROSE: He was attacked by pirates, he was attacked by bandits, he encountered all kinds of disease and storms, and he also goes in Chinese disguise, dressed up as if he were a wealthy Chinese merchant.
I don't know if it captured the imagination of the Victorians, but that certainly captured mine, that notion of cultural transvestitism.

RAZ: And this book that he publishes, the sort of diary of his exploits, makes the rounds, and by 1848, he is approached by a representative from the East India Company, at the time, one of the most important, if not the most important, multinational corporation in the world.

Ms. ROSE: The East India Company says to him: We need you to go back to China and hunt up some tea for us. They wanted really good tea stock from the very best gardens in China, and they also needed experts. They needed the Chinese to go to India to teach the British planters, as well as the Indian gardeners.

RAZ: So Fortune manages to get his seeds to India, and within his lifetime, India actually surpasses China as the world's biggest tea grower. I mean, it's a pretty astonishing turnabout in such a short period of time.

Ms. ROSE: It astonishes me. China has pretty much never really come back from that, certainly not in the Western markets. Now that Asia has such a booming economy, the Chinese are again pretty fierce tea producers. But it took a-hundred-plus years.

RAZ: Do you regard Robert Fortune as history's greatest corporate thief or the man we can thank for the tea we drink?

Ms. ROSE: I think he thought of himself as a China expert and a gardener. He didn't see himself as stealing something that didn't belong to him. He thought plants belong to everybody.

RAZ: That's Sarah Rose. She's the author of the book, "For All the Tea in China: How England Stole the World's Favorite Drink and Changed History." Sarah Rose, thank you so much.

Ms. ROSE: Thank you.

LC 3: FROM DICKENS HIMSELF, NOTES ON "A CHRISTMAS CAROL"

1.

2. audio reading
5. right-hand margin
6. classic rendition
3. reading room
4. public reading
1. animated version

2.

a. animated version
b. Christmas Eve
c. third floor
d. was not done
e. perhaps 150
f. were replaced
g. emotion to convey

Transcript: From Dickens himself, notes on "A Christmas Carol"

MELISSA BLOCK, host:
'Tis the season for the various renderings of "A Christmas Carol", by Charles Dickens. This year, there is the animated version, which you can enjoy in 3D, or if you're more inclined toward the traditional, there are assorted audio readings, such as this one, by the late British actor Paul Scofield.

Mr. PAUL SCOFIELD (Actor): Once upon a time of all the good days in the year, on Christmas Eve, old Scrooge sat busy in his counting-house.

BLOCK: Dickens himself used to perform "A Christmas Carol". But as NPR's Margot Adler reports, he didn't perform it as he had written it.

MARGOT ADLER: If you walk into New York Public Library during this holiday season, you can look into a small glass case on the third floor in the reading room. Isaac Gewirtz, the curator of the Berg Collection of English and American Literature, explains.

Mr. ISAAC GEWIRTZ (Curator, Berg Collection of English and American Literature): The most prominent item in the case is the promptbook of Charles Dickens for "A Christmas Carol'"

ADLER: And what's a promptbook?

Mr. GEWIRTZ: A promptbook is a book that prompts the reader on giving a performed reading of a text. In Dickens' day, public readings of fiction or of poetry was not done. It was considered a desecration of one's art and a lowering of one's dignity.

ADLER: But forget about dignity. Charles Dickens, according to Gewirtz, gave perhaps 150 public readings of "A Christmas Carol" over his lifetime. The first one went as long as three hours, later versions took about an hour and 25 minutes. And when you look at the promptbook, he cut out a lot. Complex sentences were replaced with simple ones.

Mr. GEWIRTZ: What's interesting though is to see how much of the atmospherics have been deleted. Scenes that set the mood in the streets of London, for instance.

ADLER: And often anything to do with the state of mind of a character that could be conveyed by tone of voice.

Mr. GEWIRTZ: You will notice that in the right-hand margins of this page there, it says tone to pathos. So he had many of these kinds of clues to himself, how to modulate his voice, what kind of emotion to convey at the time.

ADLER: So, those classic renditions of Dickens, like the one by Paul Scofield here.

Mr. SCOFIELD: Come, then, returned the nephew gaily. What right have you to be dismal? What reason have you to be morose? You're rich enough. Scrooge, having no better answer ready on the spur of the moment, said Bah again, and followed it up with humbug.

ADLER: Be advised: They may not be as traditional as you think. Dickens himself changed Dickens.

Margot Adler, NPR News, New York.

BLOCK: And you can see the edits in "A Christmas Carol", in Dickens' own handwriting at npr.org.

LC 4: THIS IS "YOUR FACE ON METH", KIDS

1.

commercial, campaign, ravage, morph, physiological, vanity, devastating, complexion

2.

a. T	**c.** F	**e.** T	**g.** F	**i.** F	**k.** T
b. T	**d.** F	**f.** T	**h.** F	**j.** F	

Transcript: This is "Your face on meth", kids

GUY RAZ, host:

Now, before Flash was born, back in the 1980s, TV watchers couldn't avoid this commercial.

(Soundbite of advertisement)

Unidentified Man: OK, last time. This is drugs. This is your brain on drugs. Any questions?

RAZ: That campaign from the Partnership for a Drug-Free America arrived just about the time the drug methamphetamine started to become a bigger problem. And since then, meth has ravaged many small towns and rural areas.

Tom Allman is the sheriff in one of those places, Mendocino County in Northern California. And he was trying to figure out a way to keep kids from even trying the drug. So he turned to a computer programmer named Laslo Vespremi, and he asked him to develop software that would digitally alter images of those kids, to show them what they'd look like after using meth.

Teenagers sit down in front of a computer screen, and one of Sheriff Allman's staffers tells them:

Mr. TOM ALLMAN (Sheriff, Mendocino County, California): We're going to take a picture of you. You're young. You're vibrant. You have great-looking skin. Your hair is there, your teeth are there. But we want to show you what you would look like after six months, one year, three years of using meth. And the software that Laslo designed morphs it into the physiological effects that meth causes: the open scabs, the droopy skin, the hair loss. If I could choose one phrase to say what this program does, it strikes at the vanity of teenagers.

RAZ: Hmm. You have been in law enforcement for almost 30 years, I understand, and it's safe to say you've seen a lot of teenagers and drug use over the years. What is it about methamphetamine that has law-enforcement officers so concerned?

Mr. ALLMAN: The addiction to methamphetamine is over 90 percent after the first-time use.

RAZ: Wow.

Mr. ALLMAN: And my goal is to just stop that first-time use. I live in a small town of Willits, where the population is less than 5,000. And I'm going to tell you, I do not know of a single person who could not relate to me of a connection they have with a friend or family member that methamphetamine has been involved with.

RAZ: Sheriff Allman, what kind of reactions have you been getting from students who have undergone this digital transformation to see themselves as meth addicts – what they might look like?

Mr. ALLMAN: The emotions we get from kids go from being scared – and some kids start crying when they see the devastating effect that meth can do to their complexion. And when I say we strike at the vanity, that's exactly what's happened. It was the way to crack the nut, to say, this could happen to you.

RAZ: Whether or not this was your intention, there is kind of a fear aspect to this program. How can you be sure that it will work, that that message will stick with those kids?

Mr. ALLMAN: Well, I can't be sure of it. And our intent was not to use scare tactics, because scare tactics don't work. And the commercial that you played at the beginning of your program of the frying egg, that didn't work, and the "Just Say No" didn't work.

So we don't know what does work. But I can tell you that the software is having more of a positive effect than anything that I've ever been involved with on the drug fight.

RAZ: That's Tom Allman. He's the sheriff of Mendocino County, and he joined me from member station KZYX in Philo, California.

Sheriff Allman, thank you so much.

Mr. ALLMAN: Thank you, Guy.

RAZ: And you can see an example of how my face was digitally altered at our Web site, npr.org.

program = A.E. / programme = B.E.

LC 5: IN BRITAIN, LIGHTS COME UP ON CLUBBERS' DRUG

1.

1. F	**3.** A	**5.** C	**7.** B
2. H	**4.** G	**6.** E	**8.** D

2.

a. C	**b.** B	**c.** A	**d.** D	**e.** D

Transcript: In Britain, lights come up on clubbers' drug

MICHELE NORRIS, host:
From NPR News, this is ALL THINGS CONSIDERED. I'm Michele Norris.
ROBERT SIEGEL, host:
And I'm Robert Siegel.
M-Cat, meow meow, drone, those are all street names for mephedrone. It's a new designer drug that has swept the British party scene and ignited a furious public debate.
Vicki Barker reports from London.
(Soundbite of music)
VICKI BARKER: About 40 teenage girls from a West London private school celebrate at a birthday party. Until a few months ago, hard liquor or cannabis might have been the strongest intoxicants smuggled into parties where parents are absent. But now, these teenagers say, a lot of those kids who do drugs are doing mephedrone, a legal high they can buy online.
These girls say they haven't done meph, but they know lots of teenagers who have.
Ms. LAURA BELL: I've known people, like, get panic attacks, get really, really panicky, have to go to hospital because they're having these, like, heart is beating really, really fast.
BARKER: Seventeen-year-old Laura Bell says many kids have assumed that the fact that meph was legal meant that it was safe.
Ms. BELL: I mean, if people are, like, raving about this thing that was incredible, that gave you a buzz that was bigger than alcohol and made you feel really, like, aware and just made you want to party, then why wouldn't you take it if there were no side effects that you knew of? Why wouldn't you take it?
BARKER: That's exactly why most politicians, and some scientists here have pushed for mephedrone to be banned: to send the signal that the drug isn't safe, and Laura agrees with them. But her friend, Jessie Farragher, unwittingly puts the case for the other camp: those scientists and drug counselors who claim outlawing meph won't solve the real problem.
Ms. JESSIE FARRAGHER: Have you heard of the Facebook group called mephedrone is turning my friends into dribbling losers? It's true. It's so true. And if it was illegal, it wouldn't matter. It's still a stupid drug that everybody does.
BARKER: Even veteran observers of Britain's party scene have been surprised at how fast meph has become the drug that everybody does. The white powder is manufactured in Chinese labs and marketed online as plant food. Not to be confused with the heroin substitute, methadone, meph is actually chemically similar to amphetamines.
It first hit Britain's dance scene around 2008. But in the past few months it has exploded across the country, with wide take-up reported among teenagers and young adults. It seemed to explode across the British media, too. There were reports 26 deaths had been linked to mephedrone. One school principal said his teachers didn't even have the legal right to confiscate it.
Both stories turned out to be inaccurate. British teachers can, in fact, confiscate any contraband, and it's not clear anyone has died solely from using mephedrone. But the public uproar led Britain's home secretary to propose making meph a class B drug on a par with cannabis and amphetamines. Bad idea, says David Nutt. He chaired the British government's drugs advisory committee, until he publicly criticized the government's decision to toughen the marijuana laws.
Mr. DAVID NUTT (Former British Drug Advisory Committee Chair): I can guarantee that as soon as mephedrone is regulated, controlled, made illegal, others will come along.
BARKER: Nutt argues recreational drugs are now so deeply entrenched in British youth culture, the phenomenon should be approached as a public health problem, not a law enforcement issue. It's both, says the man who replaced David Nutt on the panel, retired pharmacologist Les Iversen.
Mr. LES IVERSEN (British Drug Advisory Committee Chair): There's a whole group of people who have never used drugs before, suddenly is thinking that mephedrone is easily available, it's safe, it's legal. It's neither of these things now: It's not legal and it's not safe.
BARKER: In their final session before next month's elections, British lawmakers approved the ban, but users have been given a grace period. Meph technically remains legal until Friday.
For NPR News, I'm Vicki Barker in London.

LC 6: CHINA UPROOTS CHILD SLAVE LABOR RING AT BRICK PLANT

1.

a. brick; **b.** ordeal; **c.** unscrupulous; **d.** Starvation; **e.** Exploitation; **f.** kiln; **g.** Prosecution

2.

a. forced to work; **b.** paid with their lives; **c.** rid of the evidence; **d.** local communist party chief; **e.** wind of the search; **f.** not to speak; **g.** to make it out; **h.** some form of exploitation

Transcript: China uproots child slave labor ring at brick plant

LIANE HANSEN, host:
This is WEEKEND EDITION from NPR News. I'm Liane Hansen.
Our next story sounds like one from another era. It's not. The headline is child slavery. Boys as young as 8 have been sold for about $65 each to unscrupulous bosses and forced to work 14 to 16 hours a day making bricks in primitive kilns. They've been starved and beaten. Several have tried to escape and some of them reportedly paid with their lives. The horror has been going on in central China for years. Authorities only started to crack down this past Friday. Some 500 slave laborers have been rescued.
NPR's Anthony Kuhn is in Shanxi Province. Anthony, first of all, have you been able to visit any of these kilns and actually see what conditions are like?
ANTHONY KUHN: Yes, Liane. I visited the kiln that's that center of this story here in Shanxi Province. And it was pretty primitive. There was a big machine that clawed the earth away from this side of a hill and there was a row of brick kilns which – coal fire kilns which made the bricks.
Someone, apparently trying to get rid of the evidence, had destroyed the places where the workers were living, but there is still – was one building standing and I went into it and it was very depressing. It was grim and grimy and there were soiled clothes and beddings skewed around the room. And I understood from talking to the local people there that this brick kiln was run by the son of the local communist party chief and those people are now being questioned by police.
HANSEN: Have you spoken to any of the child slaves or their parents? And if so, what did they tell you?
KUHN: I spoke to parents of some of the kids by phone. Some of them had found their kids; others are still waiting for news from the ongoing search by police.

From what we understand, first of all, these parents have been through a tremendous ordeal combing this vast swath of land for their kids. Looking in iron mines, in brick kilns and coal mines. In many cases, the mine or brick kiln owners got wind of the search beforehand and found ways of obstructing search. They were told by some police that nobody was killed and so the police could do nothing about it, or they were referred to other departments. Now, the – some of the parents seem to be, sort of afraid of talking. Clearly, someone has told them not to speak and so they're in a very tough position. But we've also seen a letter from them. Some 400 parents bonded together and put a letter on the Internet about their search.

HANSEN: How did the factory owners get these young people to work for them?

KUHN: Well, from talking to the parents and the people in these villages, what we understand is that most of these people were country folk and had not had experience off the farms. They were either abducted by force or lured away by the promise of jobs at train stations, bus stations, highway underpasses, and the ones who did not escape tended to be pretty docile and inexperienced. Some of the smarter, tougher ones managed to make it out. But it's clear that after a few beatings and after a period of starvation, a lot of these men and boys would just work for food just to survive.

HANSEN: How did the owners manage to escape detection for so long?

KUHN: They were able to avoid prosecution because of official collusion, because they were in cahoots with the local officials. The particular kiln I went to – the owner was the son of the local party chief and he subcontracted out the business to another out-of-towner. He basically just said, "produce so many bricks for me a month and I'll ask no questions about how you treat the workers."

This is true in a lot of parts of Shanxi Province and neighboring Henan Province. The owners get the land and access to these natural resources from their connections with officials. And whether they are illegal or whether they are polluting, it's basically up to these officials. And local media say that officials got wind of this particular illegal plant months ago but nothing was done about until Friday.

HANSEN: Had there been arrest?

KUHN: Yes. In Shanxi Province, there have been over 120 arrests so far.

HANSEN: What's the public reaction to all of these?

KUHN: I think the overall reaction is horror and disgust. Also, I think there's a feeling of numbness particularly among the people I talked to. There's a feeling that this is a stage of what you might call primitive capital accumulation in China. Sort of like our gilded age of robber barons in the U.S. – that all this wealth that's being generated has to be generated by some form of exploitation.

HANSEN: NPR's Anthony Kuhn in China's Shanxi Province. Thank you very much, Anthony.

KUHN: Thanks, Liane.

> labor = A.E. / labour = B.E.

LC 7: BECOMING CLOSE: THE GEOGRAPHY OF FRIENDSHIP

1.

3, 5, 1, 6, 4, 7, 2

2.

a. friendships and social connections
b. undergraduate program in engineering
c. to become roommates
d. Sally was much taller/because of Sally's height
e. personality
f. more outgoing
g. proximity (or: distance), (common) race (or: heritage)
h. make up for deficits
i. trust and intimacy (or: lifelong sources of support)

Transcript: Becoming close: The geography of friendship

ARI SHAPIRO, host:

Research suggests that friendships and social connections are important for maintaining mental health. Many of us formed our most enduring friendships at a time when we were quite vulnerable: the first semester of college.

For those who arrive on campus knowing few, if any, other students, researchers say there are two strong predictors of who will end up becoming friends. NPR's Allison Aubrey reports.

ALLISON AUBREY: On the day of his 19th birthday, Bipin Sen got on a plane in New Delhi and flew to Chicago to start an undergraduate program in engineering. He'd already determined his major. What he didn't know is who he'd live with once he arrived.

Mr. BIPIN SEN (Student): I had never been to the States, never been to Chicago, and knew no one in Chicago.

AUBREY: At some point during the long flight, he exchanged glances with another passenger, a guy about his age. It turns out once they arrived, they bumped into each other at the university housing office.

Mr. SEN: Sixteen hours later and 8,000 miles across, we had our first words of exchange. He was also an incoming freshman. He was in a different program, and just after talking for a few minutes, I asked if he wanted to just be roommates for the semester.

AUBREY: Lots of friendships begin with these chance encounters. Leila Holtsman and Sally Hoffmaster met 25 years ago, when they were assigned as freshman-year roommates at the University of Virginia.

Leila recalls her first impressions were that she and Sally were not so similar. Leila says she's short, and Sally ...

Ms. LEILA HOLTSMAN: She's really tall. She's 6 feet tall. I remember being amazed by her height and thinking that alone made us really, really different.

AUBREY: And Sally says their personalities were different, too.

Ms. SALLY HOFFMASTER: I was extremely shy, and she was more – definitely more outgoing.

AUBREY: In both these cases, what drew these friends together in the first place were proximity – being in the same place at the same time – and a common race or heritage. So are these two factors really enough to spark a friendship? Bruce Sacerdote, a researcher at Dartmouth College, says the answer seems to be yes.

Professor BRUCE SACERDOTE (Researcher, Dartmouth College): I think having that shared background and that random chance meeting certainly have big impacts on who your friends are, and I think have also big impacts on who you marry, where you live, what you do.

AUBREY: Sacerdote explains a lot of sociology research points to this proximity or distance effect, including his own study. He analyzed the volume of email exchanges among students on his campus, and correlated the number of emails with factors such as race, hometown ...

Prof. SACERDOTE: Whether you went to a private or public high school, what fraternity you were in, and distance – your freshman year distance, which is by and large randomly assigned here.

AUBREY: And you found that this race and distance seemed to be critical?

Prof. SACERDOTE: Huge.

AUBREY: Yeah.

Prof. SACERDOTE: Right. They are the big determinants.

AUBREY: Of course, things such as interests and hobbies are also important. It's pretty common for friendships to be fluid. And clearly, students of different races do mix on campus. Once Bipin and his roommate developed a wider, more diverse circle of friends, they branched off in different directions.

But in the case of Sally and Leila, they became each other's rock. Sally says Leila helped her come out of her shell a bit. For instance, when they walked down the campus quad, Sally used to look down at the ground because she was too shy to make eye contact.

Ms. HOFFMASTER: And I'd be walking with her and she's like, hit me in the stomach and remind me to like, you know, look up.

AUBREY: And connect with people. Sally says it made her realize that Leila had her back, that a best friendship was evolving.

Dr. GREG EELLS (Psychologist, Cornell University): We tend to like people who kind of make up for some of the deficits we see in ourselves or help us kind of grow in ways that are not our strengths. So yeah, I think that's very typical.

AUBREY: That's psychologist Greg Eells of Cornell University. He says college roommates have a lot of face time, which can help develop trust and intimacy.

Dr. EELLS: There is something about those relationships you can form in college. It can be lifelong sources of support.

AUBREY: Leila and Sally say two and a half decades later, they're still best friends. And Sally says that when she meets someone new today, she has no problem making eye contact at all.

Allison Aubrey, NPR News.

LC 8: SORRY CHARLIE: "TWO AND A HALF MEN" MAY GO ON

1.

1. C; **2.** A; **3.** E; **4.** B; **5.** D

a. makes good on; **b.** has dropped out of; **c.** brush up on; **d.** over a barrel; **e.** swapped out

2.

a. T; **b.** F; **c.** F; **d.** T; **e.** F; **f.** F; **g.** T; **h.** F

Transcript: Sorry Charlie: "Two and a Half Men" may go on

MELISSA BLOCK, host:

Charlie Sheen is the highest-paid actor on television and the star of the highest-rated sitcom, "Two and a Half Men." But now, he's in contract negotiations, and he's indicated he's ready to leave the show if he doesn't get even more money. And that leaves some wondering: Could the series continue without him? Commentator Andrew Wallenstein says no problem.

ANDREW WALLENSTEIN: Sorry, Charlie: "Two and a Half Men" could have a future without you, unthinkable as it might sound. If you make good on your threat to go, well, we'll miss your sardonic wit.

(Soundbite of television program, "Two and a Half Men")

Mr. CHARLIE SHEEN (Actor): (As Charlie Harper) Uncle Charlie does not like to start his day with a squealing creature in his face.

(Soundbite of laughter)

WALLENSTEIN: If Sheen thinks he has CBS over a barrel, he should brush up on his TV history. It's been proven time and time again that a sitcom can go on even when the main attraction takes off.

In fact, one of the best examples of this trend involves Sheen himself. When Michael J. Fox was diagnosed with Parkinson's disease, he was forced to give up the lead role on the ABC comedy "Spin City".

(Soundbite of television program, "Spin City")

Mr. MICHAEL J. FOX (Actor): (As Michael Flaherty) By 11 o'clock, this city is going to smell like a giant foot.

(Soundbite of laughter)

WALLENSTEIN: But ABC replaced Fox with a new character played by Charlie Sheen. The ratings actually went up.

(Soundbite of television program, "Spin City")

Mr. BARRY BOSTWICK (Actor): (As Mayor Randall M. Winston Jr.) Good morning everyone.

WALLENSTEIN: Comedies have been proving their durability as far back as 1969. Remember the sitcom "Bewitched"? Dick York vacated the role of the husband after five years. But Dick Sargent assumed his character for another three. And who can forget years later when Shelley Long shocked Hollywood by dropping out of "Cheers"? She was forgotten pretty quickly once Kirstie Alley came in.

(Soundbite of television program, "Cheers")

Ms. KIRSTIE ALLEY (Actor): (As Rebecca Howe) Do you have the time?

Mr. TED DANSON (Actor): (As Sam Malone) 4:30.

Ms. ALLEY: (As Rebecca) Good because I just wanted to remember the exact moment I met the biggest jerk on earth.

(Soundbite of laughter)

WALLENSTEIN: Now you could argue, would "Cheers" have survived if Ted Danson walked away, or if Elizabeth Montgomery left "Bewitched"? You know what? I'd still say yes because one of the hallmarks of a great comedy is the way humor is distributed throughout the cast.

It's a little surprising when you think about it. Comedy is such a delicate chemistry. But the same can't be said for dramas, which almost seem to thrive on these cast defections. Just think of how "Law & Order" has swapped out actors on an almost annual basis.

Now, I'm not suggesting every comedy ever was immune to cast changes. "Seinfeld" might have seemed to be missing something if it lacked, you know, Seinfeld.

(Soundbite of television program, "Seinfeld")

Mr. JERRY SEINFELD (Actor): Not that there's anything wrong with that.

(Soundbite of laughter)

WALLENSTEIN: My bet is the writers and producers of "Two and a Half Men" are engaged in a pretty interesting creative exercise right about now. They might be wondering what brand-name actor could they bring in, and what kind of character could he play? I'd say it could be a she as well, but the show is called "Two and a Half Men."

BLOCK: Andrew Wallenstein is an editor at the Hollywood Reporter.

LC 9: TEEN TEXTING SOARS: WILL SOCIAL SKILLS SUFFER?

1.

1. C; **2.** D; **3.** A; **4.** B; **5.** D

2.

1. D; **2.** A; **3.** E; **4.** B

Transcript: Teen texting soars: Will social skills suffer?

ROBERT SIEGEL, host:

From NPR News, this is ALL THINGS CONSIDERED. I'm Robert Siegel.

MELISSA BLOCK, host:

And I'm Melissa Block.

American teenagers say e-mail is passé. And talking on the phone? Well, that's for parents. With friends, they prefer to let their fingers do the talking – actually, their thumbs.

New research out today finds three out of four teenagers now have cell phones, and they're using them to send lots of text messages.

NPR's Jennifer Ludden reports.

(Soundbite of conversation)

JENNIFER LUDDEN: As classes let out at Bethesda-Chevy Chase High School in Maryland, students are tapping on their phones before they even reach the exit. The Pew Research Center and the University of Michigan find the average teen sends about 50 texts a day, a third send double that. But even they have nothing on 17-year-old Sierra Koenick. Her grandfather once analysed her phone bill. The total: 300 texts a day. What about?

Ms. SIERRA KOENICK (Student, Bethesda-Chevy Chase High School): I mean, talking about everything. What's going on, or hey, or meet me here, or something. Usually they're actually dumb texts, not even worth it. But …

LUDDEN: But she likes sending them anyway. Asking when do you text feels like a dumb question. The answer is all the time. In fact, as I interview Koenick and two friends, they keep texting while we talk. Koenick says people often use texting to chat with or about someone who's right there.

Ms. KOENICK: Like, if it's somebody in front of you and you don't want them to know you're talking about them.

(Soundbite of laughter)

LUDDEN: Okay, so this makes me wonder if you're texting about me.

Ms. KOENICK: No, I'm not. I'm not texting them.

LUDDEN: Outside, junior Daniel Epstein and his girlfriend lounge on the steps, each with a cell phone at their fingertips. I ask Epstein about efforts to limit his texting and hear the kind of dilemma that will sound familiar to many an office worker with a crack Berry.

Mr. DANIEL EPSTEIN (Student, Bethesda Chevy Chase High School): Like, I used to keep my phone on silent. And then, you know, like at the end of the day I check it and then, like, I have, like, 10 text messages from this one person saying, like, I really need you to give me this password or something. So sometimes it's like something urgent that you have to really quickly respond to.

Ms. AMANDA LENHART (Senior Research Specialist, The Internet & American Life Project, Pew Research Center): They're really weaving this into their day. It is in some ways for teens a lot like breathing.

LUDDEN: Amanda Lenhart of the Pew Center says the report finds parents and schools struggling to set limits on teen texting. Nearly two-thirds of parents say they've taken a child's cell phone away as punishment. But that can backfire. Parents say they like using phones to track a child's whereabouts and for logistics. As for school limits, Lenhart says they don't have much impact.

Ms. LENHART: They still bring their phones to school. We found that 58 percent of teens who go to schools where the phone is forbidden say they've sent a text message in class.

LUDDEN: In Los Angeles, Harvard-Westlake High School considered an outright ban last year. Nini Halkett has taught history there for two decades. As she sees her students increasingly immersed in texting, she finds them increasingly shy and awkward in personal encounters.

Ms. NINI HALKETT (Teacher, Harvard-Westlake High School): They can get up the courage to ask you for an extension on a test or something like that on the computer, but they won't come and speak to you face to face about it. And that worries me in terms of their ability to, you know – particularly once they get out on in the workplace – their ability to interact with people.

LUDDEN: At Bethesda-Chevy Chase High, several students actually voiced the same concern. And as in Pew focus groups, teens admitted to using texting to avoid confrontation with each other or their parents – say, if you're already at the movie theater and want your mom's permission to see the film. But researcher Amanda Lenhart says teens are also strategic about when not to text.

Ms. LENHART: We heard from teens who said, you know, when I want the yes, I'll go to the phone because my parents can hear my voice and I can kind of wheedle and I can charm them, and that's how I'm going to get what I want.

LUDDEN: The art of conversation still alive and well.

Jennifer Ludden, NPR News, Washington.

BLOCK: Do you put limits on your teen's texting? Do you think texting hurts your child's social skills? You can tell us at npr.org.

LC 10: TEENS, SEX AND TV: A RISKY MIX?

1.

2. privileged high-schoolers; **5.** provocative ad; **4.** obvious culprits; **6.** reasonable assumption; **3.** dramatic repercussions; **1.** striking number

2.

a. D; **b.** D; **c.** C; **d.** A; **e.** D

Transcript: Teens, sex and TV: A risky mix?

MICHELE NORRIS, host:

From NPR News, this is All Things Considered. I'm Michele Norris. The TV show "Gossip Girl" may have a lot to answer for. A recent study provided some striking numbers about teens who watch an exceptional amount of TV with sexual content, shows such as "Gossip Girl". The study found that those teens are twice as likely to get pregnant or get somebody else pregnant as teens who mainly watch other stuff on television. NPR's Kim Masters reports now on the influence of sexual TV.

KIM MASTERS: "Gossip Girl" is probably the most notorious of the shows that involve steamy teenage sex. The show tracks privileged high schoolers from Manhattan's Upper East Side.

(Soundbite of TV show "Gossip Girl")

Mr. ED WESTWICK: (As Chuck Bass) Have sex with me.

Ms. LEIGHTON MEESTER: (As Blair Waldorf) What?

Mr. WESTWICK: (As Chuck Bass) Just once. It's all I need.

Ms. MEESTER: (As Blair Waldorf) You are disgusting, and I hate you.

Mr. WESTWICK: (As Chuck Bass) Then why are you still holding my hand?

MASTERS: But "Gossip Girl" is hardly the only show dealing in teenage lust. "The Secret Life of the American Teenager," on the ABC Family Channel, is built around a pregnancy that resulted from one brief encounter.

(Soundbite of TV show "The Secret Life of the American Teenager")

Unidentified Woman #1: Ricky does not have friends. Ricky makes friends with girls he wants to have sex with.

Ms. SHAILENE WOODELY: (As Amy Juergens) Ricky and I are just friends, and he's not going to try to have sex with me.

MASTERS: We decided to ask an actual high school student whether television shows really affect the behavior of the American teenager.

Ms. AMANDA KRZEPICKI (High School Student, Ashburn, Virginia): For me, it just really doesn't do anything. It's just entertaining to watch.

MASTERS: 15-year-old Amanda Krzepicki of Ashburn, Virginia, watches "The Secret Life of the American Teenager" with friends. She doesn't think the show affects teen behavior, but it might affect attitudes.

Ms. KRZEPICKI: Because every girl in the show – they either have a boyfriend, they're having, like, relations with some guy, they've currently had a boyfriend, or they really, really want a boyfriend.

Mr. JOSH SCHWARTZ (Co-creator, "Gossip Girl"): I think teenagers were having sex and getting pregnant long before "Gossip Girl," long before "The O.C.," long before "90210," and long before there was even television.

MASTERS: That's Josh Schwartz, one of the creators of "Gossip Girl". When the RAND study came out last month, many media reports specifically cited "Gossip Girl" as a show linked to teen pregnancy. In fact, the show didn't exist when the research was conducted. And Schwartz and his partner, Stephanie Savage, say some elements of the program are obviously based in fantasy. Even so, Savage says, "Gossip Girl" routinely shows that behavior has consequences.

Ms. STEPHANIE SAVAGE (Writer, "Gossip Girl"): The consequences may not happen in the same episode as the activity. It feels like, if you're doing activity-consequences in the same episode, that's starting to feel like an after-school special. It's starting to feel very preachy. And honestly, life isn't like that.

MASTERS: Savage says the most dramatic repercussion in the show so far came when wealthy, spoiled Blair slept with two different guys and had a pregnancy scare.

Ms. SAVAGE: This really brought her to the bottom. She was dethroned as the queen bee. She had a long journey back sort of into the good graces of her world.

(Soundbite of TV show "Gossip Girl")

Unidentified Woman #2: Blair, given you can barely manage your own messy affair, surely you're not in a position to tell anyone where they can and can't eat.

Ms. MEESTER: (As Blair Waldorf) Do you realize who you're talking to?

Unidentified Woman #3: You mean, a self-righteous (beep) who sat on her own high horse judging everyone else?

Unidentified Woman #2: Pregnant little hypocrite.

MASTERS: Blair may have suffered the wrath of her classmates, but "Gossip Girl" takes it for granted that teenagers have sex, quite a lot of sex. When a couple hooks up, they will sleep together. And you just think that's the way the world is?

Mr. SCHWARTZ: We make a big deal out of that. But we certainly create a sense of this being a significant moment in these character's lives and not something that they just kind of do out in haste.

MASTERS: So when you see that study, do you say, oh, my God, did we get teenagers pregnant? Or do you say, that's silly, or what's the reaction?

Ms. SAVAGE: Certainly, they've identified a correlation between these two things, but there's no causal effect that even they are saying. They're not saying that watching television causes pregnancy.

MASTERS: But "Gossip Girl" doesn't deserve to be singled out for outrage, according to Rebecca Collins, one of the authors of the RAND study. She says shows like "Gossip Girl" and "Secret Life of the American Teenager" may seem to be the obvious culprits, but they're not necessarily the worst offenders.

Ms. REBECCA COLLINS (Author, RAND Study): The place where you see the most sexual content, at least of the type that we looked at in our study, is in television sitcoms, the place where you might not actually be looking for it.

MASTERS: Sitcoms may not show that much sex, but they talk about it – a lot.

(Soundbite of sitcom)

Unidentified Man: You got the wrong idea. There's something you don't know about me.

Unidentified Woman #4: You're gay?

Unidentified Man: No.

Unidentified Woman #4: You're a cross-dresser?

Unidentified Man: No.

Unidentified Woman #4: Because, you know, I could really get into that.

(Soundbite of laughter)

Unidentified Man: Yes.

MASTERS: Not everyone accepts the RAND study's conclusions. Michael Males, a senior researcher for youthfacts.org, says the main factors that influence teens are the pregnancy-related behavior of adults around them, and poverty. And he says there hasn't been that much study of how teenagers use entertainment.

Mr. MICHAEL MALES (Senior Researcher, Youthfacts.org): If they consume it merely as a fantasy or as a representation of a world that is very unlike their own, which would be a reasonable assumption, then it's not going to have a lot of effect on their own personal behavior.

MASTERS: "Gossip Girl" creators Schwartz and Savage think that's clearly the case. The only thing they're not quite comfortable with are "Gossip Girl's" provocative ads, which promote the show as every parent's worst nightmare.

Mr. SCHWARTZ: I think they're funny. I think they're clever, and I think they're reflective of the tone of the show. But certainly, when you drive by a poster that says every parent's nightmare, you're like, ah man, does that mean my own parents think I'm a nightmare?

MASTERS: A son who's successful in Hollywood? For a lot of parents, that's even more of a fantasy than anything you'd see on "Gossip Girl". Kim Masters, NPR News.

LC 11: ONE TEEN'S STRUGGLE TO QUIT SMOKING

1.

1. E; **2.** A; **3.** F; **4.** C; **5.** D; **6.** B

2.

a. seen a decline; **b.** due to stress; **c.** a sort of relief; **d.** lead of their parents; **e.** share that with your; **f.** underestimate the difficulty; **g.** health effects of smoking; **h.** before age 18

Transcript: One teen's struggle to quit smoking

RENEE MONTAGNE, host:

This is Morning Edition from NPR News. Good morning, I'm Renee Montagne.

STEVE INSKEEP, host:

And I'm Steve Inskeep. It's Thursday morning, which is when we focus on your health. And today we'll report on teens and smoking. This country has generally seen a decline in youth smoking over the past decade, but that trend appears to have stalled. NPR's Patty Neighmond reports on how parents can help kids avoid that first cigarette.

PATTY NEIGHMOND: Kindra Tanner started smoking when she was 13. She says it was due to stress. Her mother had prohibited her from seeing an older boy she really liked. She was angry and upset, and one of her friends offered her a cigarette.

Ms. KINDRA TANNER (High School Student): They make you feel better when you first start. You just feel good. You feel refreshed. It's like drinking water after running all day.

NEIGHMOND: It may sound like quite a leap to compare drinking water to smoking cigarettes. But pediatrician Jonathan Klein says lots of kids he talks to view smoking exactly that way, as a sort of relief. After all, that's what one of the strongest influences in their lives, television, tells them.

Dr. JONATHAN KLEIN (Pediatrician): If you think about the actresses in "Sex and the City", for example, many of them are often using a cigarette as a relaxation device either in the context of being together and talking together or in the context of being, you know, nervous or uptight and reaching for a cigarette and a drink.

NEIGHMOND: Klein has done studies at the University of Rochester on why kids start to smoke. One reason, he says, many are following the lead of their parents. Children of smokers are twice as likely to smoke themselves compared to children of nonsmokers. So don't smoke, says Klein. And if you do smoke, quit. And if you can't, he says, share that with your children.

Dr. KLEIN: Since most smokers have tried to quit and they're still trying to quit can talk about the struggle and about why they don't want their kids to become addicted. When parents talk to their kids honestly about what their hopes and expectations are and what their values are as a family, it has a big impact on what kids decide to try and do.

NEIGHMOND: Klein says teens often underestimate the difficulty of beating a nicotine addiction. While the vast majority of smokers try to quit it at some point in their lives, less than 10 percent are ever successful. And even then, it typically takes 10 or more attempts to quit for good. Klein says, don't just tell kids, show them. You can start by pointing out scenes of real-life smokers.

Dr. KLEIN: If you look at doorways of buildings and you see, you know, addicted people, most of whom we know want to quit and have tried to quit unsuccessfully. And we see adults sort of huddling, you know, outside, waiting to go back in. But that's not the way that the use of cigarettes is shown in the movies and on TV.

NEIGHMOND: And parents can point that out too. Think of your favorite TV show, for example.

Dr. KLEIN: You'll see people holding cigarettes. You'll see people interacting with cigarettes. But you won't really see the puffs of smoke and the clouds of smoke and the smoke trailing up and irritating people in the way that it does in real life.

NEIGHMOND: Parents can help kids notice when TV and movies leave out the real health effects of smoking, like cancer and heart disease. And they can point out the impact of smoking on appearance, which may be more immediately relevant to young people. Things like yellow teeth, bad breath, wrinkles, and not benefiting from their full potential in sports. But even if parents do all this, it's no guarantee your teen won't smoke. Notice if your child seems estranged or particularly rebellious, if they have friends who smoke or if their clothes smell like cigarettes. Kindra's mother, Darlene de la Plata.

Ms. DALENE DE LA PLATA: I would smell it on her clothes, but I just kept thinking maybe that she was hanging out with people who were smoking. And I tried to make excuses, although I think on some level I probably knew.

NEIGHMOND: But when Kindra got suspended from school at 14 for smoking, her mother, a masseuse who owns a health food store in Atlanta, finally had to face it.

Ms. DE LA PLATA: That was a pivotal moment for me that I thought, wow, here I've tried to be an example, and I've tried to – you know, we've always done natural healing, natural medicine. We don't buy sodas. We don't buy junk food. We don't do any of that stuff. And this was a huge deal for me.

NEIGHMOND: De la Plata tried to get her daughter to quit. And eventually Kindra did. But it took months. Dr. Jonathan Klein says some studies suggest that after smoking just a few cigarettes, the brain actually remodels itself and makes new nicotine receptors.

Dr. KLEIN: I think the most important thing that parents can do is to really be clear with their children about their expectations for never even experimenting, never trying a cigarette.

NEIGHMOND: Nearly all adults who smoke started before age 18, and one-third had their first cigarette before the age of 14. Patti Neighmond, NPR News.

INSKEEP: And that's "Your Health" for this Thursday morning. You can get more tips to prevent teenage smoking and watch a video that lays out all the harmful ingredients in cigarettes by going to npr.org.

LC 12: CONTROVERSY OVER THE WORLD CUP SOCCER BALL

1.

a. nickname; **b.** score; **c.** to mourn; **d.** defenders; **e.** penalty kick

2.

b. mind of its own; **c.** it's the most advanced; **d.** slipped out of hands; **e.** goalies (and defenders); **f.** dropped, hit defender's hand; **g.** pick up air; **h.** because also winners complain/even winners blame ball

Transcript: Controversy over the world cup soccer ball

MELISSA BLOCK, host:

Dreadful, horrible, a catastrophe, a disaster – those words describing, in this case, not the Gulf oil spill but the official match ball for the 2010 World Cup. Like a ball you'd buy in a supermarket, complains a goalkeeper from the Brazilian team. This ball has a mind of its own, chimes in a keeper from South Africa.

The ball, made by Adidas, is called the Jabulani from the Zulu word meaning to celebrate. Ha. Well, Kevin Baxter has been trying to read the mind of that much maligned ball. He's in South Africa covering the World Cup for the LA Times.

Kevin, what is the problem with the Jabulani? What's it doing?

Mr. KEVIN BAXTER (Journalist, LA Times): Well, no one seems to know. And all those words you used to describe the ball, those are only words that you can use on a radio station like NPR. People are saying a lot stronger language when you get them off the tape recorder.

Some people think it's the way the ball was constructed. Adidas and their designers spent five years working on this ball. They say it's the most advanced soccer ball ever made. But it's not performing that way, and people knew it was going to be a problem going into the World Cup.

The most interesting thing for me, though, is it isn't just the teams that lose that complain about it. When the U.S. tied England in their first match, the tying goal was controversial. And afterwards, a lot of the U.S. players said: You know what? The goalkeeper never really had a chance. It was the ball that caused that goal to score.

BLOCK: You're talking about the game on Saturday, when the ball just slipped right out of the hands of the goalkeeper, Robert Green, and he said afterward: I don't want to make any excuses about the ball. It might have moved. I don't know.

Mr. BAXTER: Someone asked him, "Was it the ball to try to give him an out", and he wouldn't take it. He said, "I'm not going to use that as an excuse, but I will say I've never missed the ball by that much in my life."

And the guy who scored the goal, Clint Dempsey, even he said, you know, that ball is very difficult to read. It moves a lot. That might have had something to do with it.

And I mean, here's a guy that scored one of the most important goals in U.S. soccer history, and he's sitting there saying, you know what, maybe I had a little bit of help from the ball. I thought that was a remarkable statement.

BLOCK: Well, how is the ball behaving or misbehaving in this case? What's it doing?

Mr. BAXTER: Well, it just doesn't seem to move predictably, and goalies seem to be talking about it the most because goalies and defenders who have to take balls out of the air, as they leap, the ball seems to dive.

We had a situation yesterday in the Serbia – Ghana game where a Serbian defender went up to head the ball, and the ball actually dropped and hit him on the hand. He was charged with a hand ball. It turned into a penalty kick, and that decided the game, one to nothing for Ghana.

BLOCK: Well, this ball was much ballyhooed before the World Cup by Adidas. What in the design would possibly be making it behave differently than any other World Cup balls before this?

Mr. BAXTER: What it seems to be is one thing, most of the matches so far have been played at altitude. And so to help the ball fly more cleanly and more straightly at altitude, Adidas put a lot of grooves in this ball, and that seems to be the problem. The grooves seem to be picking up air and moving the ball in unpredictable ways.

And I suppose that could have been somewhat predicted if you look at what happens with a baseball pitcher when he scratches a ball or puts a dent in a ball in some way. That ball will move unpredictably. And I think these grooves are doing the same thing.

BLOCK: Kevin, aren't there complaints about the ball in just about every World Cup that comes around?

Mr. BAXTER: Yeah, that's true. And it's funny, if you go back to the first World Cup where Adidas provided the official match ball, back in the '70s, the one with the white and black geometric shapes, that was the first one that Adidas came out with. That was widely panned. People didn't like it.

It was designed primarily for TV. That World Cup, the 1970 World Cup, was the first one televised live to Europe, and people hated it. Well, now it's the most popular ball in the world. I don't think the Jabulani is going to have that kind of a lifespan, but you're right. Every World Cup, people complain about the ball, especially the losing teams, but again, what makes this World Cup different is even the winners are saying the balls are deciding games.

BLOCK: Well, Kevin Baxter, thanks for talking to us about the controversial Jabulani ball.

Mr. BAXTER: Thanks so much for the call.

BLOCK: Kevin Baxter is a sports reporter for the LA Times. He spoke with us from Johannesburg.

LC 13: SOCCER FANS URGE FIFA TO USE VIDEO REVIEW

2.

b. The "do" stresses the truthfulness of the sentence. It can be translated with "tatsächlich".

3.

a. F; **b.** F; **c.** T; **d.** F; **e.** F; **f.** T; **g.** T; **h.** F

Transcript: Soccer fans urge FIFA to use video review

MELISSA BLOCK, host:

At the World Cup in South Africa, there's been a series of blatantly blown calls by referees. And that's amplifying demands for FIFA, soccer's governing body, to adopt video technology to resolve disputes.

Jamie Trecker has been covering this impassioned debate for FoxSoccer.com.

Jamie, welcome to the program.

Mr. JAMIE TRECKER (Senior Soccer Writer, FoxSoccer.com): Hi, thanks for having me.

BLOCK: Let's talk about the first call yesterday that really brought this debate to fever pitch, and this was in the game between Germany and England. What happened?

Mr. TRECKER: Well, the Uruguayan referee, Jorge Larrionda, missed a clear goal by a player named Frank Lampard. The ball ricocheted off the crossbar behind the German goalkeeper, Mr. Neuer, and it did cross the goal line.

Everybody in the stands saw it, everybody watching on international TV saw it, and the people in the stadium saw it because they do have replay there. Unfortunately, it was a game-changing moment. Had England scored that goal and been credited with it, the game might have gone into halftime tied two-two. As most people know, England went on to lose that game four to one, and Fabio Capello, England's coach, did directly blame that blown call for taking away his team's momentum.

BLOCK: Well, one question that is raised here is whether there should be goal-line technology that would send a signal to the referee saying hey, ball crossed the goal line, that's a goal.

Mr. TRECKER: Yes, and I think there should be. There is the technology available to see if a ball did cross the line, and there's technology obviously to give people a look from different camera angles to see if the correct call was made.

BLOCK: And you did have another game yesterday, Mexico versus Argentina. Argentina was allowed a goal that was scored from an offside position and went on to win that game. Mexico was eliminated. Again, calls for why not have instant replay?

Mr. TRECKER: Yesterday, again, it was very clear. Carlos Tevez did score a goal from an offside position, and what happened on that play is one of the members of the officiating crew, the far linesman, was not in proper position to judge whether he had scored it from an offside position.

It was very clear immediately on replay that the goal should have been disallowed, and what compounded the situation was that everyone in the stadium saw it on the Jumbotron.

BLOCK: What about simply adding more refs? There's actually just one ref on the field itself. He's running something like 12 miles in a game. Why not put more people either on the field or on the sidelines?

Mr. TRECKER: Well, FIFA has never wanted to take away from the central authority of the ref. And in fact, the referees themselves have resisted the idea of having other partners on the field.

Of course, this is not new to other sports. In American football, hockey, baseball, there are a team of refs that work. The only help that a soccer referee gets is from his assistants, who run up and down the lines.

One of the things that's funny about football, however, is it is still a very patrician kind of class-oriented game. FIFA, being a rather hidebound organisation, is run by a great deal of kind of upper-class people, has always viewed the official as a central authority. And they've been more concerned with that than getting the calls right.

BLOCK: You do hear this, though, not just from FIFA but from some players, from fans and coaches, that the human factor here really separates soccer from other sports and that the free-flowing rhythm of the game, where the clock doesn't stop, that's central to what soccer is.

Mr. TRECKER: I don't think people that are pressing for goal-line technology or replay technology are asking for interruptions in the flow of the game.

Instead, what they're asking for is the fourth official, who usually just handles substitutions and other technical matters, to review controversial plays and let the flow of the game continue.

The National Hockey League provides a good example of this because, you know, there are times when a goal is scored or a goal is questionable, hockey does continue play. And then if there's a decision, an announcement is radioed to the referee in the center. He blows the whistle and restarts it.

That is an example of how world football could move forward and embrace technology and at the same time keep the essential purity of the game.

BLOCK: Well, Jamie, something tells me this debate is going to go on for a little while longer.

Mr. TRECKER: I think you're very correct.

BLOCK: Jamie Trecker covers soccer for FoxSoccer.com. Thanks so much.

Mr. TRECKER: Thank you.

BLOCK: And there is a lively discussion about this subject taking place on our soccer blog. You can join in at npr.org/cleats.

LC 14: HOMEWORK: OVERCOMING FEAR

1.

a. overcome; **b.** face; **c.** borrow; **d.** snorkel gear; **e.** triathlon; **f.** Arachnophobia; **g.** lend; **h.** cure

2.

Andrea Seabrook: F, B, H
Meg Rawlings: D, I
Lizbeth Alt: C, G

Transcript: Homework: Overcoming fear

ANDREA SEABROOK, host:

Now to your stories of overcoming fear. It's our Homework segment, and it turns out we have some seriously brave listeners like Meg Rawlings(ph) of Medford, Oregon. Her fear, her terror, actually, was water. As a child, her mother put her in swimming classes, which Meg describes as a disaster. Then at age 44, she finally had a reason to face her fear.

(Soundbite of music)

Ms. MEG RAWLINGS (Listener, Medford, Oregon): Ten years ago, my husband and I had the opportunity to go to Hawaii, and I wanted to see the tropical fish that everyone told me about. So I borrowed some snorkel gear, I got into the pool and practiced with snorkel gear.

Unidentified Man #1: Sharks patrol these waters. Sharks patrol these waters. Don't let your fingers dangle in the water.

Ms. RAWLINGS: We went to Hawaii. The water felt great, and when I came home, I thought I'd try a triathlon. I already was a runner and a cyclist. This year, I entered in the Escape from Alcatraz triathlon, which meant I had to jump off a boat that was right near Alcatraz Island, and I swam across the San Francisco Bay.

Unidentified Man #1: Swim for the shores as fast as you are able. Swim.

(Soundbite of music)

Ms. RAWLINGS: I'm not a strong swimmer, I'm not a fast swimmer, but I made it, and now I feel I've overcome my fear. It just makes me feel powerful, kind of a funny feeling to have when you're in your 50s, but it's a great feeling.

SEABROOK: And then there's Lizbeth Alt(ph) of Buffalo, New York. The thing that makes her psycho? Spiders.

(Soundbite of screaming)

Ms. LIZBETH ALT (Listener, Buffalo, New York): It seems like I would always see a spider in the bathroom. (Unintelligible), and I would, like, take a shower, and I don't know how many times I came screaming out of the bathroom, sometimes half-naked, just screaming there's a spider, there's a spider, get rid of it, get rid of it.

(Soundbite of music)

SEABROOK: Decades later, she found the perfect way to face her fear. She dragged her mother to the movie theater. The film: "Arachnophobia".

(Soundbite of film, "Arachnophobia")

Unidentified Man #2 (Actor): (As character) This doesn't make sense. They're swarming. I've never seen them this erratic.

(Soundbite of screaming)

Ms. ALT: I ended up curled up in a foetal position and hanging on to her, constantly burying my face into her arm, and at the time, I'm like 31 years old.

(Soundbite of film, "Arachnophobia")

Unidentified Man #3 (Actor): (As character) One at a time, one at a time.

Ms. ALT: It wasn't like I was cured, but it did help. Then I started to come to more grips of the fear, and now I'm not as scared of them. In fact, I can get rid of them if I have to.

Unidentified Man #3: Rock and roll.

SEABROOK: Thanks to all who faced their fears and turned in this week's Homework. For next week, we want to hear your stories of courtship, when you were wooed or were the wooer. Send your stories to homework@npr.org or call the Homework hotline. That's 202-408-5183. We may just put you on the air.

LC 15: LADY GAGA VS. ACE OF BASE

1.

1. E; **2.** F; **3.** A; **4.** B; **5.** C; **6.** D

2.

a. D; **b.** D; **c.** B; **d.** C

Transcript: Lady Gaga vs. Ace of Base

MARY LOUISE KELLY, host:

This summer, Lady Gaga has taken a little heat for her steamy single "Alejandro".

(Soundbite of song, "Alejandro")

LADY GAGA (Singer): (Singing) Don't call my name, Alejandro …

KELLY: Now, some critics say: Hang on, that sounds exactly like a dance hit from 16 years ago. Remember "Don't Turn Around" by Ace of Base?

(Soundbite of song, "Don't Turn Around")

ACE OF BASE (Band): (Singing) Don't turn around, cause you're going to see my heart breaking. Don't turn around …

KELLY: The fine line in pop music between homage and stealing. That's today's discussion from our Pop-Off Team, Maura Johnston and Jay Smooth.

Mr. JAY SMOOTH (Blogger, IllDoctrine.com): When I first heard "Alejandro" by Lady Gaga, I thought of "La Isla Bonita" by Madonna.

(Soundbite of song, "La Isla Bonita")

MADONNA (Singer): (Singing) And when the samba played, the sun would set so high ring through my ears and sting my eyes. Your Spanish lullaby …

Ms. MAURA JOHNSTON (Music Writer, IllDoctrine.com): And there was Shakira's "Whenever Wherever" from a couple of years ago. And definitely you can hear that in here, too.

(Soundbite of song, "Whenever Wherever")

SHAKIRA (Singer): (Singing) Whenever, wherever. We need to be together …

Mr. SMOOTH: You could also go with "Fernando" by ABBA.

(Soundbite of song, "Fernando")

ABBA (Band): (Singing) There was something in the air that night the stars were bright, Fernando …

MS. JOHNSTON: Every time I listen to it, I hear another influence.

Mr. SMOOTH: I mean a lot of people hear "Alejandro" and they think of the Ace of Base song from the '90s. But whenever I heard those Ace of Base songs, I felt like they were a carbon copy from a song from my childhood, "The Tide is High" by Blondie.

(Soundbite of song, "The Tide is High")

Ms. DEBORAH HARRY (Singer, Blondie): (Singing) The tide is high but I'm holding on. I'm gonna be your number one. I'm …

Mr. SMOOTH: But when "The Tide is High" came out, people who were older than me saw that as a carbon copy of the reggae songs that had preceded that. You know, you can trace that back to John Holt and the Paragons, 12 years before.

JOHN HOLT AND THE PARAGONS (Band): (Singing) I'm not the kind of man who gives up just like that. No …

Mr. SMOOTH: But when the Paragons came out, you know, many people could arguably see that as a Frankie Lymon song with a different beat underneath.

(Soundbite of song, "Diana)

Mr. FRANKIE LYMON (Singer): (Singing) Thrills I get when you hold me close. Oh, my darling you're the most. I love …

Mr. SMOOTH: All of that early reggae-ska rock steady was drawing heavily from American soul doo-wop traditions. And even beyond 20th century pop, you can go back through the history of Western music; some of the very first polyphonic compositions.

(Soundbite of a Gregorian chant)

Mr. SMOOTH: The organum and the motet were based on taking a pre-existing Gregorian chant and putting a new melody on top of it in a higher register. So that's hundreds of hundreds of years you see that going on.

(Soundbite of music)

Ms. JOHNSTON: You know, I mean this could sound very fresh to people who were born far after Ace of Base's chart moment in the States waned. Which is, you know, a fair amount of people who do listen to Lady Gaga – like, they're younger; they might not know that "Don't Turn Around" and "The Sign" were really big over here.

Mr. SMOOTH: Right. But in that case, what is Lady Gaga's responsibility for letting them know? Is she culpable?

Ms. JOHNSTON: Does she have a responsibility to sort of lay out in the liner notes of all of her records, like: I listened to this and this, a sort of bibliography, as you might say.

Mr. SMOOTH: Right. But as far as whether that constitutes stealing, I'm not sure how to feel about that. Because I recall thinking that those Ace of Base songs were so derivative themselves, I feel like to accuse Lady Gaga of stealing from Ace of Base is like saying she's stealing money from Bernie Madoff, or something.

(Soundbite of laughter)

Mr. SMOOTH: I'm not even sure – does that even count as stealing?

KELLY: That's Jay Smooth who blogs at IllDoctrine.com, and music writer Maura Johnston. And there's more from the Pop-Off Team at NPRMusic.org.

This is MORNING EDITION from NPR News. I'm Mary Louise Kelly.

RENEE MONTAGNE, host:

And I'm Renee Montagne.

LC 16: THAT NOT-SO-HEALTHY GLOW: THE DANGERS OF TANNING

1.

cancer, acne, pale-skinned, mole, melanoma, carcinogenic, ban

2.

b. ... her **white** prom dress; **d.** ... on **tanning** addiction; **e.** ... on her daughter's **back**; **f.** it was **not** her only suspicious mole; **g.** ... a **healing** response; **h.** is **not yet** banned

Transcript: That not-so-healthy glow: The danger of tanning

ROBERT SIEGEL, host:

At the end of the school year, teenage girls often head to the tanning salon, hoping to look fit and glowing in their prom dresses. But evidence is mounting that too much indoor tanning increases the risk of skin cancer.

As NPR's Patti Neighmond reports, the Food and Drug Administration is taking steps to make sure that teens take the risk seriously.

PATTI NEIGHMOND: It was right before the prom eight years ago. Seventeen-year-old Brittany Cicala was really excited. She was going with the boy she would eventually marry and her dress – well, it was beautiful: delicately beaded lace and spaghetti straps, an elegant A-line in white.

Ms. BRITTANY CICALA: Everyone around me was telling me, man, you would look so much better with a tan and your teeth would look whiter, your acne would go away.

NEIGHMOND: So pale-skinned Brittany did what lots of her friends did; she did what a lot of teens in the U.S. do. She went to a tanning salon. In fact, she went to the salon five, six, often seven days a week, and lay in the tanning bed for 20 to 25 minutes each time.

Ms. CICALA: I called myself a "tanorexic", because I would look into the mirror and never see myself as dark as other people would see me – much as an anorexic would never see themselves as thin as other people would see them. So I kept going.

NEIGHMOND: Tanorexic? Yes. That's what a study from psychologist Catherine Mosher, of Memorial Sloan-Kettering Cancer Center, recently confirmed. Mosher analyzed data from more than 420 college students, and had them answer questions typically used to screen for alcohol and substance abuse but modified to ask about tanning habits.

Dr. CATHERINE MOSHER (Behavioral Scientist, Memorial Sloan-Kettering Cancer Center): Do you try to cut down on the time you spend in tanning beds or booths but find yourself still tanning? Do you feel – ever feel guilty that you're using tanning beds or booths too much?

NEIGHMOND: Mosher found the majority of kids answered yes to one or more of these questions, which target addictive behavior. After three years of routine indoor tanning, Brittany Cicala ended up with a serious health problem.

Ms. CICALA: My mom noticed a mole on my back – about the size of a nickel – the summer of 2004. She kept bugging me about it: Brittany, that doesn't look right. You really should go get that checked out.

NEIGHMOND: But Brittany stalled and kept tanning. Then the mole started to bleed. Her doctor took one look at the mole, and scheduled a biopsy for the next morning. Brittany had melanoma, the most aggressive form of skin cancer. Two weeks later, she had surgery to remove the mole, which left a seven-inch scar. Since then, Brittany's had 34 surgeries to remove suspicious moles.

Robin Hornung is a pediatric dermatologist in Washington state. She says rates of melanoma are growing fastest among younger women, 15 to 29 years old, and researchers want to understand why.

Dr. ROBIN HORNUNG (Pediatric Dermatologist, The Everett Clinic): The question is, why is that happening? But a lot of folks would point to, perhaps indoor tanning. That's the group that makes up most of the most indoor tanners, are the young women.

NEIGHMOND: Federal officials say as many as one in five teenagers, mostly girls, have used a tanning bed over the past year. And while teens may think of a tan as a healthy glow, Hornung says it's the body's reaction to injury.

Dr. HORNUNG: We know that a tan is really your skin's response to ultraviolet light damage. DNA breaks; there are mutations in the DNA. And when you get breaking of the DNA, you actually have – a tan is, you know, kind of a healing response.

NEIGHMOND: A recent study found melanoma risk increased as much as three times if people tanned indoors more than 50 hours in their lifetime, or had more than 100 sessions in a tanning booth.

The World Health Organization recently classified tanning beds as carcinogenic, and recommended children under 18 be banned from using them. A number of countries have already put such bans in place. And the Food and Drug Administration, which regulates the tanning industry in the U.S., says it's also considering a ban.

FDA official Sharon Miller says the agency definitely plans to strengthen warning labels on the beds themselves.

Ms. SHARON MILLER (UV Radiation Specialist, FDA): We're planning to use a bulleted format and just be more direct and say that UV can cause skin cancer. You know, not draw it out and make it seem like only people who really abuse it are going to get skin cancer, because we think any exposure does contribute to your risk of skin cancer.

NEIGHMOND: The FDA may also require parents to approve tanning for kids under 18.

John Overstreet, with the Indoor Tanning Association, says bans are intrusive and represent over-regulation.

Mr. JOHN OVERSTREET (Executive Director, Indoor Tanning Association): I think the industry is a great deal more professional than it was 25 years ago.

So there's a lot of information available to these businesses that allow them to advise people about how long they should be in the tanning bed without getting overexposed.

NEIGHMOND: Meanwhile, since her own illness, cancer survivor Brittany Cicala has made skin cancer awareness her personal mission. She's testified about tanning and cancer risk at FDA hearings and at medical conferences. But by far, the most important work she does, says Cicala, is at local high schools, where she tells young girls her story about indoor tanning and cancer.

Patti Neighmond, NPR News.

LC 17: E-BOOK READERS EXPECTED TO GROW IN POPULARITY

1.

1. commuter – to commute – commuting
2. difference – to differ – different
3. access – to access – accessible
4. expectation – to expect – expecting
5. expansion – to expand – expanding
6. comparison – to compare – comparable

2.

b. lend e-books to friends; **c.** older people, (voracious) bookworms; **d.** tactile sensation; **e.** read on computer screen; **f.** on the train;
g. newspapers, magazine articles, blogs

Transcript: E-book readers expected to grow in popularity

ROBERT SIEGEL, host:
Well, now for more on e-reading, our All Tech Considered expert Omar Gallaga here. He covers technology culture for the Austin American-Statesman. Welcome back, Omar.

OMAR GALLAGA: Hi, Robert. Good to talk to you.

SIEGEL: Have you sprung for an eReader, by the way, yourself?

GALLAGA: I have not, not yet. I'm not a subway or rail commuter, but if I was, I would probably get one or if I were a student, who is juggling lots of heavy textbooks, I would probably go ahead and make the jump.

SIEGEL: Now, the Kindle is out there, the Sony machines are out there, now Barnes and Noble is going to introduce the Nook, which I gather has some new features. What's different about the Nook from other eReaders?

GALLAGA: It has, in addition to the standard six-inch eReader display, a color display right below it. So, it's got an additional second screen that will be more like a traditional LCD screen where you'll be able to see book covers in full color. And it also has a new feature called Lend Me, which allows you to lend out a copy of an e-book to a friend.

Unfortunately, you can only do that one time with one book and you have no access to that book while it's lent out. So, that's one advantage over the Kindle, but it is very limited and publishers can also opt not to allow you to lend out a particular book.

SIEGEL: Now, people talk about this holiday season as being the time when lots of people will buy these eReaders. How many do they expect and who's buying them?

GALLAGA: The last two years as e-books have kind of taken off and e-book readers like the Kindle have been introduced, it's been primarily older readers, people who are voracious bookworms. But it seems like that market is expanding. Forrester Research expects that three million e-book readers like the Kindle will be sold this year. And by the end of next year, they expect 10 million e-book readers will have been sold.

And I think some of that has to do probably with the Barnes and Noble reader, which will probably do very well.

SIEGEL: Do people in the industry talk about the inevitability of people ultimately reading with eReaders as opposed to hard copy books, I guess to have a new word for books?

GALLAGA: Well, I think so. I mean, there is definitely the trade off. You know, there is the portability and convenience of e-books versus the tactile sensation of a regular book, which there's been no duplication of that yet. You still don't have the same look and feel of books yet. But I don't think it's a fad either. I think publishers are definitely acknowledging that this is the future. And, you know, if you're comparing it to music, which was a relatively swift transition to digital music, books are definitely much more entrenched, I think, than the music industry. So, I think it's going to be a much longer transition.

SIEGEL: If I buy an eReader and I then buy lots of books, which I read on it, let's say I trade up for a different eReader or I give the eReader to my daughter, do the books convey with it? Can I keep the books somewhere else? Can I just lend a particular book and say why don't you read this, I just read it. Take a look at this one?

GALLAGA: Well, that's been a big knock against the Kindle is that if you have a Kindle and they have a Kindle, there's no easy way to lend a book or resell a book once you're done with it. But you can definitely give a device to someone and there are now ways that you can read that same e-book on, say, an iPhone or on a computer screen. Amazon just announced they're coming out with a Windows eReader application, where you'd be able to read those same e-books on your computer screen. You can already read them on your iPod or iPhone, you own that content. So, you should be able to read it in whatever format, whether it's on the e-book reader itself or on some other screen that you own.

SIEGEL: But to go back to where you began, this is a device that you, for example, associate with mobility. If you were taking a train to and from work, you would want to have this. If you're doing your reading in bed at night and your book is on the nightstand, what's the matter with a book?

GALLAGA: Well, nothing at all.

(Soundbite of laughter)

GALLAGA: In fact, that's how I tend to consume most of my books still. But I also find myself more and more reading news articles and magazine articles on my phone in bed, you know. I'm lying there with my little tiny screen and still able to digest kind of smaller content like that.

So, I think when people think of the Kindle and think of some of the other e-book readers, they think primarily about books. But these are also e-book readers for newspapers, you can also read magazine articles on these, you can also read blogs on the Amazon Kindles. So, I think definitely for shorter form content, people are going to be, you know, curled up in bed with them as well and not just these, you know, thousand-page novels.

SIEGEL: Thank you, Omar.

GALLAGA: Thanks for having me.

(Soundbite of music)

GALLAGA: And we'll be posting links to a lot of information about these devices on the All Tech Considered blog and that's at npr.org/alltech.

SIEGEL: Omar Gallaga covers technology culture for the Austin American-Statesman and for All Tech Considered.

This is NPR, National Public Radio.

LC 18: SCHOOL DESEGREGATION: AT WHICH PRICE?

1.

1. E; **2.** G; **3.** F; **4.** C; **5.** D; **6.** B; **7.** A

2.

a. F; **b.** T; **c.** F; **d.** T; **e.** F; **f.** T; **g.** T; **h.** T; **i.** T

Transcript: School desegregation: At which price?

MICHEL MARTIN, host:
This month, the nation marks an important anniversary in education and civil rights. It was 50 years ago that Central High School in Arkansas was integrated by black students, who became known as the Little Rock Nine.

Commentator S. Pearl Sharp followed their struggles as a schoolgirl herself. She says it's time to take a closer look at the lessons of their story.

S. PEARL SHARP: Education has always been pushed in the black community as the key to lifting racism's yoke off its shoulders. During the 1950s, integration was added to the plan. Growing up in a large northern city during that time, I was always clear that integration was our parents' agenda, and we children were the foot soldiers.

From elementary school through high school, my friends and I were breaking color barriers every week. We turned to being the first Negro into an art form, I danced between talking white and sounding black. I rose to the brilliance that my family expected of me, and my English Comp class, only to be shot down by the teacher who accused me of plagiarism because Negroes couldn't possibly write that well.

Still, I never experienced violence. But in 1957, on black-and-white TV, I watched kids my age facing what looked like the entire U.S. Army as they struggle to gain entrance to a Southern all-white school. The scene was Central High in Little Rock, Arkansas. Arkansas' governor, Orval Faubus, declared that blood would run in the streets if Negroes entered Central High. Only after President Eisenhower sent in the 101st Airborne did the students get inside.

Throughout the school year, they were beaten, kicked and spit on. They received lynching threats. One student's home was bombed, their parents lost jobs and businesses, and that was just the physical price tag. There was also the assault on the psyche. Up North, we cheered them and prayed for them. But secretly, I wanted to ask them if the racial madness they were going through in order to attend school with whites was worth it.

This month is the 50th anniversary of the Little Rock Nine's integration of Central High School, and I am still pondering the question. Yes, many who survived the experience say that it prepared them to be more comfortable in the larger white society. But at what price?

Segregation cost us a lot. But pursuing desegregation – which became integration, which for many became assimilation – cost us more. One of the costs was the destruction of the support system that existed on all black communities, the kind of nurturing that develops when people know they have only each other to depend on. It's a loss that slaps us in the days today with the extra high dropout rate among black students and with each child-against-child act of violence.

All of the Little Rock Nine survived the experiment. And today, they are leaders in their communities. But hundreds of children involved in integrating the schools became social or mental victims rather than victors. It is for them and for the groups today who are trying to find their entry door into the American educational system that makes me think the question is still worth exploring. When our parents put us on the train to integration without knowing the price of the ticket, did they do the right thing?

Today, school desegregation is being overturned by the same courts that initiated it. Maybe now is the time to re-examine the question of how we plan to live and to learn together.

MARTIN: S. Pearl Sharp is a writer and filmmaker living in Los Angeles. Her book, "Black Women for Beginners", has just been re-released by Random House.

LC 19: WHO WILL LIVE TO BE 100? GENETIC TEST MIGHT TELL

1.

a. longevity; **b.** centenarian; **c.** genetic marker; **d.** Genetic signatures; **e.** Dementia; **f.** Hypertension; **g.** geneticist

2.

Renee Montagne: A, G
Joe Palca: B, F
Dr. Thomas Perls: H
Dr. Paola Sebastiani: C, D
extra sentence: E

Transcript: Who will live to be 100? Genetic test might tell

MARY LOUISE KELLY, host:
This is MORNING EDITION from NPR News. I'm Mary Louise Kelly.
RENEE MONTAGNE, host:
And I'm Renee Montagne.
If there were a medical test that could tell you whether you would live to be 100, would you take it? That's no longer a hypothetical question. Scientists from Boston University report they have a first version of such a test and they're hoping it will lead to a better understanding of the genetics of why some people live longer than others. NPR's Joe Palca has more.
JOE PALCA: Fifteen years ago, scientists in Boston began the New England Centenarian Study. The criteria for participating, you had to be at least 100 years old.
Dr. THOMAS PERLS (Geneticist, Boston University): The oldest subject in our study was 119.
PALCA: Thomas Perls is director of the study. Perls says whatever other factors are involved in living into your hundreds, genes must play a role. Longevity definitely runs in families, but which genes and how they worked was a mystery. So Perls' team docked with Boston University geneticist Paola Sebastiani.
Mr. PERLS: And left it up to Dr. Sebastiani to solve the genetic puzzle.
PALCA: OK. And so, Dr. Sebastiani, did you solve it?
(Soundbite of laughter)
Dr. PAOLA SEBASTIANI (Geneticist): I think we went step ahead. Maybe we haven't solved it completely.
PALCA: Sebastiani took samples from the centenarians and looked for differences between their DNA and the DNA of normal-aged people. As she reports in the journal "Science", she was able to develop a computer model that used 150 genetic markers, specific bits of DNA scattered around the 23 pairs of human chromosomes, to predict who would be able to join the centenarian club.
Dr. SEBASTIANI: And the accuracy of this model is 77 percent.
PALCA: The model also allowed Sebastiani to identify genetic signatures: gene patterns that were present in subgroups of centenarians with particular characteristics. For example, the subgroup who lived the longest was also the group most likely to have delayed onset of diseases that typically affect older people.
Dr. SEBASTIANI: For example, dementia, cardiovascular disease, hypertension.
PALCA: In other words, Sebastiani says not only did these people live long lives; they lived long, healthy lives.
So have you tested yourself for your genetic signature using these markers?
Dr. SEBASTIANI: Not yet.
PALCA: Neither has her colleague Thomas Perls.
Dr. PERLS: Actually the various authors of the paper feel that this really isn't quite ready for prime time.
PALCA: First, the test isn't 100 percent accurate. But second, what would you do with the information? OK. May you'd do a better job of saving money if you knew you were going to live to 100. But Perls says consider the flip side.

If people knew they were unlikely to live to 100 they might stop watching their weight or exercising or start doing dangerous things like ...

Dr. PERLS: Jumping out of an airplane and being a real risk taker, because I'm not going to live a long time, versus maybe I shouldn't be such a risk taker.

PALCA: Perls and Sebastiani agree that the real value of this study should be what it will tell scientists about the genetics of aging.

Dr. SEBASTIANI: At the moment this is a statistical analysis. And a lot of work has to be done to then understand what is the biology, what is the contribution of all these different genetic markers. So this is the first step.

PALCA: Geneticist Richard Myers of the Hudson Alpha Institute for Biotechnology agrees.

Dr. RICHARD MYERS (Hudson Alpha Institute of Biotechnology): This is sort of the first hint of regions of the genome that might be important for extreme longevity. And it's – you have a hint, and that's better than having nothing.

PALCA: But it does mean understanding the genetics of longevity will take a while, maybe even 100 years. If we live that long.

Joe Palca, NPR News, Washington.

LC 20: THIS YEAR, SMART PHONES ARE HOLIDAY MUST-HAVE

1.

Black Friday, wireless carrier, Cyber Monday, bricks-and-mortar stores

2.

b. has on their list; **c.** shoot actual marshmallows; **d.** rumours swirling (rumors: AE); **e.** commit to a two-year; **f.** search for deals; **g.** trust unfamiliar sites; **h.** get your password

Transcript: This year, smart phones are holiday must-have

ROBERT SIEGEL, host:

This is ALL THINGS CONSIDERED from NPR News. I'm Robert Siegel.

MELISSA BLOCK, host:

I'm Melissa Block. And it's time now for All Tech Considered.

(Soundbite of music)

BLOCK: From Zhu Zhu hamsters to smart phones, there is a whole universe of holiday gifts out there with computer chips inside. And Omar Gallaga joins us to talk about tech related presents for the holidays. Omar talks with us most Mondays from Austin, Texas, where he is the technology culture reporter for the Austin American-Statesman. Omar, welcome back.

Mr. OMAR GALLAGA (Reporter, Austin American-Statesman): Hi, Melissa. Happy tech holidays.

BLOCK: Thanks and same to you. And every year, there seems to be some kind of gadget that everybody has on their list. Last year, GPS units were really hot. What is being talked about as the most popular stuff this year?

Mr. GALLAGA: You know, over Black Friday and with all the search trends online we are seeing lot of stuff related to smart phones, eBook readers like the Amazon Kindle and Barnes and Noble Nook are very sought after this holiday season, and anything to do with HD TV and Blu-ray. I mean HD TVs have gotten so cheap now that they are getting pretty ubiquitous, but anything that you can connect to an HD TV like a game console that does HD or a Blu-ray player that plays Netflix movies over the Web, that stuff is very popular. And then lots of sales of netbooks, laptops and desktops over Black Friday, so the computer segment is definitely not dying off. So – and also we got some information from Google that Marshmallow Shooters and Magic Ears are two of the most trended holiday items this year. Marshmallow Shooters are sort of like Nerf guns that shoot actual marshmallows.

BLOCK: Yeah. Okay.

Mr. GALLAGA: And Magic Ears are a kind of ear-bud headphones that are very popular.

BLOCK: Omar, you mentioned smart phones in there and there was news over the weekend – big news over the weekend – that revolved around a rumor that Google is coming out with its phone and there's a lot of speculation about when exactly that will be. What have you heard?

Mr. GALLAGA: Yeah, there's been a lot of rumors swirling over the weekend about Google's phone called the Nexus One. Now this is the phone built by the company HTC for Google and they have issued these phones out to their employees to try out Google apps that they're developing. Now, previously Google had been doing the Android platform which means Google developed the software that is on phones like the Motorola Droid and the HTC Hero, but this would actually be a Google phone, a phone that Google would sell directly to consumers on its Web site.

And now, what we know so far, and again this is a lot of speculation and rumors, this would not be on a particular wireless carrier. It would have GSM built in, so it would have to be on either T-Mobile or AT&T's network, but the idea would be that Google will sell it to you directly without a wireless carrier involved. So, this could be pretty revolutionary because smart phones like the iPhone and the Motorola Droid are so popular this holiday season, some people might want to think about waiting a little bit till early next year and see what Google does before you commit to a two-year contract on a phone.

BLOCK: Okay. Well, for people who aren't waiting but are shopping now, maybe shopping online at the last minute, where can they find the best deals?

Mr. GALLAGA: You know, most people assume that that a lot of best deals were on Black Friday or on Cyber Monday a couple of weeks ago. In fact, today is going to be possibly one of the best holiday shopping days of the year because there's still enough time to get stuff shipped to you and there's a lot of – the big retail online sites are offering special deals right up to Christmas. So, offers.com, pricegrabber, shopper.com, those are all really good sites that aggregate prices – are really good places to start if you just want to do some comparison shopping and see what prices are available online. Even Twitter is a good place to search for deals that are coming directly from companies like Dell or like travel through Jet Blue. I mean, they post their stuff directly to Twitter. I think the biggest tip though is definitely look at the shipping dates. Look – make sure that stuff's going to get to you by the date you want it to and have a plan in case it doesn't. A lot of people are doing comparison shopping on the Web, but still going to the bricks-and-mortar stores to actually make their purchase.

BLOCK: And if you are swiping your virtual credit card online this week, what are some of the best ways to protect yourself?

Mr. GALLAGA: Well, the things you would do any other time of year when you're doing online shopping, you want to keep your virus and spyware software up to date. Don't trust unfamiliar sites that are not retailers that you're comfortable shopping with. Don't buy anything from eBay, from someone who has no reputations score and someone that has no feedback from other users. And also, you know, watch out for emails. I mean, you might get a good holiday deal email that might send you to somewhere that you're not looking to go, that there might be a phishing scheme to get your password or your credit card information.

BLOCK: Omar, thanks so much.

MR. Gallaga: Thanks for having me, and we'll of course be posting links to a lot of these deals, sales information and tips on the All Tech Considered blog at npr.org/alltech.

BLOCK: Great. Omar Gallaga covers technology cultures for the Austin American-Statesman and for All Tech Considered.

RC 1: 50 CENT: MILLIONAIRE RAP STAR

Task 1

addiction – to be addicted to; criminal – to commit a crime; poverty – to be poor; signature – to sign; amazement – to be amazed; producer – to produce; success – to be successful; talent – to be talented; decision – to decide; adolescence – to be an adult; introduction – to introduce; management – to manage

Task 3

1. F His childhood and early ...
2. F Consequently he was brought ...
3. T In order to support ...
4. F Unfortunately he permanently had ...
5. T As far as music ...
6. T When he was involved ...
7. T Rap superstar Eminem, who ...
8. F By now it has ...
9. T He is a rather ...

Task 4

1. gun – a weapon that fires bullets
2. murder – to kill somebody
3. tough – a person who is rough, not kind and gentle
4. arrest – what the police do with a person who has done something wrong
5. steal – to take something that doesn't belong to you without asking
6. boot camp – a place with strict discipline for young criminals
7. shooting – a crime in which someone is killed with a gun

RC 2: ROBIN HOOD – BRITAIN'S BEST KNOWN MYSTERY MAN

Task 2

Answer B best summarises the article.

Task 3

1 D; **2** A; **3** F; **4** C; **5** H; **6** E; not used: B, G

Task 4

1. Robin Hood is called a "noble" thief because he stole money from the rich people to give it to the poor ones.
2. Names like Robin or Robert were very popular in the Middle Ages and so it's almost impossible to trace back Robin Hood with his first name. There were simply too many people being called Robin or Robert.
3. Nowadays Robin Hood has appeared in at least six blockbuster movies.
4. People compare Robin Hood with Santa Clause because the one is as popular as the other and like Santa Clause, every child also knows Robin Hood.
5. People believe that he lived during the time of King Richard the Lionheart (1157–1199).
6. The King's men were never able to catch Robin Hood because in the forest the gang appeared and disappeared like ghosts and they were never really seen.

Task 5

1. poor – wealthy; **2.** courageous – afraid; **3.** fictional – real; **4.** significant – unimportant
5. numerous – few; **6.** countless – limited; **7.** deny – admit; **8.** different – same

RC 3: TYPICALLY AMERICAN – STARBUCKS COFFEE

Task 1

1. coffee beans
2. caffeine
3. beverages
4. rainy
5. half
6. species
7. bitter
8. roasted
9. taste
10. density

Task 2

1. chain – a group of stores belonging to the same company
2. to be based in – the place where a company has its headquarter
3. panini – small soft sandwiches filled for example with ham and cheese
4. pastry – sweet stuff like cookies or brownies
5. mug – a colloquial (slang) expression for cup
6. tumbler – a colloquial (slang) expression for glass
7. nappy – first layer of cloth worn by babies
8. scholarship – it grants you access to university without paying for it

Task 4

1. (flavoured) coffee, (meeting) friends, (green) logo, (nice) ambiente
2. Seattle, Washington, US
3. sandwiches, panini, pastry, snacks, ice cream, salad (4 Wörter daraus)
4. mugs, tumblers, books, music
5. little money/money problems/father changing jobs/father job hopper
6. individual design/shops individual characteristic/shops no longer unified

RC 4: HAVING NO MONEY DESTROYS YOUR LIFE

Task 2

1. C; 2. A; 3. B; 4. D; 5. D; 6. C; 7. B; 8. A

RC 5: WHEN MOUNTAINEERING TURNS INTO AN OBSESSION

Task 1

1. Mount Everest (8844 m)
2. K2 (8611 m)
3. Kangchenjunga (8586 m)
4. Lhotse (8501 m)
5. Makalu (8462 m)
6. Cho Oyu (8201 m)
7. Dhaulagiri (8167 m)
8. Nanga Parbat (8126 m)

Task 2

1. mountaineering – to climb (high) mountains
2. glacier – part of a very high mountain where there is only ice, also in summer
3. crampon – metallic pieces you put on your shoes to have good grip on snow and ice
4. altitude – height
5. altitude sickness – the feeling of being sick when you are on very high mountains
6. rope team – at least two people walking on a glacier and being connected with a rope

Task 4

1 F; 2 B; 3 H; 4 D; 5 A; 6 G; not used: C, E, I

RC 6: SWEATSHOPS – THE PRICE FOR YOUR CLOTHES IS HUMANITY

Task 1

1. sweatshop – a factory with very poor and unfair working conditions
2. developing country – it's another term for 3rd world country
3. health insurance – makes it possible for you to go to the doctor without paying for it
4. abortion – killing and removing your unborn baby from your body
5. employer – the person who is your boss and who pays your wages/salary
6. refugee – a person who has fled to another country
7. to complain – to nag all the time/to talk about all the things you don't like
8. customer – a person who goes shopping somewhere and buys something
9. a widespread problem – a problem that affects many other areas as well

Task 3

1. F As the name already ...
2. T First of all, most ...
3. T Many of them end ...
4. F So usually they neither ...
5. F Furthermore, women are regularly ...
6. F Popular brands like Nike ...
7. F During the last years ...

Task 4

Sweatshops are not a **new** phenomenon. On the contrary, they have been existing for quite some time. In earlier times, however, the problem was largely **denied** and governments hardly cared for the workers' rights. Fortunately this has changed and the workers' well-being and the observation of their **rights** are a major concern nowadays. It's also no longer possible for a worker not to have a **health insurance**. This ensures that once you fall ill or you have to go to a hospital, you don't have to pay extra for it.

But still, regular **controls** are necessary to make sure that the big companies really stick to the rules. For the company it's of course much **cheaper** to have their goods manufactured in a sweatshop and because of this the profit they can make afterwards is enormous.

Nevertheless, it should be the **human being** that counts most and not the profit and the money.

RC 7: PLASTIC SURGERY – AN ADDICTION?

Task 1

1. to be addicted **to** something – von etwas abhängig sein, süchtig sein
2. to be responsible **for** something – für etwas verantwortlich sein
3. to long **for** something – sich nach etwas sehnen, etwas wollen
4. to crave **for** something – sich nach etwas sehnen, etwas wollen
5. to carry **out** something – etwas durchführen, ausführen
6. to be discontent **with** something – mit etwas unzufrieden sein

Task 2

1. cosmetic surgeon
2. anaesthesia
3. hurting pain
4. dissatisfied
5. liposuction
6. lifting
7. wrinkles
8. injecting
9. beauty ideal
10. pain killers
11. accident
12. risky

Task 4

1 B; **2** D; **3** A; **4** G; **5** E; **6** H; not used: C, F

RC 8: WHAT MAKES TEENAGERS REALLY HAPPY?

Task 1

Individuelle Lösungen!

Task 2

1. party-pooper (slang) – somebody who has never fun and always worries about possible problems
2. kidney and liver – inner organs of the human body
3. coward – somebody who is always afraid and frightened and doesn't take any risks
4. dehydration – if you don't drink enough and your body doesn't have enough water
5. peer pressure – you are forced to always do what your friends do, even if you don't want

Task 4

1. all life long/life-long venture/your whole life
2. gives feelings of security/safety and well-being/can rely on somebody/somebody cares for them
3. being part of group/develop social skills
4. no social interaction/no social contacts/no contacts – feeling lonely/lack in social interaction
5. afraid of bad image/afraid to be excluded/non-acceptance of friends/forced to do things
6. curiosity, experience this feeling/nosey, feeling being high/peer pressure
7. wrong drug, don't stop/wrong drug and overdo/wrong drug no limit
8. if you sweat/sweat, not enough water/don't drink enough/dancing, sweating, no drinking
9. damage liver, kidney, coma/life-threatening and coma

RC 9: IMPOSSIBLE TO BE HAPPY – YOUTH UNEMPLOYMENT

Task 1

1. unemployment – the state of not having a job and not receiving any money
2. to be employed – to have a job and earn money regularly
3. employer – the person who is your boss
4. wages/salary – the money you get for your work
5. to have a paper route – to deliver newspapers to people's houses
6. to employ somebody – to give somebody a job

Task 3

1. F When just considering America ...
2. T There are basically two ...
3. F The problem is that ...
4. F Banks no longer gave ...
5. T They had to do ...
6. F Sometimes the difficulty of ...
7. T Furthermore, teens from poor ...
8. F Fortunately teens have realised ...
9. T In the end, this ...
10. T Today, 83% of 16–19 year olds ...

Task 4

Jobs for 13 year old teens: deliver magazines, deliver newspapers, work as a baby-sitter, work at your parents' company, wash your dad's car, mow your neighbour's lawn

Jobs for 14 year old teens: work in a grocery store, work in a restaurant, work at a gas station (ACHTUNG: das britische Wort hierfür ist *petrol station*!), work at a baseball park

Jobs for 16 year old teens: work in an office, sell cinema tickets, give tutoring lessons, give swimming lessons

Jobs for 18 year old teens: work as security guard, do any work at night, deliver parcels by car, animate tourists

RC 10: HAPPY AND LUCKY: BEYONCÉ – TODAY'S BIGGEST POP STAR

Task 1

1. achievement – positive things you have already reached in your life
2. inauguration – celebration that officially turned Obama into the president of the USA
3. medical equipment – things doctors and nurses need in hospitals for surgeries
4. to appear on TV – to have a gig on TV
5. to rename – to change a name
6. an award – a prize for the things you have achieved in your life
7. to rehearse – to train/to practise
8. to sign – to write your name below an important document
9. to release an album – to put an album on the market/ready for the audience
10. to be involved in sth. – to be part of something/to be associated with something

Task 3

1 E; **2** A; **3** F; **4** C; **5** H; **6** B; not used: D, G

Task 4

Number C best summarises the article.

Task 5

Number B best describes the place where such an article is most likely to be published.

RC 11: ELECTRONIC WASTE: A 21ST CENTURY PROBLEM

Task 2

3	This is basically due to the fact that people in rich countries regularly need new computers and mobiles.
7	Unfortunately they don't know how dangerous that is, for the humans as well as the nature.
5	But the people in these poor countries don't know how to recycle e-waste correctly.
1	The problem that these days too much waste is produced is not new.
4	The useless electronic stuff is shipped to Third World Countries where it is recycled.
9	But they won't stop doing that as they urgently need the money to support their families.
8	They expose themselves to poisonous fumes and risk to get cancer or other incurable diseases.
6	What they do is to burn the stuff to separate the plastic from the metal.
2	What is new, however, is the fact that the amount of electronic waste has risen dramatically.

Task 3

Eva Meyers: B; Jacob Ronald: C; Marc Sleigh: C

RC 12: WHAT'S AN NGO? ... TALKING ABOUT AMNESTY

Task 1

The following sentences hold true for Amnesty International:
They fight to stop violence against women.
Amnesty defends poor people's rights.
It's their goal to abolish death penalty.
Amnesty protects the rights of immigrants.
They are against any kind of torture.
They care about the rights of refugees.

Task 2

1. Amnesty International is a well-known **human** rights organisation.
2. As it is **independent** from the government, Amnesty is a non-governmental organisation.
3. It was founded in the **United Kingdom** in July 1961.
4. Amnesty's **haedquarters** are in London.
5. They have about **2.2** million members and supporters worldwide.
6. Their methods range from media attention to **lobbying** and campaigns.
7. Amnesty's motto is as follows: *It's better to light a* **candle** *than to curse the darkness.*
8. It's characteristic for Amnesty that they are a **non-profit** organisation.
9. Peter Benenson, a labour **lawyer**, founded Amnesty International.

Task 4

1 F; **2** D; **3** A; **4** C; **5** G; **6** E; not used: B, H

RC 13: AMNESTY INTERNATIONAL: DID YOU KNOW THAT ... ?

Task 1

1. If you work on a voluntary basis, you don't get any money for the things you do.
2. People who work for free mostly do that out of very idealistic reasons.
3. If you have an idealistic attitude, you believe that you can make the world a better place.
4. In case you join Amnesty International you usually have to pay a membership fee.
5. Amnesty members are fully convinced that their help and support is needed and helpful.
6. If you donate money, you give it to a charity organisation to help.

Task 3

1. T He called on people ...
2. F There was an enormous ...
3. F Then the prisoner is ...
4. T The hundreds of thousands ...
5. F The money available is ...
6. T Donations are extremely important ...

7. F They are young and ...
8. T You may find politicians ...
9. T And their motivation is ...
10. F Today there are more ...
11. F Jeremy, in "real life" ...

RC 14: FACING MULTICULTURAL BRITAIN

Task 1

ADJECTIVE	NOUN	GERMAN TRANSLATION
to be patient	patience	Geduld
to be tolerant	tolerance	Toleranz
to be adapted	adaption	Anpassung
to be poor	poverty	Armut
to be persecuted	persecution	Verfolgung
to be abundant	abundance	Überfluss

Task 3

1 H; **2** G; **3** A; **4** D; **5** B; **6** F; not used: C, E

Task 4

Nowadays the number of immigrants living in Great Britain is very **high**. They come from **different** developing countries but their reasons to immigrate are very **similar**: they hope to live a **better** life, to be able to nourish their families and to **find** a good job. Sometimes immigrants also had to leave their country because of **war** or religious/political **persecution**. However, once they arrived in the **new** country, they often have to deal with a very different life. They have to get used to **different** morals and customs. They also have to learn the new **language** which is sometimes more difficult than originally expected. Quite often immigrant families stay there for the rest of their **life/lives**.
Their **children** grow up being so-called second generation immigrants. They usually have a much **easier** life than their parents but they also have to face and handle certain **problems/prejudices**. Unfortunately **discrimination** is still widespread, not only in the UK but also in many other countries.

RC 15: NEW LAWS TO REGULATE ALCOHOL CONSUMPTION

Task 1

drink alcohol regularly, get addicted to drinking, risk severe health damages, being under the influence of alcohol, dead drunk (= sinnlos betrunken sein), a bunch of drunks (= ein Haufen Betrunkener), to sober up (= ausnüchtern), alcohol consumption, to be intoxicated (= mit Alkohol vergiftet sein), to feel sick

Task 3

1. C; **2.** D; **3.** B; **4.** D; **5.** A; **6.** A; **7.** A; **8.** C

RC 16: PLAGUE OF COCAINE

Task 1

1. to struggle – to strongly fight/to have difficulties with something
2. customs – an area you have to pass when entering a foreign country
3. prearranged – something that was fixed and planned some time ago
4. plainclothes police – policemen not dressed in uniforms but casual clothes
5. to be delighted – to be extremely happy
6. port – harbour
7. money-laundering – to whitewash black and illegal money
8. to confiscate – to take something away
9. an eldorado – a very nice and pleasant place where you feel comfortable
10. to fight vigorously – to fight very hard and with full enthusiasm

Task 3

1. three suitcases/lots of luggage/three heavy suitcases/to unload her suitcases

2. because of her job/job as flight attendant/she worked for airline
3. everything was prearranged/already arranged/driver already got instructions
4. to be less striking/to be less noticeable/no suspicion/less suspicious
5. smuggling Cocaine between countries
6. problem of America/American problem/problem of Americans/America/United States
7. Eine Auswahl von vier der folgenden Wörter: ship/boat/animals/fruit/humans/children
8. long coastlines – big demand/endless coastlines – big market

EXTRA READING – SHORT STORY: LEAVING

Task 2

1. Moira was informed about the accident at 4 in the morning and at that time she was very sleepy and confused as the telephone had woken her up.
2. The sneakers are important for Moira because she only bought them one week ago together with her daughter Kate. And now Kate is in hospital.
3. She saw a man standing next to the hospital's entry. He was smoking a cigarette and didn't seem to feel comfortable.
4. She took the stairs because she was too impatient and too nervous to wait for the elevator.

Task 3

Die korrekte Nummerierung der Sätze lautet von oben nach unten: 5, 8, 2, 9, 4, 10, 1, 6, 3, 7

Task 4

1. accountant, middle-aged, divorced
2. like friends/good, friendly relationship/they're on good terms/not like mother – daughter
3. risk of being hurt/afraid to be hurt/no hurt again/afraid to be unhappy
4. Eine Auswahl von drei der folgenden Wörter: dark/medical machines/bed/silent/sterile
5. drank too much, collapsed/too much alcohol, collapse
6. strong rain/raining strongly/heavy rain/raining heavily/raining cats and dogs

Task 5

1. B; **2.** B; **3.** D; **4.** A; **5.** C; **6.** D; **7.** A; **8.** C

WRITING
INFORMAL (PERSONAL) LETTER

Exercise 1

heading	12 Holloway Circus Birmingham B1,1	return address
	26 January 2011	date
salutation **comma**	Hi Jenna,	
text	Thanks for your birthday card – I really love the CD you sent me. I'm listening to it right now! What's your favourite track? Mine is number 9 – it's so powerful.	introduction
	Anyway, I'm writing to tell you that my parents want us to move. They've actually already bought a cute house in Brighton! The neighbourhood seems to be okay – loads of families with kids of my age. The house itself is fantastic! I'm finally going to have my own room – you know my little sister can be a real pest sometimes. Well, in the future I'll just shut the door if she gets too bad. Cool, isn't it? The garden is awesome too. We're going to have our own apples and raspberries. Yummy! The only thing that bothers me a bit is that I'll have to leave all my friends behind. But there are some cool youth clubs in Brighton – I guess I won't have troubles finding new friends. And there are still e-mails, letters and cell phones. At least, for us, nothing will change ☺.	main body
	That reminds me of Phil! He is fetching me in a minute to talk about the move ... He wants us to keep a long-distance relationship – but I'm not sure if this will work out. Well, I'll keep you in the loop on that matter in the next letter.	conclusion
closing	Hugs and kisses, *Anna*	signature
postscriptum	PS: Give my love to your sister! A. P.	

Exercise 2

INFORMAL	FORMAL	INFORMAL	FORMAL
Hi Sophie!	**Dear Ms Jennings,**	See ya on Monday.	**I'm looking forward to seeing you on Monday.**
Thanks (Thx) for your letter!	**I want to thank you for your letter.**	Best wishes,	**Yours faithfully,** (Name des Empfängers ist bekannt.) **Yours sincerely,**
Sorry (Sry) for not answering your last letter.	**I apologise for not answering your letter.**	There are some things that really annoy me!	**I would like to mention some aspects annoying me.**

FORMAL (BUSINESS) LETTER

Exercise 1

1. D; **2.** E; **3.** B; **4.** A; **5.** C; **6.** D

Exercise 2

	286 Wisteria Lane Portland, OR 97205	return address
recipient's name and address	Mr. Michael Kelzo Colorful Inc. 476 Strong Road Springfield, OR 97477	
greeting	Dear Mr. Kelzo, 24 March 2011	date
subject line	Subject: Request for fabric sample	
opening	I am writing to enquire about the new set of fabric samples as advertised in your leaflet sent out in February.	
main message	We are a manufacturer of high-quality upholstery, operating in 10 states of the U.S.A. As we are interested in expanding our product range, we are currently looking for trendy fabrics. Accordingly, your advertisement has caught our attention. We would be grateful if you could send us a sample of your collection.	
close	We are looking forward to hearing from you.	
closing phrase	Yours sincerely,	
	Jonathan Frazer Jonathan Frazer Product Manager	signature

Exercise 3

OPENING (beginning a letter)	REFERRING (expressing reference)	CLOSE (ending a letter)
A, B	D, H	C, E, F, G, I, J

E-MAIL

Exercise 1

Maria forgot to mention the level of her English skills.

REPORT

Exercise 1

Introduction
The aim of this report is to assess the success of this year's study trip to Ireland and to recommend any improvements.

Host families
Although the families that students stayed with were very hospitable, students sometimes did not feel integrated with the families. It would be preferable if host families had children of the students' age in order to propel interaction.

Programme
The programme concentrated highly on cultural activities and accordingly included many visits to museums. Students mentioned that they would have preferred seeing more of the countryside and learning more about Irish lifestyle. I recommend that future trips should offer a larger variety of activities, like city trips, coach trips to the surrounding areas and evening entertainment like cinema visits or theatre shows.

Language school
While students got on very well with their teachers, students pointed out that the outline of their English classes did not meet their expectations. For future classes, it might be advisable to focus more on speaking than on writing activities.

Conclusion
To sum up, this year's trip was a great success, despite the reservations mentioned above. If the changes mentioned above can be put into effect, we will be looking forward to going on a further trip.

Exercise 2

Introductions: A, E, F, H
Positive aspects: G, N
Recommendations and suggestions: C, D, J, K, L
Conclusions: B, I, M

MODEL TASKS

Task 1 Formal letter/e-mail

To:	info@camp-for-kids
From:	Steve Saunders
Subject:	Application: Camp-for-kids

Dear Sir or Madam,

I recently saw your advertisement requesting coaches for your summer camp in Canada, and I should very much like to become a part of your team for the following holidays.

I have already gained some experience in working with children, as I am a group leader in our local scouts club. I therefore am prepared to face the challenges a camp-holiday with 8-to-14-year-olds holds. Not only am I communicative, outgoing and fun-loving, I also do know how to take the responsibility for young people. Another important aspect which qualifies me for the advertised position is the fact that as a member of our school's athletics club, I train daily to stay physically fit. These qualities, together with my skills acquired as a scouts guide, will make me the perfect candidate.

However, I have two queries about the project. Firstly, how will the journey to the campsite be organised? And secondly, when exactly will the project start?

Please feel free to contact me if you have any further questions. I am looking forward to hearing from you soon.

Yours sincerely,

Steve Saunders

Task 2 Formal letter (letter of complaint)

452, Willington Street
Milton Keynes MK41WN
England

12 November 2012

The Manager
Living TV
62 Broadcast Boulevard
London W2 2TH

To whom it may concern,

Subject: Complaint about "Britain's next top model"

I am writing to express my dissatisfaction with your show "Britain's next top model", as broadcast every Thursday on your TV station.

I have to state that Living TV, being one of the most popular TV stations in Britain, has a devastating consequence on the morals, behaviour and health of our youth.
As the girls you present in the show are role models for thousands of teenagers in Britain, you must be more careful in choosing your candidates. At the moment, young girls in front of the TV sets are told that a woman is reduced to a beautiful body which you should openly display. What about brains and character?
Another aspect which strikes me as extremely problematic is the way the girls are treated in the show. The jury's criticism mainly focuses on lowering the candidates' self-esteem with shockingly rude remarks about their appearance and performance. I do miss the principle of respect in your show!
My final point of criticism focuses on the concept of beauty itself which you propel in your show. Stop telling teenagers that they must be underweight to be considered beautiful. You should rather favour an image of fitness and individual beauty than one of starved uniformity.

I am of course aware of the fact that your format is designed to entertain with controversial strategies. Nevertheless you must keep in mind that it is our nation's youth which is at stake! Please re-think your concept considering some of my suggestions.

I am looking forward to hearing from you.

Yours sincerely,
Andrea Sachs
Andrea Sachs

Task 3 **Personal letter**

452, Maritime Street
Santa Cruz, CA 95060

6 April 2012

Hi Geoff,

How are things going back in England? I am doing just fine in my new town. Santa Cruz is in fact quite cool! Imagine, I had my first surf lesson last week. Yeah – I didn't manage well at first – but I'm gonna make it, I'm sure. Now that I've got such a cool board, I will have to ride it, won't I?

Anyway – the reason I am writing to you is the following: You remember Bethany? I wrote about her in my last letter. She's that cute girl who is in my Trigonometry class. Imagine: She invited me to her birthday party. I was so excited!! My first party in the States. I had a certain picture in my mind from all those "teen movies" and series. But I can tell you one thing: I just was so wrong. First of all: The party started in the afternoon. We spent three boring hours in her family's living room, playing computer games. How boring. Her parents kept watching us suspiciously – I thought they were able to read my mind ... But no way: No close dancing, no kissing, not even holding hands. So I thought: Okay – let's rock the house. A big mistake: When I turned up the volume, Beth's mum gave me an angry glance and turned the volume down. So at least the food was great – but that's not what I expect from a "successful" party. Geoff – I really miss ours!

So – thanks for reading my complaints. I have to stop writing now because I want to call Beth ... I am going to give us another try. Perhaps I can talk to her in private.

See ya dude,
Zac

Task 4 **Personal e-mail**

To:	monamoon42@hotmail.com
From:	jolenedarling23@gmail.com
Subject:	Help!

Dear Mona,

I was deeply shocked when I read your last e-mail. And I have to tell you – I know exactly how you feel. Last year, a guy in my class faced the same problem.

I've known Rick since kindergarten. His great passion was music: Rick started playing the drums as a kid and at the age of fifteen he joined a band. And: They really made it. After four months they released their first single. Our local radio station played their songs up and down. Then – suddenly: the break-up. Their lead singer left the band: no more hits, Rick was devastated. He lost all the joy in his life, withdrew from his friends. He looked more and more like a wreck: thinning hair, sick skin, dull eyes. First, I thought it was just the shock, but I soon realised that there was something more behind his decay: METH. That drug is quite popular in our town, and it quickly does its job: You use it once – you get hooked on it. And it destroys your body, mind and soul. First I panicked – then I stepped up for his life. I talked to Rick's parents, informed the headmaster of our school. Rick was sent to a detox centre. We all worked together – supported Rick, comforted him, gave him what he needed: a perspective. Rick was lucky: He got a second chance. I hope he will take it.

Please Mona – don't give up. Address the problem – talk about it. Make people aware of it. But always keep in mind: This drug is a monster. A monster which sometimes wins the fight.

All my thoughts are with you,

Jolene

Task 5

Individuelle Lösung

Task 6 **Article**

150 years ago – life was ...?

Can you imagine a life without running water, no hot baths, no TV or radio? Not really? I could not either – but nevertheless I did it: I spent four weeks in the 19th century house, a TV show which shows you what life was like 150 years ago. If you want to learn more about that adventure, read on!

When I arrived at the set, I had to change my cosy jeans for a stubborn woollen dress that felt itchy on my bare legs. I had to wear woollen socks under my sturdy boots, which gave me blisters after only an hour of wearing them. The house itself looked great: an old Victorian mansion with high ceilings, colourful tapestries, cosy looking fireplaces and impressive furniture. But I was not supposed to enjoy all these things: I was the housemaid who had to sweep the floors, cook the meals and keep the house clean and warm. My room, however, was small and shabby and always cold. I shared it with the two other maids. At first, I was horrified: Three spoilt girls crammed into that tiny cave? But I can tell you one thing: Hard times make good friends. The days were rough – but we had a cool time nevertheless. We found ways to treat ourselves with little bites of sweets from the kitchen (Jane, one of the girls, was the cook's favourite), we giggled and laughed all the time. And I even had a typical 19th century romance with the stable boy: secret glances, backdoor kisses, cute little presents – it was so romantic. Time passed quickly – and after the four weeks I of course felt happy to get back to my comfortable 21st century home – but I somehow miss the simple life that makes you appreciate small happy moments so much more.

So – 150 years ago, life was definitely not easy. What I have learned from that adventure is: I am happy to live a modern life – but I could do with a bit of 19th century romance.

Task 7 Article

Summer, sun, sea, relaxing on the beach. No, I am not talking about my last holidays. I am talking about our school trip!

Monday, 8 a.m.: Twenty-four eager faces cannot wait to see the train coming in. There it is: Vienna – Cannes. A long journey – and we were all looking forward to it.

In Cannes, we met our host families. While our spoilt Gina had to stay with a rather stressed looking mummy and her four kids, I shared a 240 m² villa with a great couple. I am just a lucky devil. That would be a great week, wouldn't it? Sure – French classes from nine to twelve – but then we would have enough time to enjoy the great French weather at the Côte d'Azur. And by the way – our French teacher was great! A 24-year-old French beauty – with a hilarious sense of humour. I really learned a lot that week … French is a beautiful language ☺. After school, we made various trips: We learnt how to make perfume in Grasse (no, not like Monsieur Grenouille), we went shopping in Monaco, relaxed in Nice and had coffee in St. Tropez. Walking down the Promenade des Anglais in the sunshine, you feel like a star. In the evenings we relaxed on the beach and just had a great time.

So, if your teachers ask you: Where do you want to go on your next school trip: France is the answer!

Task 8 Report

Introduction
The aim of this report is to assess how satisfied young people are with life in our town as well as to give some recommendations how to improve various aspects.

Safety
The majority of young people say that they feel very safe. What could be improved, however, is the situation at the train station at night, as some girls do not feel comfortable when arriving in the dark. Better lightening could fight that problem.

Shopping
Most teenagers complain that our town does not offer attractive shopping facilities. They would be happy if the range of clothes and shoe shops could be widened.

Sports areas
What our teenagers mention as very positive is the range of sports and recreation facilities offered in our town. They especially appreciate the large indoor and outdoor pool as well as the skatepark and the tennis court. What could be improved is the offer of sports clubs. Especially girls would love to join gymnastics, judo and karate courses.

Nightlife
An aspect that definitely needs improvement is nightlife. Most teenagers would appreciate a youth club that offers facilities for meeting and socialising at the weekend.

Conclusion
All in all, young people enjoy living in our town. However, improvements with regard to shopping facilities as well as nightlife would definitely raise satisfaction among teenagers.

Task 9 Report

Introduction
The aim of this report is to assess the implementation of e-books and e-readers at our school and to give recommendations for the future.

Positive aspects
The replacement of traditional school books with e-books has had various positive consequences. Students primarily praise the reduction of weight they have to carry each day. Moreover, they appreciate the fact that they quickly have all the information they need at hand. E-books have several attractive features, like e-dictionaries or access to wikipedia. What students consider as especially helpful is the fact that some books can be read out loud.

Negative aspects
Of course, students also mention some negative aspects of e-books. First, a majority of students claims that they miss the possibility of taking notes in the books themselves. Secondly, some students have problems getting used to the handling of e-readers. They prefer browsing through actual pages to turning electronic sites.

Conclusion and Recommendations
Summing up, I want to mention that the majority of students speak in favour of replacing school books with e-books. They, however, note that a possibility of taking notes in the books should be offered. This would, of course, require an improvement of the e-reader technology.

Task 10

Individuelle Lösung

Task 11 Opinion essay

"12-year-old boy nearly died from alcohol poisoning"
"13-year-old girl found unconscious because of alcohol abuse"

Headlines like these dominate our daily newspapers. In order to fight the growing problem of teenage alcohol abuse, politicians are discussing the question whether to raise the age of legally purchasing alcohol from 18 to 21. But would this action really fight the problem?

Let us reflect on the situation in a country where the age limit of buying alcohol is 21: the United States. Of course, it cannot be denied that you just cannot find any young people drinking alcohol publicly in the streets or in pubs. But does that mean that American teenagers do not drink any alcohol?

No! They find ways of purchasing it and then have secret house-parties. As American teenagers have never learnt to deal with alcohol in a sensible and responsible way, they exaggerate their alcohol consumption at those parties.

So, the answer to the question whether raising the age of legally purchasing alcohol to 21 would fight the problem of teenage alcohol abuse is: No. As illustrated in the paragraph above, teenagers will find ways to get alcohol, and as they are not used to dealing with it, they will end up in hospital. But of course, there are other ways to fight teenage binge drinking. The first action that should be taken is stricter controls at bars, in supermarkets and any places where alcohol can be purchased. As long as 13-year-olds can still buy hard liquors at the next petrol station, any new laws that should help to fight teenage binge-drinking are completely useless. Moreover, young kids should be informed of the consequences of alcohol abuse at an early age. Parents and teachers have to face their responsibility in making kids familiar with and aware of the damage excessive alcohol abuse can cause. Only when our kids learn to deal with alcohol in a responsible way will we be able to avoid alcohol excesses.

So, summing up, I want to mention the following: Let us not delay the problem of teenage alcohol abuse, let us talk about it and fight it now!

Task 12 und 13

Individuelle Lösung

GRAMMAR

TENSES

Exercise 1

Hi Mark,

Sorry that I **haven't been able** to write earlier, but things **have been** quite crazy recently. You know, the first four weeks of my holidays **turned out** to be quite rushed because I **had to** work in my father's company. However, in August, I **had** the most amazing time in my life. But, let me tell you from the start. On my last Friday afternoon at work, I **was sitting** in front of my computer, **keying** in some receipts for my father, when he suddenly **appeared** in my room. After he **had praised** me for my excellent work he **showed** me two tickets for Ibiza! I **couldn't believe** my ears when he **told** me that those tickets **were** for my best friend Dave and me. The following Monday at nine, Dave and I **were sitting** on the plane, **talking** about our plans for the following week. We **would relax** on the beach, meet some cute girls and party all night long. Sounds good, ey? The first two days, we really **whooped** it up! One party after the other, lazy afternoons on the beach, the hot sun shining down on us: HEAVEN. On the third day, Dave and I **were lying** in the sun, nearly dozing off, when I **felt** an ice-cold hand on my back. I **didn't know** what was going on, so I screamed, "Dave, what **are you doing**?" But ... that **wasn't** Dave! When I **looked up** I saw that the most beautiful girl I **had ever seen was looking down** at me. I remembered that I **had met** Amy the night before, but I thought that she had a crush on Dave. Amy said, "Hi Ben! I **have been thinking** about you all day long. I (**have**) **lost** your numbers, but now that I **have found** you, I **won't let** you go!" Quite bold, isn't she? You bet – I **didn't mind** her talking so frankly. Anyway, Amy and I **spent** a wonderful time in Ibiza ... and who knows? She only **lives** twenty minutes from my house ...

Sorry, but I have to stop writing now. Mum **is calling** me for dinner.

See ya, Ben

Exercise 2

Margo: Jimmy, how **are** you? I really **haven't seen** you for ages! What **have you been doing** within the last few months? I'm curious so tell me please!

Jimmy: Hey Margo! It's nice to see you! You **look** good. Well, there's a lot to tell you. Did you know that I **lost** my job two months ago?

Margo: No, I **didn't hear** about that! Why? What **went** wrong if I may ask?

Jimmy: Oh, the company **had gone** bankrupt and so I **had to** look for another job.

Margo: And **have you already found** something new?

Jimmy: Luckily yes! Actually it was much easier than I **had expected**. At first I **thought** I would have to write hundreds of letters of applications but in fact I immediately **found** something new.

Margo: Oh that's great! So where **are you working** right now?

Jimmy: I **am** responsible for online marketing at a German company for outdoor sports. I really **enjoy** doing that because, you know, I **have always been** keen on doing sports myself. Actually I **was** surprised that I **got** this job so easily and quickly because after I **had sent** my CV, they immediately **invited** me for a personal conversation and about six weeks later I **had** my first working day.

Margo: That's super, Jimmy! Congratulations! And what exactly **do you have to do** at that job? Can you explain that to me?

Jimmy: Well, at the moment I **am working** on improving the online Internet presentation of the company. And one of my next projects **is going to be** to facilitate online shopping possibilities for the customers. But it **is going to take** some time until I can work on that one.

Margo: Sounds like a real challenge! Hey Jimmy, what about meeting for a cup of coffee next week?

Jimmy: Definitely! If you **give** me your number, I **will call** you at the weekend. I really look forward to **seeing** you more often.

Margo: Great! Here is my card. Just let me know when you have time! Bye Jimmy!

Modal verbs

Tricia: Hi Marla! Nice to see you. I'm sorry that I **couldn't go/was not able to go** to the cinema with you yesterday. I **had to help** my mum.

Marla: What **did you have to do**?

Tricia: First, I **had to** iron tons of clothes and then I **should have cleaned** my room. But when I was ironing one of my shirts, I burnt my finger. So, I **couldn't go on/wasn't able to go on**.

Marla: Poor you. You know you have to be careful when you iron things. You **might have got** badly hurt.

Tricia: I know, I know. I'm glad that nothing really bad happened. I simply **should have paid** more attention to what I was doing. The next time I iron shirts I **will have to be** more careful. That's it.

Marla: I'm glad I **haven't had to do** much housework recently. Two weeks ago, my mum **could convince/was able to convince** Ms Jennings, our cleaning lady, to work for us every day. Since then, all of us **have been able to relax**. You know, before Ms Jennings came, my father, my brother and I **had had to work** at least an hour a day to help our mum. That was quite hard.

Tricia: I remember! So, now that you have enough time, I guess that you **will be able to come** to my party next Saturday?

Marla: I'm not sure. I think that I **will have to look after** my little brother because my parents want to visit some friends.

Tricia: Oh Marla. You **should talk** to your parents again and tell them that you need some time for your friends. Tell them that you **were not allowed to go** to Lucy's party last week because you **were supposed to study** for your Maths test.

Marla: I know, Tricia, I know. But I think that my parents were quite right last week. I really **could have studied** more before the weekend. But I didn't. So, I **had to face** the consequences and stay at home.

Tricia: You sound like your own mother, Marla. Come on. You are fifteen years old. Give it a try.

Marla: You're right. By the way – do you know where Rick is? He **should have joined** us an hour ago. He said that he wanted to do some homework, but he **must have finished** by now.

Tricia: Right. I don't know. Let's call him ...

CONDITIONALS

Conditional 0

Exercise 1

3. Wenn das „if" am Anfang steht, werden Bedingung und Folge durch einen Beistrich getrennt.

Exercise 2 and 3

1. If you heat snow, it melts. **B**

2. If I am happy, I listen to music. **A**

3. Please ask if you have a question. **C**

4. If you run fast, you sweat. **B** (**A**)

5. If the baby is hungry, it cries. **A**

Conditional 1

Exercise 4

1. If you forget your girlfriend's birthday again, she won't want to see you.

2. I won't be able to help you if you don't tell me about your problem.

3. Jane will help you if you ask her. I'm sure.

Conditional 2

Exercise 5

1. I would not call her today if I were you.

2. If I won a million euros, I could finally make a round-the-world trip

3. If Eric had time, he would go to the movies with you. But he unfortunately has to work.

Conditional 3a

Exercise 6

1. If I had cleaned my room yesterday, I could go swimming with you now.

2. Peter would play in a successful band if he hadn't stopped practicing playing the drums.

3. Jake and Angie would be married now if she had not cheated on him.

Conditional 3b

Exercise 7

1. Jim wouldn't have lost his key if he had put it in the drawer.

2. If I had told Alicia the truth, she wouldn't have shouted at me.

3. We would have caught the bus if it hadn't taken you so long to get dressed.

Mixed conditionals

1. If I had a plane, I would fly to Paris every Sunday. (Conditional 2: unwahrscheinlich)

2. If we catch the 11:30 train, we will arrive on time. (Conditional 1: wahrscheinlich)

3. If I hadn't broken my leg, I would go skiing this weekend. (Conditional 3: unmöglich, Auswirkung in Gegenwart)

4. If my mum wakes me before 11 on Sundays, I tell her to go away. (Conditional 0: allgemeine Situation)

5. If I had an older brother, I would ask him to do my homework. (Conditional 2: unwahrscheinlich)

6. If Trisha had asked Pete, he would have invited her to the party. (Conditional 3b: Auswirkung in Vergangenheit)

7. If you put salt into water, it doesn't freeze at 0 degrees. (Conditional 0: natural law)

8. If Kim doesn't hand in her essay today, she will get an F. (Conditional 1: wahrscheinlich)

9. If I hadn't thought of buying cream, I wouldn't have been able to mix those great cocktails. (Conditional 3b: Auswirkung in Vergangenheit)

10. If Jim hadn't forgotten his calculator, he could (would be able to) do his homework now. (Conditional 3a: Auswirkung in der Gegenwart)

11. If I was/were better at playing poker, I would join your game. (Conditional 2: unwahrscheinlich)

12. If it rains, I won't go swimming. (Conditional 1: wahrscheinlich, dass es regnet)

13. If I had closed the window, the wind wouldn't have blown away my essay. (Conditional 3: Auswirkung in Vergangenheit)

14. If you go shopping, please don't forget to buy strawberries.

15. If my cat caught a mouse, I would try to save it. (Conditional 2: unwahrscheinlich, dass die Katze eine Maus fängt)

REPORTED SPEECH

Aussage

Exercise 1

1. Reporting verb: suggested = past simple ▶ Zeitensprung: Mum suggested that I could take the car because she didn't need it.

2. Reporting verb: remarked = past simple ▶ Zeitensprung: Sabrina remarked that she had been reading her favourite magazine when she suddenly had felt cold.

3. Reporting verb: has said = present perfect ▶ kein Zeitensprung: Dad has just said that he doesn't want to drive to town. He thinks that we should take our bikes.

4. Reporting verb: will say = will-future ▶ kein Zeitensprung: Barbara will say that she is sure that it is going to be sunny.

5. Reporting verb: replied = past simple ▶ Zeitensprung: Greg replied that he hadn't seen Melissa for a year and that I didn't have to worry.

6. Reporting verb: complains = present simple ▶ kein Zeitensprung: My girlfriend always complains that I spend too much time with my friends."

7. Reporting verb: mentioned = past simple ▶ Zeitensprung: Melissa mentioned that it was sunny and that they might go to the beach.

Frage

Exercise 2

Umformulierte Regel: Leite die indirekte Ergänzungsfrage mit dem Fragewort ein (when, where, why, how long, how much, who, which, what, …).

Exercise 3

1. He asked me if I had called him at ten.

2. Douglas will ask Sally where she wants to go on holiday.

3. Mum asked us if we had forgotten to lock the door.

Mixed exercises

Exercise 4

Dear Adrienne,

Imagine what happened yesterday! I was sitting in the school cafeteria, when I suddenly saw Brian standing next to me. He greeted me and asked me how I was. I answered that I felt great. Then he asked me if he was allowed to take the seat next to me. Of course I offered him to go ahead. After a short silence, I asked him if he had already done his Maths homework. He replied that he had tried it the day before, but he had not been able to do some of the exercises. I asked if he wanted me to help him, but he refused politely. Brian hesitated shortly and then told me that what he was trying to ask me was … and there he paused. I encouraged him to go on, but then Jane interrupted us and asked Brian to pass her the salt. I gave it to her and then asked Brian what he wanted to ask me. You won't believe it, but Jane interrupted us again. This time she wanted us to pass her the mustard. I gave it to her and told her quite impatiently not to constantly interrupt us. Finally Brian asked me if I wanted to go to the movies with him that evening. I happily responded that I was so happy he had finally asked. Brian expressed that that was cool and asked me when I wanted to go. I suggested going that night and wanted to know if he had already seen *Inception* with Leonardo DiCaprio. Brian replied that he hadn't and offered that he would fetch me at seven. I accepted happily and Brian said bye.

Suddenly, Jane shouted at me angrily. She asked loudly what I had done and wanted to know if I hadn't known that Brian had been dating Veronica for three weeks. Surprised, I ordered her to stop shouting and wanted her to tell me what she was talking about. Jane claimed that Brian had asked out Veronica after the school dance. She mentioned that they had been seeing each other quite a lot since then. Jane exclaimed that she couldn't believe Brian had asked me out. She insisted that Brian was one of the most awful cheaters at school and advised me not to trust him. Of course, I answered that I didn't believe her. I begged her to stop talking badly about Brian because I had been looking forward to that moment for months. Jane explained that she just wanted to warn me and that she didn't want to be blamed in case Brian disappointed me. I thanked her but told her that I would see Brian anyway. Jane replied that that was up to me.

Of course I asked Brian about Veronica. He informed me that Jane hadn't told me the truth. He only saw Veronica once, but they didn't get on.

I will keep you in the loop.   Love, Kim

Exercise 5

  1. Alan observed that Gerry hadn't washed his car for a while.

  2. My mum urged my father to buy the bigger car.

  3. My sister denied that she had taken my blouse.

  4. Mathew admitted that he had copied his homework from Tina.

  5. Roland called Vanessa his darling.

  6. Lilly admired that Patrick and Hannah were dancing so beautifully.

  7. Emma implored her boyfriend not to leave her because she couldn't live without him.

  8. Steven advised Ralph to take the stronger car.

  9. I regretted that I hadn't been able to join the party the day before. I really had wanted to.

10. Anthony claimed that his motorbike was much faster than mine.

11. Mike promised Jennifer that that would be the best day in her life.

12. Samantha greeted Bianca.

13. Georgiana complained that she wouldn't be able to see me all summer if I worked in Spain.

14. Cynthia suggested going swimming.

PASSIVE VOICE

Exercise 1

ACTIVE	PASSIVE
The landlady serves *breakfast* from 7 to 10.	**Breakfast** is served from 7 to 10 (by *the landlady*).
They are repairing *the old bridge*.	**The old bridge** is being repaired (by *them*).

The estate agent sold *the house*.	**The house** was sold (by *the estate agent*).
Someone has stolen *my bike*.	**My bike** has been stolen (by *someone*).
The painters will paint *the wall*.	**The wall** will be painted (by *the painters*).

Im Passiv wird das Objekt zum Subjekt. Das Subjekt, der Handlungsträger, kann, muss aber nicht, als „by-agent" am Ende des Satzes erwähnt werden.
(**Subjekte** sind fett, *Objekte* kursiv gedruckt.)

Exercise 2

| **BILDUNG** | to be (in der entsprechenden Zeit) + past participle
Subjekt wird zum **Objekt**.
Objekt wird zum **Subjekt**. |

Exercise 3

TENSE	ACTIVE	PASSIVE
Present simple	The gardener mows the lawn twice a week.	**The lawn is mowed twice a week.**
Present cont.	**The mechanic is repairing our car.**	Our car is being repaired.
Past simple	**They built the house in 1756.**	The house was built in 1756.
Past cont.	Someone was following us.	**We were being followed.**
Present perfect	**I haven't fed the cat today.**	The cat hasn't been fed today.
Past perfect	They had closed the restaurant.	**The restaurant had been closed.**
Will-future	**They will release the album next month.**	The album will be released next month.
Going-to fut.	They are going to release the film in April.	**The film is going to be released in April.**
Conditional	They would invite Sally.	**Sally would be invited.**

Exercise 4

1. The dog has been fed twice today.

2. Tweety's cage must be cleaned more carefully.

3. Dinner should have been served at eight.

4. The film is going to be shot in Mexico.

5. The poem ought to be learned/learnt by heart.

6. The birds have been being observed for two months now.

7. My keys had been stolen.

8. A new skyscraper will be built.

9. I was being interviewed when I was hit by a tomato.

10. The water couldn't be turned off.

11. My lost dog has been found.

12. The baby elephant can't be seen today.

13. The car wasn't sold yesterday.

14. The bear would have been caught if better traps had been taken.

15. The zoo is not closed before seven.

Exercise 5

Steve: Hi Donna. How **are things going**?

Donna: Great!

Steve: Why **wasn't** Claire at the last training session?

Donna: Haven't you heard? She **has been thrown/was thrown/had been thrown** out for stealing.

Steve: No! When **did that happen**?

Donna: Yesterday evening. She **was seen** taking money from someone's bag in the changing room.

Steve: Who by?

Donna: The sports club manager. She **was checking** the changing rooms when she **found** Claire there with Karen's bag.

Steve: Oh no! What **was done** about Claire then?

Donna: When Claire **was being interviewed** she said she **had been asked** to fetch some money for Karen. However, after Karen **had been questioned** it became clear that the sports club manager **had not been told** the truth. Karen **had not said** a word to Claire about fetching the money.

Steve: That's a terrible story. But I think that Karen **shouldn't have left** her money in the locker!

Donna: Sure. She **has just been told** the same by the manager.
Now, Claire promised that she **was definitely not going to do** such a stupid thing again.

Steve: Who knows. What do you think Claire **will do** now?

Donna: I really don't know. This is the second club she **has had to leave** so far, isn't it?

Steve: Yes, as far as I know. I wonder what **could be done** to help a person like her.

Donna: Maybe she **should be sent** to a psychologist. I hope she **won't be arrested** for something worse one day.

Steve: Yes, I'm afraid she **won't be able to change** all on her own.

ADJECTIVES AND ADVERBS

Adjective or adverb?

Exercise 1

1. beautifully/prettily
2. badly
3. fantastic, happily
4. quite/rather/pretty/fairly
5. carefully
6. well, good
7. hard, hardly
8. straight ahead, right
9. quietly
10. lately/recently
11. deeply
12. closely/carefully

Comparison of adjectives and adverbs

Exercise 2

1. more carefully
2. much faster
3. worse
4. much higher
5. extremely interesting
6. latest, less exciting, last
7. faster, the fastest
8. more happily/more gaily
9. bad, worse
10. cleverer/more intelligent
11. further/more
12. harder, better
13. sadder
14. the most horrible/the most terrible
15. more heavily

Word order of adjectives

Exercise 3

1. marvellous darkblue leather
2. numerous tiny black
3. horrible 150-year-old Victorian mahogany coffee
4. some delicious ice-cold cherry-flavoured Belgium
5. disgusting old muddy boat-shaped basketball

Compound adjectives

Exercise 4

1. dog-tired
2. crystal clear
3. dead-slow
4. foolhardy
5. jet-black
6. pitch dark
7. stone-deaf
8. skin-tight
9. flat broke
10. wide awake
11. stark naked

RELATIVE CLAUSES

Exercise 1

Jane: Der Relativsatz „who lives in London" gibt eine wichtige, einschränkende Information über den Bruder. Jane muss also mehrere Brüder haben.
Der beifügende Relativsatz in Klammern gibt eine unwichtige Information über Marys Bruder. Sie hat also nur einen.

Exercise 2

1. The River Thames, whose name is derived from the Celtic name *Tamesas,* flows through London.
2. Malcolm kept on talking for hours, which annoyed us a lot.
3. The school (that/which) my cousin teaches in offers twenty different sports clubs. The school in which my cousin teaches offers twenty different sports clubs. (Die zweite Version, in der die Präposition „in" vor das Relativpronomen gezogen wird, ist die formalere. Hier darf „that" NICHT verwendet werden!)
4. The girl with whom I danced at prom night asked me for a date. The girl (that) I danced with at prom night asked me for a date.
5. My sister's husband, who plays in a rock band, often takes me to cool concerts.
6. The coach and the dolphin that you can see on *this* picture always do a great show. (Zwei Bilder mit Delfin und Trainer: who ist nicht möglich!) The coach and the dolphin, who you can see on this picture, always do a great show. (Nur ein Bild!)
7. I went to see the doctor, who told me to stay in bed for a week.
8. There are some phrases in this text which/that are difficult to translate.
9. My father, who never wants to spend a lot of money, bought an apartment that is too small.

Exercise 3

1. Boris always orders the most expensive steak <u>which</u> costs him a lot of money. Richtig: , which
2. The bike <u>what</u> I saw in the shop costs 3000 dollars. Richtig: that/which
3. Lenny showed me a photo of his dog, <u>that</u> he loves very much. Richtig: , which
4. ✓
5. My mother <u>who has just left the house</u> will call you back. Richtig: My mother, who has just left the house, will call you back. (nur eine Mutter: non-defining relative clause)
6. My cat Scratchy, <u>that</u> is sleeping in my lap, is digging her claws in my thigh. Richtig: which
7. Pluto <u>which is the second largest dwarf-planet in the Solar System</u> is a member of the Kuiper belt. Richtig: Pluto, which is the second largest dwarf-planet in the Solar System, is a member of the Kuiper belt.
8. You are all <u>what</u> I need. Richtig: that

GERUND

admit, deny, regret, suggest
e.g.: Peter admitted having eaten all the pudding. Peter admitted that he had eaten all the pudding.

1. I admit having taken the car without asking you before.
2. We are looking forward to seeing you next weekend.
3. I just couldn't resist eating the chocolate cake.
4. You should really give up/stop/quit smoking.
5. I really appreciate your supporting my sister's dream of becoming an actress. (formal)
   I really appreciate you supporting my sister's dream of becoming an actress. (informal)

1. I don't think that Marco is capable of doing something cruel like that.
2. Your husband is annoyed at your constant nagging/moaning/complaining.
3. Sandra is disappointed at not having won.
4. You are wrong in thinking that I don't love you.
5. He is notorious for never giving up.
6. Elias is not keen on going skiing with us.
7. I'm tired of/I'm fed up with always having to make up for your mistakes.

1. I can't stand sleeping in a room with closed windows.
2. Bella can't help staring at Edward.
3. There is no point in blaming me. It's no good/use blaming me.
4. How about/What about having an ice cream in the park?
5. It's a waste of time looking for Lucky. He will come home.
6. It's no use/good addressing him. He is busy flirting with Jessica.
7. I feel like going for a walk.
8. This film is worth seeing.

Gerund or infinitive?

The correct rules are: 3. and 5.

The correct rules are: 2. and 5.

1	2	3	4
C	D	A	B

stop to = innehalten, um etwas zu tun
start to = losgehen, losfahren, um etwas zu tun

1	2	3	4	5	6
F	C	A	E	B	D

1. He stopped to let the cat cross the street.
2. I couldn't avoid dropping the glass.
3. Your bad mark means studying harder.
4. He resented her lying at him.
5. We apologise for having forgotten to water the flowers.
6. He just didn't stop staring at me.
7. Alan talked Maria into going to the movies with him.
8. I will never forget kissing Julie under the palm trees.
9. We must not forget to lock the door.
10. Thank you for helping me with the Maths homework.
11. I tried to tell you the truth, but you didn't listen.
12. There is no knowing what she is going to do next.
13. I have never meant to tell Nadja about us.
14. Joan doesn't mind wearing a uniform.
15. Please remember to send us a postcard from your holiday.
16. Let's start to finish on time.

LANGUAGE IN USE

Task 1

0	1	2	3	4	5	6	7	8	9	10
C	A	D	C	C	A	D	B	A	C	B

Task 2

0	1	2	3	4	5	6	7	8	9	10	11	12	13
G	P	E	B	M	L	A	H	K	I	C	N	F	D

Not used: J, O

Task 3

Text	Answer	No.
The **current** summer of 2010 was characterised for US president Barack Obama with an enormous victory. It was a victory he had been fighting for desperately and a victory hardly anybody had believed to really **be** happen. It was the victory in the **all** health care debate, which was also a personal triumph for Obama as no other American president **who** had ever reached that goal before. But what exactly does that mean in **the** detail?	current	1
	OK	2
	be	3
	all	4
	who	5
	the	6
It will help millions of **some** Americans to find affordable health insurance for the first time. Up to that point every inhabitant of the United States **who** was responsible himself/herself for having a sufficient health insurance. This, of course, was a problem for those who did not have enough money. Quite often they were not insured at all and when they had to visit a physician, the **same** trouble started. The summer 2010, however, changed **it** everything. Yet it also divided as **of** never before a nation that still today teaches its children that America was built on self-reliance and suspicion of a strong government.	some	7
	who	8
	OK	9
	OK	10
	same	11
	it	12
	of	13
	OK	14
Americans **who** were simply not used to relying on the government as they have always tried to come to terms with their own affairs. When the White House press secretary announced **of** the changes related to health care he even did that with the words, "Freedom dies a little bit today". For **yet** sure, Europeans cannot understand **about** how health insurance benefits can be seen as a limitation of personal freedom. But then, people in **the** Europe have never had a system comparable with the one in the United States.	who	15
	OK	16
	of	17
	yet	18
	about	19
	the	20
	OK	21
As is always the case when a fight is won, not everybody is **not** happy with the new regulation. Obama critics announced that the president would have to pay a high price for **your** reforms that force Americans for the first time to buy health insurance or else pay a fine. And also the Democrats were not reluctant with their criticism. According to them Obama will be punished by the voters for expanding the state rather than **being** reward him for this achievement. In any case, the public **does** remains sceptical.	not	22
	OK	23
	your	24
	OK	25
	OK	26
	being	27
	does	28
The impact of **the** Obama's health reforms will be felt by American society for decades. Within the first six months new rules outlawing the worst insurance company abuses **which** were set up and within the next four years benefits and tax credits should **not** reach poor and indigent families.	the	29
	OK	30
	which	31
	not	32

Task 4

1 involves
2 environment
3 dependency
4 create
5 suffered
6 flooding
7 is concerned
8 expand
9 restore
10 safety
11 responsibility
12 intends

Task 5

0	1	2	3	4	5	6	7	8	9	10
D	B	D	C	A	C	B	B	D	A	C

Task 6

0	1	2	3	4	5	6	7	8	9	10	11	12	13
J	L	O	F	C	E	K	N	P	B	H	I	D	A

Not used: G, M

Task 7

1 into
2 to
3 than
4 as
5 them
6 on
7 more
8 by/due to/because of
9 be

Task 8

0	1	2	3	4	5	6	7	8	9	10
C	B	A	A	D	C	B	A	D	C	D

VOCABULARY

SYNONYME

Task 1

1. Lucy is never **rude**. In fact she's one of the nicest and friendliest people I know.
2. Mum always instructs me to **hoover** my room but somehow I never do it.
3. I can tell you, my little brother Joseph tells so much **nonsense** when the day is long.
4. Yesterday I really had to **rush** not to miss the bus to school. That would have been a complete **disaster** and the teacher would have been angry with me.
5. Caroline's best friend Melissa has never had a husband so consequently she is **unmarried**.
6. Unfortunately doing home-exercises for school is **obligatory** for children and teens.
7. Peter completely **misread** his girlfriend's behaviour and so she was angry.
8. When I have to write an English exam I usually make **numerous** stupid mistakes.
9. In the film I have watched recently Leonardo DiCaprio played a **generous** rich guy.
10. Mark's excuse was absolutely **plausible** so Sue forgave him his strange behaviour.

Task 2

ENGLISH WORD	SYNONYM
numerous	many
home	domestic
unmarried	single
stupid	silly
nonsense	rubbish
misread	misinterpret
behave	act
disaster	catastrophe

ENGLISH WORD	SYNONYM
generous	beneficial
unusual	uncommon/strange
hoover	vaccum clean
rude	impolite
obligatory	compulsory
rush	hurry
respond	answer
plausible	believable

Task 3

annoying	if your younger brothers and/or sisters permanently go on your nerves
sunrise/sundawn	the moment the sun starts shining in the morning
survive/outlive	if you don't die but go on living
rue/regret	feeling sorry for something you have done or said to somebody
perhaps/maybe	if you are uncertain whether to do something or not, being hesitant
chop/cut	you can do it with any food and afterwards you have small pieces
organic/biologic	if you don't have any artificial substances or additives in food
apparent/obvious	if something is absolutely clear to everybody
unstated/unspoken	if something is not said, not expressed, not articulated with words
isolated/lonely	being completely on your own and not having any friends or family
propose/suggest	to present an idea to somebody, to make a suggestion
knowingly/deliberately	if you do something with full knowledge and intention

HOMONYME

Task 1

1. I think tomorrow's **weather** will be very bad: lots of rain and thunderstorm.
2. Pat has really grown strong. She must have put on a lot of **weight**.
3. Marcus is really keen on fish but he can't stand **meat**. Not even chicken.
4. If you want to go to the London Eye, you have to go **through** Hyde Park.
5. I was walking through the supermarket's **aisles** for 10 minutes before I found what I was looking for. That was really a **waste** of time.
6. Apart from a really pretty face top models need to have a slim **waist**.
7. Gilian never knows **whether** to put on blue jeans or black ones.
8. Paula and Lory have a *Jour fixe*. This means they always **meet** on Monday evening.
9. When David **threw** the ball to Jason he unfortunately hit the window and broke it.
10. Yesterday morning Melanie overslept and so she almost **missed** the bus.
11. I'm not very good at English so I usually need a lot of **practice** and training.
12. When I was in Ireland I was surprised that there was always **mist** in the morning.

Task 2

1. Patience	**8.** sell
2. practice	**9.** knights
3. ate	**10.** Where
4. marry	**11.** vary
5. sale	**12.** sea
6. rode	**13.** which
7. scent	**14.** their

Task 3

1. Somehow I feel very weak and tired today.

2. I haven't done the English homework, too./I have also not done the English homework.

3. It's very impolite to stare at somebody. Please stop doing it.

4. I liked the scene best in which/where she threw the cake into his face.

5. I hope that one day there will be peace on earth.

6. Please put on your shoes and wait for me in front of the door.

7. If I were rich, I would have a maid. (Achtung: Vergiss nicht auf den Beistrich!)

8. Drew read the text aloud so that everybody could hear it.

COLLOCATIONS

Task 1

Das Verb, das jeweils **nicht** passt, ist:

1. to break	**8.** to reload	**15.** work up	**22.** to deserve	**29.** to make the worst of
2. to postpone	**9.** to deny	**16.** to withdraw	**23.** to ignore	**30.** to drop
3. to reduce	**10.** to abandon	**17.** to perform	**24.** to fix	**31.** to demand
4. to save	**11.** to destroy	**18.** to cancel	**25.** to discover	**32.** to extract
5. to release	**12.** to forget	**19.** to commit	**26.** to resist to	**33.** to refresh
6. to describe	**13.** to find	**20.** to refuse	**27.** to ensure	**34.** to buy
7. to forget	**14.** to grow	**21.** to provide	**28.** to go in	**35.** to review

ADJEKTIVE

Task 1

ADJECTIVE	OPPOSITE	ADJECTIVE	OPPOSITE
active	**lazy**	innocent	**guilty**
afraid	**brave/courageous**	interested	**bored, uninterested**
after	**before**	keen	**uninterested, ignorant**
alike	**different**	kind	**cruel, nasty**
alive	**dead**	lazy	**active, busy**
apart	**together**	less	**more**
asleep	**awake**	loud	**silent, quiet**
awful	**delicious, nice, pleasant**	major	**minor**
bad	**good**	many	**few (some)**
best	**worst**	narrow	**broad, wide**
beautiful	**ugly**	native	**foreign, strange**
calm	**excited/vivid**	occasionally	**frequently, seldom**
cheap	**expensive**	occupied	**vacant**
clean	**dirty/filthy**	pleasant	**unpleasant**
dangerous	**safe**	polite	**impolite**
desperate	**hopeful**	poor	**wealthy, rich**
early	**late**	quick	**slow**
easy	**difficult, hard**	rough	**gentle, smooth, soft**
elementary	**advanced**	rude	**polite**
false	**true, correct**	similar	**different**
far	**near**	serious	**funny**
fat	**slim, thin**	solid	**liquid**
generous	**mean**	tight	**loose**
guilty	**innocent**	trivial	**important**
healthy	**ill, sick**	urban	**rural**
heavy	**light**	voluntary	**compulsory**

TESTING SECTION

TEST 1

RC

Task

Die korrekte Nummerierung der Sätze lautet von oben nach unten: 5, 2, 9, 8, 6, 4, 1, 7, 3

Language in Use

1 revealed	**4** worse	**7** has been conditioned	**10** combined
2 be considered	**5** has declined	**8** expect	**11** fail
3 disastrous	**6** inactive	**9** ironic	**12** be limited

Grammar

Task 1

1. If Pete drove more carefully, I would go with him.
2. If we had not forgotten to invite Sady, she would not be angry.
3. If you tell me your secret, I will not say a word.
4. If you drop a stone into water, it sinks.
5. If Sue had paid more attention, she would not have broken her arm.
6. If Dana had not sold her car, we could drive to Italy.

Task 2

1. Simon implored me not to tell dad about the car. (begged me)
2. Sharon asked Anthony if he had gone to Spain the summer before.
3. My sister asked me if she could borrow my blue dress that night.
4. Robby advised/recommended Anna to take the bus because it was faster than the train.
5. My neighbour commanded his dog to get the stick. (told, ordered)
6. My brother asked me if I was going to visit granny that weekend.
7. Miranda asked Joe if he had heard the noise. She wanted to know what he thought it was. Then she suggested to better go and see.

LC

1. they are complete strangers	**3.** same-sex couples	**5.** they spread the word	**7.** public areas (bars, restaurants)
2. it saves time	**4.** white, well-educated	**6.** online dating was stigmatised	

Transcript: Computers are becoming Cupid's best weapon

MICHELE NORRIS, host:

A question: How did you meet your romantic partner? Friends have long been society's top matchmakers, with help from parents and co-workers, but they're all losing ground to the Internet. A new study finds nearly a quarter of couples meet online.

As NPR's Jennifer Ludden reports, the Web may soon become the number one way Americans find a mate.

JENNIFER LUDDEN: Technology hasn't shaken up the dating scene this much since the invention of the telephone. But Michael Rosenfeld of Stanford University says even that doesn't compare.

Professor MICHAEL ROSENFELD (Department of Sociology, Stanford University): The telephone made it easier to be in contact, but only really with the people you already knew. That is, you wouldn't pick up the phone and call somebody you didn't know, it would be awkward.

LUDDEN: But Rosenfeld says those connecting online are most often complete strangers, not even friends of friends. Though, of course, dating sites reveal a great deal about them.

Dr. NICOLE ADAMS (Psychologist): You know level of income, life goals, interests, likes, dislikes.

LUDDEN: Nicole Adams is a 35-year-old psychologist in New York and has been dating online while going through a divorce.

Dr. ADAMS: You also kind of want to weed out the real ...

(Soundbite of laughter)

Dr. ADAMS: ... crazy people, for lack of a better term.

LUDDEN: Sure, she says, people used to trust family and friends to consider all that and come up with a good match.

Dr. ADAMS: But nobody really, really knows what I like, except me.

LUDDEN: Adams says she appreciates being able to reach out to people she'd never encounter in her own social circles, including those from different religions and ethnicities. Then she says there is this very practical aspect: Web dating saves a lot of time.

Adams says if she does meet someone through friends or family, even if sparks don't fly, she's more likely to suffer through a few more dates and let him down gently.

Dr. ADAMS: Whereas online dating, you don't have any of that pressure. If you meet him and something happens to him, mm, next. Thanks a lot, it's been real.

LUDDEN: Ouch. But the smaller the pool of potential partners, the more important those Web contacts may be. Researcher Rosenfeld found a whopping 61 percent of same-sex couples meet online.

Prof. ROSENFELD: So the Internet is friend to everybody who is looking for something that's hard to find. And that's true whether you're looking for parts for a '57 Chevy or a partner who has some attributes that are uncommon.

LUDDEN: On the other hand, a recent Duke University study finds online daters are disproportionately white and well-educated; partly because fewer minorities have a computer at home. But that study also predicted Web-dating will continue to grow, as online access expands and successful couples spread the word.

Stanford University's Rosenfeld says it's all easing a social stigma.

Prof. ROSENFELD: It used to be that people who met online had a separate story that they thought was more palatable. It seemed a little seedy and unseemly, and for some reason people used to think that it was more upstanding to say I met him in a bar.

LUDDEN: Bars, by the way, along with restaurants and other public areas are still the third most likely place for couples to meet. Although Rosenfeld says when you speak to people, it turns out many met there after first encountering each other online.

Jennifer Ludden, NPR News.

TEST 2

RC

Task

1. C; **2.** G; **3.** A; **4.** E; **5.** D; not used: F, B

Language in Use

Let's for a minute not talk about **the** Burger King's tasty hamburgers,	the	1
cheeseburgers and fries. Let's rather spend a minute thinking about the financial	OK	2
crisis the fast food company is **all** currently facing and trying to handle. While only	all	3
a few years ago the Miami-based chain **which** ranked worldwide second and had a	which	4
booming business, things have obviously changed and the single restaurants and	OK	5
franchise partners now have to deal with a significant drop **as** in sales and profits.	as	6
The reasons for this phenomenon are numerous and **to** easy to explain.	to	7
To begin with, Burger King's rather narrow business philosophy has not changed	OK	8
for quite **of** some time. Consequently the food they have on offer no longer	of	9
corresponds with **the** customers' wishes. Consider the following example: Burger	the	10
King's biggest rival **at** McDonalds has managed to enlarge and diversify its	at	11
product range, now also **not** including various salads, wraps, paninis and even	not	12
coffee shop areas. And this development is a good and necessary because due to an	a	13
extended understanding of healthy food and healthy eating habits **like** the current	like	14
market demands such changes and adoptions. Burger King, in contrast, still sticks	OK	15
to traditional food only offering burgers, fries and fizzy drinks. It goes without	OK	16
saying that **if** by doing so they lose a significant number of customers to	if	17
McDonalds, which is one main reason for the permanently decreasing profits. This	OK	18
tendency **which** specially holds true for working class mothers who rather drive	which	19
their kids to **the** McDonalds after the soccer training than to Burger King where the	the	20
children are soon fed up with the small choice of products **on** available.	on	21
But Burger King's customers **who** have also changed due to the recession. Again,	who	22
prosperous families rather **likely** shift to McDonalds while the proportion of blacks	likely	23
and Hispanics eating at Burger King restaurants constantly rises **up**. The problem	up	24
here is only, that these two population groups were particularly **and** hard hit by	and	25
unemployment and have therefore only little money to spend **it** on food. Sounds	it	26
like the perfect vicious circle.	OK	27
Burger King's full dilemma is manifested at **the** Wall Street. While fast food still	the	28
enjoys enormous popularity in the USA, the company has been losing **a** support	a	29
from various investors since a profit warning **of** a few months ago. And indeed,	of	30
sceptical investors really feel discontent and remain hesitant. As **if** it seems today,	if	31
McDonalds will enlarge its profits and become even more prominent and popular.	OK	32

Grammar

The history of the hot dog

The history of the hot dog **can be traced back** to Ancient Greece and **must be linked** to the creation of sausages in general. Accordingly, the term "sausage" **is mentioned/was mentioned** in Homer's *Odyssey*, which **was written** in the late eighth century B.C. The first cook of sausages, however, **is claimed to** have been the Roman Emperor Nero's cook who **stuffed** a pig's intestines with meat and then **tied** them into separate sections. Thus, the "wiener" **was born**. Several other stories and myths **are entwined** around the creation of the hot dog sausage. One of them says that the butcher's guild in Frankfurt **introduced** a spiced and smoked sausage in 1852. This thin sausage **was called** "Frankfurter" after its hometown. As the sausage's shape **reminded** people of a "dachshund", it **was called** the dachshund sausage. When German emigrants **moved** to the United States, the sausage and its name **were taken** with them. In the 1860s, German immigrants then **started** selling "frankfurters" and "wieners" in milk rolls with sauerkraut on pushcarts. In 1867, Charles Feltman **founded** the first Coney Island hot dog stand in Brooklyn. From that moment on, various forms of hot dogs **spread/have spread** all over the U.S.A. Today, the hot dog **is known** all over the world. Numerous variants **have been created**, like the famous chilli hot dog, or the corn dog. Hot dogs **are appreciated** as a quick, delicious snack that **meets** nearly everybody's taste. When you are in LA, drop in at "Pink's", the city's most famous hot dog stand. But don't come hungry – every hot dog **is prepared** fresh and individually for you – and the queue always holds a huge crowd. But it **will be** worth the wait – I promise.

LC

1. D; **2.** C; **3.** D; **4.** B; **5.** D

Transcript: Hearing loss increases in U.S. teens

This is NPR news ...

ROBERT SIEGEL, host:

More and more American teenagers are suffering hearing loss. That's according to a new nationwide government survey. As NPR's Patti Neighmond reports, it's not clear why, but there is suspicion that wearing earbuds to listen to music may be to blame.

PATTI NEIGHMOND: To understand the extent of hearing impairment we're talking about, we're going to play you some tones that will give you an idea of the amount of hearing loss these kids experience. First this is a high-frequency tone at a normal listening level.

(Soundbite of tone)

NEIGHMOND: Now we're going to lower the volume a little.

(Soundbite of tone)

NEIGHMOND: And teenagers with healthy hearing can hear that drop in volume, but lots of these kids couldn't. Now we're dropping the volume even more.

(Soundbite of tone)

NEIGHMOND: And this where one in five of the kids tested, aged 12 to 19, had difficulty hearing. Researchers say that over the past 15 years, there's been a 30 percent increase in the number of teenagers suffering hearing loss in this range.

Dr. Gary Curhan of Brigham and Women's Hospital in Boston was one of the researchers who analyzed the government data. He says the hearing loss is slight, but studies show even mild hearing loss affects academic performance.

Dr. GARY CURHAN (Brigham and Women's Hospital): They may be able to hear that somebody's whispering but may not be able to understand it, and there have been some people who study hearing loss who distinguish between whether they actually can hear and understand the sounds and whether it's intelligible versus just detectible.

NEIGHMOND: One of those hearing specialists is Dr. Alison Grimes, who sees patients and does research at the Audiology Clinic at Ronald Reagan UCLA Medical Center. She says we've known for centuries that loud noise damages the ear.

Dr. ALISON GRIMES (Audiology Clinic, Ronald Reagan UCLA Medical Center): We know that musicians are at higher likelihood of having hearing loss, whether it's rock musicians or classical musicians. We know that when we go to a concert and we walk out of a concert three hours later, our ears feel full and stuffy, and our ears ring. Those are signs of temporary or possibly permanent damage to hearing from exposure to loud noise.

NEIGHMOND: The study didn't explore why more teens today are suffering hearing loss, but Grimes says there's a pretty likely culprit.

Dr. GRIMES: Probably exposure to MP3 players to personal listening devices to music would be the suspicion that most of us have.

NEIGHMOND: Grimes says most hearing experts agree if you can hear the music from a teenager's earbuds, it's too loud, and for the teenager, it's likely destroying the tiny hairs in the inner ear that respond to particular pitches and help transmit sound to the brain.

Dr. GRIMES: If pieces of that transmission are missing, then the sound that goes up to the brain is not going to be the clear sound that we need to be able to hear to understand speech.

NEIGHMOND: Grimes says research shows the louder the noise and the longer you're hearing it, the greater the risk of hearing loss, and that's why there are standards for noise on the job, and when the noise gets to a certain level, workers are required to wear ear protection and have annual hearing checkups. But for loud music plugged into the ear, the research isn't clear yet. However, Grimes says there are recommendations.

Dr. GRIMES: Lower volume is safer, and if a person is going to listen at a higher volume, it's a good idea to take to turn it off and take out the earphones for, say, 10 or 15 minutes every hour, give your ears a rest.

NEIGHMOND: For more specific guidance, Grimes suggests going to the American Academy of Audiology website, turntotheleft.org.

Patti Neighmond, NPR News.

TEST 3

RC

Task

1. rising (higher) number of immigrants/more immigrants from India
2. parents choose future spouse (partner)/parents decide for children
3. search your own partner/it's your own decision/parents don't search partner
4. torn between cultures/uncertain about their culture/insecure what to do
5. violates human rights/children forced to marry/involves physical-emotional pressure
6. based on long-lasting qualities/no spontaneous decision/should be more persistent
7. don't know your partner/it's a risky business/hardly know your spouse
8. their motivation is crucial (essential, important)/motivation decides about success

Language in Use

0	1	2	3	4	5	6	7	8	9	10	11	12	13
I	P	C	N	H	K	L	M	G	B	O	F	J	E

Not used: A, D

Grammar

Task 1

1	incredibly cool	8	quickly
2	finally	9	smoothly
3	dreadfully boring	10	hardly
4	long-desired	11	overwhelmingly powerful
5	brightly	12	peacefully
6	sparkelling	13	better
7	brand new black and white Swiss	14	simply

Task 2

1. Benjamin, whose car, (which) he had only bought two months ago, had been stolen, called the police.
2. We put super glue in Emmet's shoes, which he didn't find funny.
3. The girl whose dog, which she loved like mad, had run away was crying.
4. The boy (who/that) we met yesterday at the party and whose number you lost called me a minute ago.
5. My friend who lives in Australia and whose job is studying crocodiles has just married. (no commas: you have more than one friend)

LC

1. a bit of experience
2. found guilty of
3. is suing
4. more appropriate laws
5. pointed out
6. a new urgency

Transcript: 15 percent of teens with cells receive "sexts"

ROBERT SIEGEL, host:

Sexting is a provocative word for a relatively new activity that teens do and get in trouble for. They send sexually suggestive or nude photos over a cell phone. A new study by the Pew Research Center finds nearly one in six teens has received these pictures.

NPR's Laura Sydell reports that educators and lawmakers are struggling with how to deal with sexting.

LAURA SYDELL: The study showed that only four percent of teens between 12 and 17 actually send suggestive photos. Fifteen percent say they have seen sexy photos on phones.

Ms. AMANDA LENHART (Senior Research Specialist, Pew Internet & American Life Project): That doesn't actually even take into account teens who see it over somebody's shoulder, who hear about it in the hallways of the school.

SYDELL: Study author Amanda Lenhart.

Ms. LENHART: Teens told us that this is something they have quite a bit of experience with. This is part of their daily lives.

SYDELL: Schools and communities are struggling to stop sexting. Law enforcement has been stepping in. Lenhart worries they've been overreacting. She points to the case of Phillip Alpert. When he was 18 years old he had a fight with his 16-year-old girlfriend one night. In a fit of rage, he forwarded a naked photo of her to their friends and family. Alpert was prosecuted and found guilty of sending out child pornography. At 19, he's now a registered sex offender.

Ms. LENHART: It doesn't make sense that somebody who's done what he has done would actually be listed on a public listing along with rapists and other people who harm people and children in ways that are so much greater.

SYDELL: In another case, a group of 13-year-old girls took pictures of themselves at a slumber party dressed only in bras and towels. The photos made their way to the local district attorney. He threatened them with prosecution. And now the ACLU is suing the DA for violating the girls' First Amendment rights. ACLU attorney Vic Walczak.

Ms. VIC WALCZAK (Attorney, ACLU): What kids are doing today is no different than what they were doing 10, 20, 30, 40 years ago. What's different is the technology has changed and it's now more visible.

SYDELL: The parents won their case in federal district court, but prosecutor George Skumanick is appealing. NPR could not reach Mr. Skumanick. A few state legislatures are trying to make more appropriate laws. Vermont and Utah downgraded the penalties for minors and first-time perpetrators of sexting. But the real battle may be trying to get teens to think before they act.

As DA Skumanick pointed out in an earlier interview, sexting can be dangerous. Two girls killed themselves after naked pictures leaked out at their schools and they were taunted by peers. Recently, LG electronics started a YouTube campaign with James Lipton, the host of "Inside the Actors Studio". Lipton stands by a teenage boy who's about to send out an erotic phone picture of himself to his girlfriend Zoey.

Mr. JAMES LIPTON (Host, Inside the Actors Studio): Zoey is a Twitter addict and the last thing he needs is tweets about his feats. Before you text, give it a ponder.

SYDELL: Getting teens to think before they act is a fight that's gone on for generations. Unfortunately, in this digital age, it may be taking on a new urgency.

Laura Sydell, NPR news.

TEST 4

RC

1. D; **2.** A; **3.** D; **4.** C; **5.** A; **6.** B; **7.** B; **8.** C

Language in Use

1 of	**4** children's/kids'	**7** was	**10** lots/a lot
2 to	**5** anything	**8** that/which	**11** hardly/rarely/seldom/not
3 for	**6** of	**9** with	**12** to

Grammar

1. I apologise for not having thought of your birthday.
2. I won't pardon your constant ignoring me anymore.
3. We forgot asking our parents to fetch us from the party.
4. Today I prefer not to take dessert.
5. Has Serena really stopped seeing/dating Aden?
6. Patience is so looking forward to telling you the news.
7. I'm fed up with waiting for him to call me.
8. The advantages of texting can't be denied./There's no denying the advantages of texting.
9. I regret not having helped Gina with painting her room.
10. How about/What about watching a film in the drive-in?
11. I admire his gift of always finding a parking space.
12. It's fun sitting here, watching the guys surfing.
13. I have been fined for parking here.
14. We will never get accustomed to/used to wearing those uniforms.

LC

1. C; **2.** A; **3.** D; **4.** C; **5.** B

Transcript: Impact of child obesity goes beyond health

RENEE MONTAGNE, host:

The health risks of being overweight or obese are well-documented. Extra pounds increase the likelihood of diabetes, heart disease and certain cancers, even among children. New research also documents significant social and economic consequences of being chronically overweight or obese since childhood. NPR's Patti Neighmond reports.

PATTI NEIGHMOND: Philippa Clarke, a researcher at the University of Michigan, wanted to know what happens to people who've been overweight or obese since adolescence. She compared one group of 40-year-olds, who were normal weight at high school graduation but who gained weight gradually over time, to another group of 40-year-olds, who were overweight since age 19.

Ms. PHILIPPA CLARKE (University of Michigan): We found that those people who are persistently overweight were more likely to not have gone on to have any further education beyond their high school degree, to be receiving welfare or unemployment compensation at age 40, and to have no current partner.

NEIGHMOND: Clarke says her study didn't address why, but she speculates these adults probably experienced discrimination as children – discrimination that diminished their self-esteem and in turn, their aspirations.

Other research supports that theory. Yale psychologist Kelly Brownell has done research showing that overweight kids are far – are more likely to report being teased.

Mr. KELLY BROWNELL (Psychologist, Yale University): Teasing that comes directly from teachers, in some cases; certainly, from peers; sometimes even by their own families. This gets internalized so overweight children feel inferior, feel like there's something defective with themselves and therefore, they tend not to aspire. And this isn't true in all cases, but a lot of them tend not to aspire to such heights because they don't believe they deserve it.

NEIGHMOND: Brownell says his studies have shown that overweight people are 26 times more likely to report discrimination than their normal-weight counterparts. And Brownell says discrimination against overweight individuals has increased significantly over the past decade despite the fact that more adults are becoming overweight.

One of the reasons, he says, may be that people think overweight adults have only themselves to blame. They should eat less and exercise more. But Brownell says blame is simply unreasonable, particularly when it comes to children and weight and especially in low-income neighbourhoods, where markets are often inadequate, and places to exercise are nearly nonexistent.

Mr. BROWNELL: The social climate and our toxic food environment is so disastrous that more and more people are having trouble resisting it. And that's really what's explaining the high prevalence of obesity. So it's unfair to put people in an environment where weight gain is a very, very strong possibility and then to blame them for having the problem.

NEIGHMOND: Changing the environment is a key to solving the problem. Pediatrician Joe Thompson is a specialist in childhood obesity at the University of Arkansas College Of Medicine. Over the past decade, Thompson says, the state's made changes in schools to promote an environment where it's easier for kids to make healthy choices.

Dr. JOE THOMPSON (University of Arkansas College of Medicine): In Arkansas, we've actually tried to change the offerings in our school cafeterias, and tried to restrict some of the less nutritious available foods in vending machines and others – throughout the school campus.

NEIGHMOND: And Thompson says those efforts have paid off.

Dr. THOMPSON: The rate of the epidemic has slowed nationwide, and we have actually shown a halt to the epidemic.

NEIGHMOND: Supporting research findings that suggest the best way to confront the medical and social effects of being overweight or obese is to prevent it in the first place.

Patti Neighmond, NPR News.

LC: Impact of childhood obesity goes beyond health

Hörübung:
Mediathek

Task **Multiple choice**

Find the best endings to the sentences. Tick the correct box.

1. Consequences of obesity

A on the health of people are not well enough documented. ❏

B on children are to be investigated. ❏

C on social and economic aspects have newly been studied. ❏

D on the life of children will be studied in the years to come. ❏

2. People who are persistently overweight

A have a relatively low level of education. ❏

B feel less shy about their body than people who gained weight gradually over time. ❏

C have a higher risk of suffering a heart disease-related death. ❏

D do not tend to live on welfare. ❏

3. Overweight children do not show a high level of ambition in their later life

A because they have never experienced competition and success. ❏

B because the teasing they experience causes depressions. ❏

C because the discrimination they experience has negative effects on their learning habits. ❏

D because they feel like they are not worth success. ❏

4. Discrimination against overweight people

A has decreased in the last years because more people are overweight. ❏

B has increased in the last years because people feel plagued by overweight people. ❏

C has increased because people think they are to be blamed themselves for their weight. ❏

D has decreased when it comes to overweight children. ❏

5. Child obesity

A can be blamed on the children themselves. ❏

B can only be fought by changing children's environment and habits. ❏

C can probably never be successfully fought. ❏

D can only be fought by propelling children's self-esteem. ❏

2 Punkte pro richtiger Antwort ☐ / 10

Gesamtpunkte ☐

Note	Punkte
Sehr gut	40–44
Gut	35–39
Befriedigend	29–34
Genügend	22–28
Nicht genügend	0–21

TITELVERZEICHNIS DER HÖRÜBUNGEN IN DER MEDIATHEK

Titelnummer	Zeit	Buch Seite	Titel
1	3:30	7	Struggling to overcome anorexia
2	4:34	8	The tea thieves: How a drink shaped an empire
3	3:18	9	From Dickens himself, notes on "A Christmas Carol"
4	3:40	10	This is "Your face on meth", kids
5	3:50	11	In Britain, lights come up on clubber's drug
6	4:59	12	China uproots child slave labor ring at brick plant
7	3:52	13	Becoming close: The geography of friendship
8	3:08	14	Sorry Charlie: "Two and a Half Men" may go on
9	4:02	15	Teen texting soars: Will social skills suffer?
10	5:23	16	Teens, sex and TV: A risky mix?
11	5:06	17	One teen's struggle to quit smoking
12	4:22	18	Controversy over the world cup soccer ball
13	4:17	19	Soccer fans urge FIFA to use video review
14	3:27	20	Homework: Overcoming fear
15	3:48	21	Lady Gaga vs. Ace of Base
16	5:30	22	That not-so-healthy glow: The dangers of tanning
17	4:23	23	E-book readers expected to grow in popularity
18	3:48	24	School desegregation: At which price?
19	3:40	25	Who will live to be 100? Genetic test might tell
20	4:26	26	This year, smart phones are holiday must-have
21	4:04	145	Computers are becoming Cupid's best weapon
22	3:43	149	Hearing loss increases in U.S. teens
23	3:17	154	15 percent of teens with cells receive "sexts"
24	3:35	159	Impact of childhood obesity goes beyond health